THE VICTORIAN THEATRE

THE
VICTORIAN THEATRE
1792-1914

A SURVEY

BY

GEORGE ROWELL

Special Lecturer in Drama, University of Bristol

SECOND EDITION

CAMBRIDGE UNIVERSITY PRESS

CAMBRIDGE

LONDON · NEW YORK · MELBOURNE

Published by the Syndics of the Cambridge University Press
The Pitt Building, Trumpington Street, Cambridge CB2 1RP
Bentley House, 200 Euston Road, London NW1 2DB
32 East 57th Street, New York, NY 10022, USA
296 Beaconsfield Parade, Middle Park, Melbourne 3206, Australia

© George Rowell 1978

First published by Oxford University Press 1956
Reprinted 1967
Second edition first published by Cambridge University Press 1978

Printed in Great Britain at the
University Press, Cambridge

Library of Congress Cataloguing in Publication Data
Rowell, George.
The Victorian theatre, 1792–1914.
Bibliography: p.
Includes index.
1. Theater — England — History — 19th century.
2. English drama—19th century—History and criticism.
3. Theater — England — Bibliography. I. Title.
PN2594.R65 1978 792'.0941 78–2900

ISBN 0 521 22070 X hard covers
ISBN 0 521 29346 4 paperback

CONTENTS

PREFACE TO THE SECOND EDITION — vii

PREFACE TO THE FIRST EDITION — viii

LIST OF ILLUSTRATIONS — ix

1. THE NEW THEATRE — 1

    Theatre and Audience (3)—'*Major*' *and* '*Minor*' *Houses* (8)—*Staging Methods* (14)—*The Interior Scene* (18)—*Stage Machinery and Lighting* (20) —*Acting Styles* (22)

2. THE NEW DRAMA — 31

    The Romantic Poets and the Theatre (32)—*The Demand for Spectacle* (38)—*Gothic Drama* (43) —*Native Melodrama* (46)—*Bulwer-Lytton and Boucicault* (51)—*Taylor and Reade* (57)—*The Eclipse of Comedy* (63)—*Burlesque* (66)

3. THE RETURN OF RESPECTABILITY — 75

    Robertson's Plays (75)—*Robertson's 'Stage-Management'* (78)—*Auditorium and Audience* (82)—*Robertson's Successors* (84)—*Gilbert and Sullivan* (92)—*Irving at the Lyceum* (95)— *Irving's Repertory* (98).

4. THE ERA OF SOCIETY DRAMA — 103

    An Age of Actor Managers (104)—*The Playwright's Progress* (107)—*The Plays of Oscar Wilde* (109)—*Arthur Wing Pinero* (112)—

Henry Arthur Jones (118)—*Society Dramatists* (126)—*Intellectual Drama: Shaw* (128)—*The Court Theatre Seasons, 1904–7* (133)—*Social Drama* (135)—*The Repertory Movement* (138)—*The Production of Shakespeare* (140)—*Melodrama and Musical Comedy* (142)—*The Development of Society Drama* (145)—*Changes* (148)

AFTERWORD 1978   151

The Crown and the Theatre (151)—*The Provincial Theatre* (153)—*Comedy and Farce* (156)—*Comic Acting* (158)—*Late Victorian Melodrama* (159)—*The Playwright's Right to Pay* (160)—*A Century of Dramatic Critics* (162)— *Victorian Plays in Revival* (164)—*Retrospect and Prospect* (166)

PLAY-LIST, 1792–1914   171

A BIBLIOGRAPHY OF THE ENGLISH THEATRE, 1792–1914   179

INDEX   225

PREFACE TO
THE SECOND EDITION

In its new edition this book comes of age, and under the imprint of another publisher. The choice of the period 1792 to 1914 (rather than that of 1837 to 1901 suggested by the original title) has been clarified by the addition of the relevant dates. Minor errors have been corrected in the text, and an Afterword added to rectify some of the omissions and false emphases which the past two decades have revealed. The debt to other workers in the field which this Afterword owes is some measure of the attention the subject has received since the book first appeared.

Another such measure is the new Bibliography. The book was conceived as a brief overall survey, in which limitations of space were offset to some extent by as complete a Bibliography as could then be assembled. Additions to this were printed as an Appendix to the 1967 reissue. For this second edition the relevant publications of the past ten years have been included, and the whole Bibliography collated for ease of reference. It may be noted that the number of works appearing since 1956 is only slightly smaller than those undertaken before that date. Since opinion loses currency by its very nature, there could be more lasting value in this Bibliography than in what precedes it.

1978   G.R.

PREFACE TO
THE FIRST EDITION

Strictly speaking, a survey of the Victorian theatre should begin in 1837, the year of Queen Victoria's accession, and end in 1901, the year of her death. Such divisions are inevitably arbitrary, and where a natural division suggests itself it is often convenient to accept it, and perhaps pardonable to leave the title unqualified.

Such a natural division exists in the case of the Victorian theatre, many of whose characteristics were established well before 1837, and which underwent no noticeable change in 1901. The choice of 1792 for the start of this survey and of 1914 for its end are explained in the following pages. If the chapter of theatre history which they cover appears well enough defined, it may yet be granted the style of 'the Victorian theatre' in the teeth of chronology.

1955   G.R.

ILLUSTRATIONS

The Development of the Victorian Theatre

1A. DRURY LANE IN 1792: The Drury Lane built by Wren in 1674 stood until 1792. The interior was much altered, particularly by Robert Adam in 1775, but the original building remained. Most of the alterations were designed to increase the capacity, by adding a second gallery, enlarging the boxes, and reducing the apron-stage. Even so, the capacity of Drury Lane, as seen here, cannot greatly have exceeded 1,000. This drawing was made by William Capon, the scenic artist shortly, before the theatre's demolition. (*Reproduced by permission of the University of Bristol Theatre Collection*) *facing p.* 2

1B. DRURY LANE IN 1794: The new Drury Lane, designed by Henry Holland and opened in 1794, held at least three times as many spectators as its predecessor. The capacity of the new house has recently been estimated at 3,611. Five tiers can be seen in this print, and the auditorium is far more ornately decorated than before. Nevertheless, the various tiers still encircle the pit in the Georgian manner. This print was published by Richard Philips in 1804, five years before the theatre was burnt to the ground. (*Reproduced by permission of the University of Bristol Theatre Collection*) *facing p.* 2

A 'Minor' Theatre

2. ASTLEY'S ABOUT 1792: Astley's, like the Surrey Theatre, began as a riding school, became a circus and ultimately a theatre. The building shown here (erected in 1783 and demolished in 1794) was still partly a circus tent, and the painted foliage was added to justify the title 'Royal Grove'. At one end, however, a stage was erected, and scenes alternated from there to the ring, which had easy access from the stage. The next Astley's was a permanent building. (*Reproduced by permission of the University of Bristol Theatre Collection*) *facing p.* 3

Transition

3A. THE FUTURE PRINCE OF WALES'S: This print of the Regency Theatre, later to become the Prince of Wales's, was first published in *Theatrum Illustratum* by Robert Wilkinson in 1825. It shows the Georgian playhouse in the process of transformation into the Victorian theatre. The proscenium door and balcony, with a reduced apron-stage, are retained, and the scenery (apparently for *Othello*) is of the conventional wing and back-scene type. But there is a suggestion that the first tier of boxes is interrupted, and that the pit continues at the back under the second tier. The Regency Theatre had a chequered career and many different names until rechristened the Prince of Wales's by Marie Wilton in 1865. (*Reproduced by permission of the University of Bristol Theatre Collection*) *facing p.* 18

3B. THE GAIETY IN 1869: The opening of the Gaiety in 1869 marked another step in the development of the Victorian theatre. This sketch, from the *Illustrated London News* of January 1869, shows that the stage was now virtually cut off from the auditorium. Orchestra-stalls provided with backs occupy the first five rows of the pit, but the pit-benches can be seen behind them. There is a similar division of the first tier. Three rows of seats are open, in the manner of the modern dress-circle, but behind these come boxes somewhat on the Georgian pattern. The whole auditorium is elaborately decorated and follows the fashionable curving lines of the Victorian theatre. (*Reproduced by permission of the University of Bristol Theatre Collection*) *facing p.* 18

The Victorian Theatre

4. THE ST. JAMES'S IN 1900: Although opened in 1835, the St. James's underwent varied fortunes until taken over by George Alexander in 1891. In 1900 the interior was reconstructed. This picture, first published in the *Sketch* in February 1900, shows the final appearance of the Victorian theatre. The proscenium-arch has developed into an elaborate picture-frame, sharply dividing the stage from the auditorium. The greater part of the pit is occupied by upholstered orchestra-stalls which extend under the first tier, both at the sides and at the back. The various tiers are no longer partitioned into boxes but are open and overhang the pit. The only surviving boxes are two, on either side of the proscenium-arch, evidently for ceremonial occasions. The decorations, though rich, are less gaudy than those of the mid-Victorian theatre. (*Reproduced by permission of the University of Bristol Theatre Collection*) *facing p.* 19

A Century of Shakespearean Production

Macready's Lead

5A. 'HENRY V' AT COVENT GARDEN, 1839. BEFORE HARFLEUR: (Etching by George Scharf, published in *Recollections of the Scenic Effects of Covent Garden Theatre*, London, 1839.) Scharf's series of scenes from Macready's productions at Covent Garden between 1837 and 1839 provide the best evidence yet discovered of Macready's work as a producer, since they were evidently made during or immediately after a performance. Much of the vigour of the production and splendour of the setting is preserved in this drawing. The composition of the set is far harder to deduce. The arch on Stage L. is presumably a wing; so, probably, are the fortifications on Stage R. Much of the mid- and far-distance, including most of the troops, must be painted on a back-drop. (*Reproduced by permission of The Theatre Museum*) *between pp.* 74–5

5B. BACK-CLOTH FOR AGINCOURT: Clarkson Stanfield's original design for this back-cloth, squared-up ready for the scene-painter, is preserved in the Victoria and Albert Museum, and gives a striking impression of the panoramas, particularly the cloud-formations, for which he was famous. (*Reproduced by permission of The Theatre Museum*) *between pp.* 74–5

Charles Kean's Archæology

6. 'THE WINTER'S TALE' AT THE PRINCESS'S, 1856: The Shakespearean and other productions of Charles Kean at the Princess's between 1850 and 1859 were notable for their splendour and for the pains taken to ensure historical accuracy of setting and costume. This design for Act II, Scene 1 of *The Winter's Tale* is styled 'Court of the Gynæconitis, or Women's Apartments', and in a note for the souvenir of the production Kean wrote: 'Among the Greeks and their Sicilian cousins it used to be the custom for the females to have rooms of their own, apart from the rooms of the men. The scene represents the court or principal hall of Hermione's apartments. In the centre of the hall, surrounded by four rows of columns, is the Peristyle or open court, one of the principal features in ancient Grecian or Roman architecture, and which we see revived in the beautiful Pompeian House in the Crystal Palace.' The design was by H. Cuthbert, one of a group of artists who worked for Kean at the Princess's. It makes effective use of the diagonal setting-line much favoured by Kean in order to conceal the narrowness of the proscenium-opening. The series of water-colour sketches of Kean's productions, preserved in the Victoria and Albert Museum, and from which this is taken, were made as a record, and it is impossible to be certain how much of the set is backcloth, and how much border and wings. (*Reproduced by permission of The Theatre Museum*)   *between pp.* 74–5

Irving at the Lyceum

7. 'MUCH ADO ABOUT NOTHING', 1882: (From the oil-painting by Sir Johnston Forbes Robertson.) This picture of the Church Scene fully conveys the sumptuousness of Irving's Shakespearean productions, in which the chief scenes were given elaborate built-up settings, skilfully devised and painted (in this case by William Telbin the Younger). Irving is clearly recognizable as Benedick, centre, and Ellen Terry as Beatrice; at stage right is Forbes Robertson himself, who played Claudio in this production. Others in the picture are Don Pedro (William Terriss) on Benedick's right, Hero (Jessie Millward) kneeling, Leonato (James Fernandez) at her side, Father Francis (Tom Mead) on steps, and Don John (Charles Glenny) back to altar. (*Courtesy of The Walter Hampden–Edwin Booth Theatre Collection at the Players*)   *between pp.* 74–5

Tree at Her Majesty's

8. 'KING JOHN', 1899. THE FIGHT NEAR ANGIERS: Tree's series of Shakespearean productions at Her Majesty's developed to the full the methods of staging popularized in the Victorian theatre. The settings were greatly elaborated and details stated rather than implied. The battle between the English and French near Angiers in *King John* happens off-stage. Tree, however, introduced a special tableau, depicting this battle. The photograph shows how the crowds massed on the stage were increased by painting faces and figures on a series of 'cut-outs' at the back. The settings for this production were by Hawes Craven, but Joseph Harker was entrusted with the tableau. (*Reproduced by permission of the University of Bristol Theatre Collection*)   *between pp.* 74–5

The Reaction

9. 'A MIDSUMMER NIGHT'S DREAM' AT THE SAVOY, 1914: The three Shakespearean productions by Granville Barker at the Savoy between 1912 and 1914 marked a conscious rejection of the methods of the Victorian actor-managers. The settings were neither elaborate nor especially accurate historically. The Wood near Athens, seen in this photograph, was represented by the designer, Norman Wilkinson, by means of painted curtains, which were heavily criticized, as were the gilded trappings of the fairies, also seen here. The aim was to suggest the scene by simple but imaginative means, not to portray it realistically. (*Reproduced by permission of The Theatre Museum*)   *between pp.* 74–5

Pantomime

10. BEHIND THE SCENES: This sketch, first printed in the *Magazine of Art* in 1889, was made by William Telbin the Younger, one of a large family of Victorian scenic artists. It conveys much of the atmosphere of the Victorian theatre: the heavily gilded pillars of the proscenium-arch, the limelight from the fly-gallery, the gas floats. The system of scene-changing is shown in some detail: as the Good Fairy descends by a trap-door, one pair of flats opens to reveal the next scene. The upper grooves, in which the flats slide, are prominently shown, including the pivoted portion which can be raised out of sight when not required. (*Reproduced by permission of the University of Bristol Theatre Collection*)   *between pp.* 74–5

11. IN THE WINGS: A sketch published in the *Graphic* in 1869 and drawn from an unusual angle, which provides a view across the stage. The cast of the pantomime can be seen waiting their cue. The upper grooves and limelight are again prominent, and two sets of gas-wings (known as 'ladders') provide side-lighting. (*Reproduced by permission of the University of Bristol Theatre Collection*)   *between pp.* 74–5

12. BENEATH THE STAGE: A sketch from the *Illustrated Sporting and Dramatic News* of 1874, showing a stage-trap in action at the Princess's. The Clown, about to make his entry, stands on the platform, which is raised by counter-weights. The top-hatted stage-hand holds the rope whereby cues are given to and by the stage-manager. A chorus-girl and a thirsty theatre-dresser are leaning against a winch. A member of the orchestra and the stage cat can also be seen. (*Reproduced by permission of the Raymond Mander–Joe Mitchenson Theatre Collection*)   *between pp.* 74–5

The Interior Scene

13. 'THE MINISTER AND THE MERCER'. DRURY LANE, 1834: The prompt-book for this play by Alfred Bunn is preserved in the Enthoven Collection at the Victoria and Albert Museum, and contains a number of sketches and plans of the settings, which were carried out under Clarkson Stanfield's direction. This pen-and-ink sketch of the scene for Act II, the Mercer's shop, shows an interesting combination of traditional and novel features. The greater part of the set consists of the familiar wings, the back scene is evidently a pair of flats, and the lack of borders seems to

have exposed the upper grooves. At stage right, however, an elaborate staircase has been built, with a door at its head, both of which the script requires to be practicable. The use of different acting-levels has begun. (*Reproduced by permission of The Theatre Museum*) facing p. 130

14. SCENE FROM 'COURT FAVOUR', 1836. VESTRIS AND MATHEWS AT THE OLYMPIC: Little evidence of the scenic reforms of Madame Vestris and Charles Mathews has survived. The scene from *Court Favour* by J. R. Planché, published in *Webster's Acting National Drama*, Volume II (London, 1838), claims to be 'an engraving by Pierce Egan the Younger, from a drawing taken during the representation'. At any rate, there appears to have been a practicable ceiling cloth instead of a border, and there is some suggestion of enclosing the sides of the stage by means of raking-pieces, in place of the traditional wings. If so, this is a step, at least, towards the evolution of the box-set. The stage directions for this scene run: '*A handsome apartment at* SIR ANDREW ALLSIDE'S; *glass doors in centre opening on a terrace with flight of steps R.S.L. leading down into garden, over the wall of which are seen the towers of Westminster Abbey; folding-doors on each side between first and third wings.*' Mathews and Madame Vestris are recognizable in the parts of David Brown and Lucy. (*Reproduced by permission of the Raymond Mander–Joe Mitchenson Theatre Collection*) facing p. 131

Robertson and the Bancrofts

15. 'OURS' AT THE PRINCE OF WALES'S, 1866: This sketch from the *Illustrated London News* of 20 October 1866 is evidently an 'artist's impression' of the Crimean scene (Act III) from *Ours*. However, it does convey the wealth of detail achieved in the staging of Robertson's plays, and shows how the atmosphere of the hut was obtained by fully enclosing the scene. One famous piece of stage-management, throwing in snow at the door, is also shown. Charles S. James was responsible for the scenery. (*Reproduced by permission of The Theatre Museum*) facing p. 146

Alexander at the St. James's

16. 'JOHN GLAYDE'S HONOUR', 1907: Both the style and the staging of Society drama are reflected in this photograph of a scene from Altred Sutro's play. Act IV, an artist's studio in Paris, is an elaborately constructed interior, designed by Joseph Harker, with a practicable balcony and a suitable backing seen through the window. Furnishings and properties are much in evidence. The situation depicted is equally typical. The husband (Alexander) confronts his young wife (Eva Moore) in the studio of the handsome artist (Matheson Lang) with the following words: 'JOHN. I shall divorce her—you can get married. I shall make provision for her, that she never may want. Take her, and help her —to lie and betray no more. (MURIEL *covers her face with her hands.* TREVOR *stands tongue-tied, bewildered. Without looking at her, without looking at him,* JOHN GLAYDE *moves slowly to the door, and goes. His steps are heard on the stone outside, then the clang of the gate; neither of the two stirs. The curtain slowly falls.*)' (*Reproduced by permission of The Theatre Museum*) facing p. 147

THE NEW THEATRE

Every spectacle demands its audience—the nursery performance, with its conscripted parents and friends, no less than the circuses which the Romans were given with their bread. Actors can continue to act and playwrights to be heard only at an audience's pleasure. The history of any theatrical epoch is therefore the history of its audience's wishes, as interpreted by the playwrights, actors, and managers of the day. This back-stage collaboration may give an audience something that it does not expect, and so contribute to theatrical evolution; but it can never force on an audience something that it does not want.

In nineteenth-century England the audience shaped both the theatre and the drama played within it; for patronage, the only card with which a manager may sometimes outbid public taste, was at its lowest ebb at Victoria's accession. Polite society, when it patronized the theatre at all, favoured the opera; a large section of that society, however, shunned the theatre altogether and sought entertainment from the circulating library. Into the gap left by the withdrawal of the upper classes there rushed the masses of a capital whose population almost trebled between 1811 and 1851. To accommodate them the theatres multiplied their numbers and trebled their size. To penetrate these vast spaces the actors broadened their style. To satisfy the audience the bill was lengthened from three to four, five, and even six hours. To fix their attention the artist and machinist contrived ever greater wonders.

The playwright's place in the Victorian theatre was, at the outset, that of handyman to the company. He existed to make their performance possible, rather than they to interpret his work to an audience. The evolution of the Victorian theatre shows the audience and dramatist advancing hand-in-hand. As the audience's behaviour improved, so did the playwright's position. When Stalls and Dress Circle claimed their place in the theatre, the author's royalties and copyright came too. At the end of the Victorian period Society had taken the theatre to its heart once more and the playwright's status was fully restored.

These conditions make the history of the Victorian theatre and of Victorian drama inseparable. No other period in English theatre history illustrates so clearly the fact that a play exists fully only in performance. Many plays of the period, famous in their day, appear scarcely intelligible on the printed page, so great is their reliance on the actor's powers of projection and on the machinist's skill, to which a mass of highly technical stage directions testifies. To recreate from the text a performance of a Victorian play calls for imagination strongly disciplined in the theatrical practice of the day; and for the same reason a study of Victorian drama entails a study of the Victorian theatre.

Lacking literary values, the Victorian theatre has been largely neglected by both critics and historians. Such neglect is certainly justified if the place of Victorian drama in the modern repertory is the test. Yet in theatre history the nineteenth century is a period of great importance. Its opening witnessed the disappearance of the Georgian playhouse, small, intimate, founded on long-established conventions of staging and writing. The first half of the century saw the English theatre expand its resources to the full. Legal as well as physical obstacles were overcome in the evolution of a type of spectacle at its zenith by the middle of Victoria's reign. This expansion was followed by a concentration of effort from which emerged the modern English theatre as we still know it: a playhouse of modest size, a stage framed by the proscenium-arch, lit by electricity, backed by canvas walls, conducted with the restraint and attention to detail which characterize modern English acting and production. For this theatre the later Victorian playwrights evolved a drama serious in tone, realistic in method, and general in appeal— three principles still strong in English dramatic writing.

The lasting interest of the Victorian theatre is therefore its

1. *Drury Lane*

ABOVE: *in* 1792. BELOW: *in* 1794

2. Astley's about 1792

rôle as the cradle of the modern theatre; and it is the aim of this study to trace the stages of its evolution.

Theatre and Audience

In the playhouse of to-day the orchestra-stall commands the highest purse and the greatest prestige. Save for ceremonial occasions it takes precedence over the obsolescent box. But that part of the auditorium now held by the orchestra-stall is the battleground of the theatre: disputed territory, passing from hand to hand as the forces which have shaped playgoing as a social pursuit advance, retreat, and re-deploy. In the Elizabethan age the 'standing room' around the platform-stage was packed with groundlings, paying for admission with their patience as well as their pennies. In the Banqueting House at Whitehall the floor-space in front of the stage was kept clear of spectators, so that when the masque was done the masquers could descend and invite their audience, the Stuart court, to join in a dance. When in the tennis-court playhouse of the Restoration this area became the pit, the fashionable found their seats there, and Samuel Pepys was willing and proud to stake his claim to a pit-bench, before hurrying to the next tavern for a mid-day meal. Even in Garrick's day playgoers of quality vied for a seat in the pit, content to rub shoulders with butcher or barber to see Garrick play Lear.

By the outset of the nineteenth century, however, butcher and barber had driven their fashionable clients from the pit to the boxes, or in many cases out of the playhouse altogether. The 'Old Price' riots which inaugurated John Philip Kemble's reign at the rebuilt Covent Garden in 1809 mark the triumph of mob-rule in the English theatre. It had been troubled with numerous riots before, but such troubles had either involved personalities, before and behind the curtain, or nationalities, as in the anti-French riots which beset Drury Lane in 1755. In 1809, however, theatre-rioting became a species of class-war: foremost among the grievances of the rioters was Kemble's conversion of the third tier into boxes to shelter the gentry driven from the pit, and the rise in price of admission to the pit from 3s. 6d. to 4s. So effective and varied were the means of protest adopted by the rioters that for sixty-seven nights not a word of the entertainment offered by the Company could be heard in the theatre. Ultimately Kemble had to concede the substance of their demands, and make an abject apology for good measure. Small wonder that for the next fifty years polite society quitted the theatre for the opera house and the play for the novel. Their gradual return to the playhouse will be a main theme of this study, but it was a process that could not be accelerated. The Bancrofts' attempt to complete it by abolishing the last surviving pit-benches in favour of orchestra-stalls at the Haymarket in 1880 provoked a first-night demonstration. The spirit of the O.P. Rioters died hard.

That spirit had already made itself felt in the Georgian theatre. Playgoing habits underwent significant changes under the Hanoverians. The early afternoon performances of the Restoration theatre had presupposed a wholly leisured audience of independent income. Even in Queen Anne's day a five o'clock curtain must have largely excluded the working man from the theatre. But before the eighteenth century was far advanced the playbills were announcing that the entertainment was 'to commence at six' and around six it commenced for another century and a half. The patron who could not get to the theatre by six was admitted at eight for half-price, and since the barber's appetite was larger than his courtier-client's, a farce or Harlequinade had to be added to the main piece, so the performance lasted for four or even five hours. The famous encounter at Drury Lane in 1817 between Edmund Kean and the newly 'discovered' Junius Brutus Booth, who rashly accepted an offer to play Iago to Kean's Othello, was only part of a bill which included, besides *Othello*, 'a new pastoral ballet, composed by Mr. Byrne, called *Patrick's Return*', and for good measure *The Follies of a Day*, Holcroft's version of *The Marriage of Figaro*. But the bill at Drury Lane was meagre compared with those offered at some of the newer theatres. At Sadler's Wells in 1825, for instance, the following was promised:

The amusements will consist of a romantic tale of mysterious horror and broad grin, never acted, called the *Enchanted Girdles, or Winki the Witch and the Ladies of Samarkand*. A most whimsical burletta, which sends people home perfectly exhausted from uninterrupted risibility,

4

called *The Lawyer, The Jew and the Yorkshireman* with, by request of 75 distinguished families, and a party of 5, that never to be sufficiently praised pantomime, called *Magic in Two Colours, or Fairy Blue and Fairy Red, or Harlequin and the Marble Rock*. It would be perfectly superfluous for any man in his senses to attempt anything more than the mere announcement in recommendation of the above unparalleled representations, so attractive in themselves as to threaten a complete monopoly of the qualities of the magnet; and though the proprietors were to talk nonsense for an hour, they could not assert a more important truth than that they possess the only Wells from which you may draw wine, three shillings and sixpence a full quart. Those whose important avocations prevent their coming at the commencement will be admitted for half price at half past eight. Ladies and gentlemen who are not judges of the superior entertainments announced are respectfully requested to bring as many as possible with them who are. N.B.—A full moon during the week.[1]

Probably the ladies and gentlemen whose taste was so roughly dismissed contrived to bring with them, not a companion but a store of vegetables.

On the provincial theatre the pattern of change in the course of the eighteenth century, though different, was no less marked. That the tradition of aristocratic patronage of the strolling player did not survive the Interregnum is suggested by such evidence of his condition as has appeared. The close-knit society of the Restoration period found its theatrical entertainment at the London playhouse rather than at its own country seats; and for the next hundred years the strolling player must have had a furtive, even persecuted, existence, acting where he could, what he could, for such poor rewards as an aiding and abetting audience could provide. With the passing of the Licensing Act of 1737 even a well-disposed Justice of the Peace could not protect the player from the greed and malice of the Common Informer. At last the squire and the shopkeeper picked up the patron's mantle discarded by the nobleman. With the issue of Royal patents to a number of provincial theatres after 1750 the country actor found himself again secure from interference, and this security seems soon to have spread to

[1] Playbill printed in Hone's *Every Day Book* (1841) and quoted by J. W. Cunliffe in *Modern English Playwrights* (New York, 1927), p. 2.

playhouses not entitled to call themselves Theatres Royal. The opening of the new century saw the provincial theatre in process of reorganization; for the squire was withdrawing his support, and the days of the small country theatre were numbered. But in the swiftly-growing industrial areas the factory-workers clamoured for entertainment, and it was in such towns that the provincial player of the nineteenth century earned his pay. Mob-rule was established in the provinces, no less than in the capital.

This increase of popular support made its most noticeable mark on the size and shape of the playhouse. When Wren had laid down the pattern of the Restoration theatre with his designs for Dorset Garden in 1671 and Drury Lane in 1674, he had not forgotten its origin in a tennis-court. The intimacy of his Drury Lane depended as much on its overall length, 112 feet, as on the disposition of proscenium-doors and an apron-stage projecting 17 feet into the auditorium. Although much altered and extended, it was the shell of Wren's Drury Lane which Garrick handed over to Sheridan's keeping in 1776. But by 1791 the pressure of popular playgoing imposed an intolerable strain on the old building, which was then demolished. The vast new building erected in its place and opened in 1794 embodied all the characteristics of the new theatre. Provided with five tiers instead of the former three, the seating capacity has been estimated at over 3,500, and the depth of the stage, 92 feet, was only 20 feet short of the overall length of Wren's Drury Lane. Since Covent Garden, originally built by John Rich in 1732, was also greatly enlarged in 1792 by Henry Holland, the architect of Drury Lane, the transformation of the theatrical scene was complete. That scene was soon to suffer another change, for in September 1808 the shell of Rich's Covent Garden was burnt down, as was the magnificent new Drury Lane in February 1809, so that for much of that year both London's great playhouses were in ruins. The pattern of the new theatre was soon restored, however. Both the new Covent Garden, to which the O.P. Rioters gave a baptism of clamour, and the new Drury Lane, finally rebuilt in 1812 through the exertions of Samuel Whitbread, the brewer, held audiences of over 3,000.

This great increase of capacity was achieved as much by internal arrangement as by overall dimensions. The principle of

the tiered box still held, and the overhanging balcony has not
yet been traced earlier than at the Adelphi Theatre of the 1820s.
But the number of tiers multiplied above the two or three of the
Georgian playhouse to four, five, and even six. Moreover, the
shape of the theatre was changing in addition to its size: the
elongated horseshoe which was the Georgian playhouse's inheritance from the Restoration tennis-court gave place to the
familiar near-circle of the Victorian theatre. Such a change in
ground-plan not only provided space for further boxes in each
tier, but, more importantly, increased the provision of pit-
benches. It was the pit-benches, too, which took possession of
the space yielded by the retreating apron-stage, a retreat which
completed the process of attrition long practised on the proscenium-doors and balconies. These survivals of the Elizabethan
stage façade had played an important part in the Restoration
theatre, Davenant's playhouse in Lincoln's Inn Fields having
three doors and balconies on either side of the proscenium. The
growth of the Georgian audience had gradually engulfed the
additional units, but so long as the apron-stage remained an integral part of the acting area, one door on each side provided
the access essential to the staging of the play. Now, with the
gradual withdrawal of the action behind the proscenium-arch,
the proscenium-door lost its function. Its last use was for players
taking calls at the end of the performance, and eventually it disappeared altogether. The actors at Drury Lane in 1812, miss-
ing the familiar contact with their audience, called for the proscenium-doors to be restored. Their cry was taken up by James
and Horatio Smith in their *Rejected Addresses*, parodying the
unsuccessful entries in the competition for an address to be
spoken at the opening of the new theatre. The Smiths put forward the ghost of Dr. Johnson as the actors' advocate:

The children of Thespis are general in their censure of the architect in
having placed the locality of exit at such a distance from the oily irra-
diators which now dazzle the eyes of him who addresses you. I am,
cries the queen of terrors, robbed of my fair proportions. When the
king killing Thane hints to the breathless auditory the murders he
means to perpetrate in the castle of Macduff 'ere my purpose cool', so
vast is the interval he has to travel before he can escape from the stage,
that his purpose has even time to freeze. Your condition, cries the

muse of smiles, is hard, but it is cygnet's down in comparison with mine. The peerless peer of capers and congées has laid it down as a rule that the best good thing uttered by the morning visitor should conduct him rapidly to the doorway, last impressions vying in durability with first. But when on this boarded elongation it falls to my lot to say a good thing: to ejaculate 'Keep moving', or to chaunt 'hic hoc horum genitivo', many are the moments that must elapse ere I can hide myself from public vision in the recesses of O.P. or P.S.

. . . Let the actor consider the line of exit as that line beyond which he should not soar in quest of spurious applause; let him reflect that in proportion as he advances to the lamps, he recedes from nature, that the truncheon of Hotspur acquires no additional charm from encountering the cheek of beauty in the stage box.[1]

For a time the actors had their way and the proscenium-doors at Drury Lane were restored. But the tide of theatrical presentation was flowing strongly away from the audience and no body of actors could long hold it back. What changes were effected in the fields of staging and acting must be considered later.

'Major' and 'Minor' Houses

For comparison between the old and the new theatre Drury Lane and Covent Garden, the two 'patent' playhouses, naturally suggest themselves. In the public mind, if not in strict law, it was in these foundations that the patents granted by Charles II to the King's Men under Killigrew and the Duke's Men under Davenant came to rest, though Davenant's patent wandered far before John Rich finally opened Covent Garden in 1732 and completed the diarchy of the Georgian theatre. By the end of the eighteenth century that diarchy, though reinforced by several Licensing Acts, had been seriously challenged. The King's Theatre in the Haymarket, long established as the home of opera and ballet, could point to a licence granted in 1705 by Queen Anne. The Little Theatre in the Haymarket, a challenge to authority from its opening in 1720 and particularly vigorous under Fielding, finally earned for its manager, Samuel Foote, a patent dating from 1766 to present plays during the summer recess. This privilege subsequent managers exercised so widely

---

[1] Horace and James Smith: *Rejected Addresses* (London, 1812), p. 57.

that eventually the Haymarket's seasons fell little short of those at the other patent theatres.

Another challenge to patented privilege came from places of entertainment which, like Sadler's Wells pleasure gardens or Astley's Amphitheatre, on Surreyside, near Westminster Bridge, originally made no claim to present plays. Lying mostly on the eastern or southern fringes of the capital, these centres served the needs of the rapidly increasing workers of the new industrial age. Those needs also increased rapidly; by 1765 the Sadler's Wells grounds comprised some sort of theatre and by 1782 Astley's had a rival in the Royal Circus, soon to become the Surrey Theatre. It is clear that the entertainment provided was at first of the simplest, consisting largely of dancing, tumbling, and riding. Accounts survive of the crude banners brought on to eke out the action. If the management was often short on spelling and ungallantly scrawled: 'Blow up the courser's aunt' for 'Blow up the corsair's haunt', or 'Lead her to the bridal halter', the audience were probably little the wiser. But these entertainments could not remain for ever mute. Spectacle calls for song, if not speech. The amphitheatres on Surreyside began to sport stages at one end of the ring on which essential episodes could be played out between the 'turns'. Such innovations disgusted a true-bred rider like the famous Ducrow of Astley's, who put the playwright and his dialogue severely in their place:

'Cut the cackle and come to the 'osses. I'll show you how to cut it. You say "Yield thee, Englishman!" Then you (indicating the other) answer "Never!" Then you say "Obstinate Englishman, you die." Then you both fights. There, that settles the matter; the audience will understand you a deal better, and the poor 'osses won't catch cold while you're jawing.'[1]

Nevertheless the audience demanded its cackle, and that demand posed a difficult legal problem: were the patent theatres' privileges infringed? As early as 1787 John Palmer had opened his Royalty Theatre with a full-blown performance of *As You Like It.* His site, Wellclose Square, near Goodman's Fields, was already established as a centre of theatrical revolt

---

[1] H. Barton Baker: *The London Stage* (London, 1904), p. 387.

through the building of at least one theatre nearby before the Licensing Act of 1737. Lying outside the City of Westminster's boundaries, it was not subject to the Lord Chamberlain. But the patent theatres appealed to the City of London magistrates, the appropriate authority, and Palmer was silenced. The pieces presented by these new minor theatres, therefore, constituted a wider though less direct challenge to theatrical monopoly. The need which they met gave birth to the term 'burletta', a form of entertainment which was held not to infringe the patent theatres' exclusive right to present legitimate drama. The task of finding a definition for burletta, however, defeated even George Colman the younger, when Reader of Plays to the Lord Chamberlain. He first defined a burletta as 'a drama in rhyme which is entirely musical; a short piece of recitation and singing, wholly accompanied more or less by the orchestra',[1] and when pressed by his superior to be more explicit could only falter:

I think that you may fairly say that it is easy sometimes to say what is not a Burletta, tho' it may be difficult to define what a Burletta is, according to the legal acceptation of the Term, Burletta, Five or six songs in a Piece of one Act for example, where the songs make a natural part of the Piece (*and not forced into an acting piece*, to qualify it as a Burletta) may be perhaps considered so far a Burletta, as not to be refused by the Chamberlain, tho' there always remains the question, whether a Burletta must not be in verse, and the whole sung, not *said*; which makes the question dangerous.[2]

Clearly music and action were integral parts; but before long spoken dialogue was not only admitted but began to predominate. In the 1830s the inclusion of five songs per act was held to redeem any amount of spoken dialogue, and by the early 1840s an occasional chord on the piano seems to have been all that was required. Thus modified, pieces from the regular repertory could be and were played at the minor theatres. Drury Lane actors like Edmund Kean and Elliston appeared on Surreyside, and the Lord Chamberlain began to issue burletta licences not only to plays but to theatres opened within his jurisdiction, like the Olympic and the Adelphi.

[1] *Random Records* (London, 1830), p. 146.
[2] Note preserved at the Lord Chamberlain's Office and printed by Allardyce Nicoll in *Early Nineteenth Century Drama* (Cambridge, 1955), p. 138.

The patent theatres' monopoly of legitimate drama had, in fact, become unworkable. It was not merely that the inhabitants of London's new districts demanded their own theatres and their own entertainment. The playgoers of Drury Lane and Covent Garden demanded identical entertainment. Legitimate drama, the repertory of proven plays which with occasional additions had served the Georgian theatre, yielded to the demand for spectacle and sensation. Pantomime and ballad-opera were already firmly established at the two patent theatres; now melodrama, equestrian drama, aquatic drama, and every kind of 'show' conquered even these sanctuaries of English drama. The situation was well summed up by Planché when, in *The Drama's Levée*, he made Legitimate Drama and Illegitimate Drama the sons of Mother Drama, who was beginning to wish they had never been born:

Enter LEGITIMATE DRAMA *in a Roman toga.*

L. DRAMA. He whom they own Legitimate is here.

DRAMA. You naughty boy! when I'm so very poorly;
  You have been fighting with your brother surely.

L. DRAMA. I have; because of him I can't get fed,
  Whilst he is almost sick with gingerbread.

DRAMA. Will you ne'er cease this ruinous debate?
  Where's that audacious Illegitimate?

(*Enter* ILLEGITIMATE DRAMA *in a dress half harlequin and half melo-dramatic.*)

I. DRAMA. Behold! (*Striking an attitude.*)

DRAMA. Unnatural son!

I. DRAMA Is't thus I'm styled?
  I always thought I was your *natural* child.

L. DRAMA. He puns! He'll pick a pocket the next minute!

I. DRAMA. I shan't pick yours, because there's nothing in it!

L. DRAMA. That is because you robb'd me long ago!

I. DRAMA. Come, who began to rob, I'd like to know?
  When I was quite a child in leading string,
  Before I'd learnt to speak, or anything
  But dance my dolls to music, didn't you
  Begin to vow they were your playthings too?
  Stole from the nursery of my best hopes,
  My rocking horses and my skipping ropes,

11

And took my harlequins from loss to save you,
And now you blame the *punches* that I gave you.

They continue to bicker until DRAMA sadly concludes:

Unless between themselves they soon agree,
Those boys, I feel, will be the death of me!
They so confound me that though I'm their mother,
I vow I sometimes can't tell one from t'other.

The effects of this change of taste on dramatic writing will be considered later. Its effect on the organization of the English theatre was to undermine the prestige of the two patent houses. Far from inhibiting the actions of the minor theatres, they were themselves inhibited by the obligations they had inherited of presenting at least some legitimate drama. Macready's tenure of Covent Garden from 1837 to 1839 and of Drury Lane from 1841 to 1843, and the Mathewses' management of Covent Garden from 1839 to 1842 represented a last attempt to preserve the traditions of the patent theatres. Powerless to check their rivals' growth, the proprietors of Drury Lane and Covent Garden had also to tolerate new theatres springing up all over London. In outlying districts vast amphitheatres appeared, such as the Pavilion, Whitechapel, in 1828; the Standard, Shoreditch, in 1835: and the Eagle Saloon in the City Road, with its Grecian Theatre, about 1838. South of the Thames the Royal Circus had become the Surrey Theatre in 1810, and the Coburg, opened in 1816 and complimenting by its title Princess Charlotte's husband, tactfully changed its name to the Royal Victoria in 1833, four years before the accession. Now the minors began an invasion of the inmost citadel. After housing the burnt-out Drury Lane company in 1809, the Lyceum, at which entertainments had been staged even before 1800, received a licence which put it, as a summer theatre, on much the same footing as the Haymarket. The Olympic was built as an outpost of Astley's in 1806, and farther along the Strand appeared the Sans Pareil (soon to be the Adelphi) also in 1806, and in 1832 the Strand Theatre itself. Then in 1835 the St. James's was built not far from the Lord Chamberlain's office at St. James's Palace. The veil of the temple had been rent and not even legal pretence could conceal the fact. Several attempts to abolish the patents were made before, in 1832, a Bill to this effect passed the Commons, only to be thrown out by the House of Lords, with their traditional fondness for lost causes. In 1843, however, the Theatre Regulation Act abolished whatever legal basis the monopoly of the patent theatres had possessed. Soothsayers prophesied a further outbreak of theatre-building, but in fact the demand was already satiated. Between 1843 and 1860 not a single important new theatre was opened in London, for it needed another change in playgoing habits to bring about that development. Meanwhile Covent Garden was permanently transformed into an opera house (in 1847) and Drury Lane drifted uncertainly towards melodrama and pantomime.

If the opponents of the Theatre Regulation Act proved inaccurate in their predictions, its advocates certainly did not see all their dreams come true. There was little change in the bills of the former minor theatres after 1843, partly because of the inconsistency with which the monopoly had been interpreted, but more because the type of entertainment offered by them before 1843—melodrama and burlesque—was what their audiences continued to demand. One immediate consequence of the abolition of the patents, all the more remarkable for its uniqueness, was the management from 1844 to 1862 of Sadler's Wells by Samuel Phelps, a disciple of Macready. In this theatrical wilderness Phelps presented a chiefly classical repertory, handsomely mounted, which ultimately covered all but four of Shakespeare's plays. His courage eventually inspired a transpontine rival, William Creswick, whose performances of Shakespeare at the Surrey in the 1850s marked another gain for the legitimate drama. More spectacular was the management of Charles Kean at the Princess's from 1850 to 1859. The contribution of this management to the literature and production methods of the Victorian theatre will require later examination. Perhaps its chief importance lay in the attraction to an insignificant playhouse of an audience which regularly included the Royal family, to see a repertory combining Shakespeare with 'gentlemanly' melodrama. Kean's achievement was a definite reversal of the trend of Victorian playgoing.

Staging Methods

The staple fare of the early Victorian theatre was spectacle, and spectacle, whether in the form of melodrama, opera, ballet, extravaganza, pantomime, or Shakespearean pageant, demanded a far more elaborate style of staging than the Georgian theatre had afforded. The pattern of English staging had been firmly established by Restoration practice. In superseding the Elizabethan playhouse the indoor Restoration theatre with its changeable scenery had naturally borrowed largely from the Court Masque of the early Stuarts. From the Masque was taken the principle of shutters, opening centrally and moving in grooves set above the stage and in the stage itself. Both interior and exterior scenes employed wings to complete the setting, and varied the shutters with an occasional scene 'in relief', made up of wings, cut-outs, and a backcloth. The use of backcloths, however, was governed by the lack of flying-space above the stage, a feature inherited from the tennis-court theatres of the early Restoration period.

The system of shutters or 'flats' in grooves, universally adopted in the Georgian theatre, had the advantage of great flexibility, and by employing visual scene-changing before the audience's eyes it materially speeded up the tempo of the play. By standardizing the position of pieces of scenery according to the grooves they occupied, it must also greatly have reduced rehearsal time, and thus made possible the constant changes of bill which survived from the Georgian into the Victorian era. In the course of the eighteenth century, too, several refinements were added to the established system of staging: in particular, sunken footlights, giving greater control; directional lighting by means of oil lamps placed in the wings; and coloured lighting by wrapping the lamps with coloured materials. Moreover, several artists of the late eighteenth century extended the possibilities of the scene in relief. The Alsatian artist, De Loutherbourg, who worked for Garrick at Drury Lane, was particularly active in employing cut-out profiles, raking-pieces set at various angles, and elaborate backcloths—an alternative arrangement to flats and wings, increasingly distinguished by the term 'Set Scene'. It was these means which William Capon at the end of the century employed on the more thorough and detailed setting of Shakespeare's History plays, exploiting the fashionable taste for Gothic in his designs for the Kembles at Drury Lane and later at Covent Garden.

Nevertheless, the scenery employed in the Georgian theatre was essentially a background for the actors. Although it was possible to make entrances from the wings, the principal access, so long as the apron-stage remained the main acting area, lay through the proscenium-doors. Even the detailed settings of De Loutherbourg and Capon, therefore, should be visualized as set in the framework of the Georgian proscenium-doors and boxes, the Georgian apron-stage, and above all the Georgian audience itself. It was this blending of styles which made acceptable Garrick's playing Lear in a tie-wig and brocaded coat, or Othello in a suit of English regimentals. For this reason the audience saw no contradiction in an actor's taking pains with the details of his own costume at the expense of the company's ensemble.

The nineteenth-century audience's taste for the spectacular called for two main developments of Georgian stagecraft. One was the further modification of the fixed flats and grooves system in favour of a more varied system of settings, better suited to the elaborate pieces to be mounted. The development of the scene in relief, already noted, entailed far more flying-space above the stage than the Georgian playhouse had afforded, for the Georgian compromise of rolling or tumbling backcloths did not meet the full demands of spectacular drama. Ultimately, too, spectacle called for different acting levels to be built up on the stage, although the traditional grooves seem to have checked this development, at least until the middle of the century. The second major development necessary was the integration of all the components of the stage-picture within a single, neutral framework. To this process the disappearance of the apron-stage and with it the proscenium-doors contributed greatly. On the unification of the stage-picture itself two forces were at work: one was the desire for greater artistic consistency in setting and costume, the other was the inspiration of archæology, the urge to wrap both stage and players in historically authentic clothing. A trend towards unity of style has already been noted in the work of De Loutherbourg and Capon.

It found fuller expression during Macready's management of Covent Garden (1837–9) and Drury Lane (1841–3). Macready's initiative in purging Shakespeare's text of 'improvements' (especially by restoring the Fool in *King Lear*) and purging the auditorium of scandalous conduct, has been fully recognized. Less acknowledgement has been made to his innovations in production, aided by the artist Clarkson Stanfield, whose skill in panorama was employed on the elaborate dioramas which Macready used to illustrate, for instance, the transitions from England to France in *Henry V*. Stanfield, pre-eminently a seascape painter, provided many imposing backcloths and clearly brought not only his powers as a painter but also his mechanical ingenuity to the production of the opera *Acis and Galatea*, in 1842, particularly to the scene representing the coast of Sicily, in which the seas delighted the audience

. . . as they come swelling towards us, the waves breaking as they come, the last billow actually tumbling over and over with spray and foam upon the shore, and then receding with the noise of water over stones and shells, to show the hard, wet sand, and, in its due time, roll and break again.[1]

The *Examiner* critic may have been of an impressionable nature, but even his imagination cannot obscure mechanical and scenic dexterity of a high order. No one was more conscious than Macready of the dangers which might spring from the Pandora's box which the new theatre with its elaborate equipment constituted. In the last years of his acting career, before his retirement in 1851, he turned his back on management, concerning himself only with his own performance. His horror of Charles Kean's productions at the Princess's, though much of it may have sprung from the vanity which he never conquered, also arose from a sense of guilt. As he later confessed to Lady Pollock, when discussing Kean's production of *The Winter's Tale*:

'Evidently,' said he, 'the accessories swallow up the poetry and the action.'

[1] Reprinted by William Archer in *William Charles Macready* (London, 1890), p. 99.

'True,' I said, seeking to comfort him; 'but don't take it to heart. You are out of it all now.'

'Do you know,' said he, 'why I take it so much to heart? It is because I feel myself in some measure responsible. I . . . have set an example which is accompanied with great peril, for the public is willing to have the magnificence without the tragedy, and the poet is swallowed up in display. When I read such a description as this of the production of a great drama, I am touched with a feeling of something like remorse. Is it possible, I ask myself. Did *I* hold the torch? Did *I* point out the path?'[1]

Aptly enough, it was a professional antiquarian, James Robinson Planché, ultimately Somerset Herald as well as playwright and designer, who gave the antiquarian movement in the theatre its lead, with his work for Charles Kemble's *King John* in 1823, and in his *History of English Costume*, published in 1834. But the antiquarian spirit in the Victorian theatre is most closely associated with the designs of Frederick Lloyds, Thomas Grieve, and William Telbin for the productions of Charles Kean at the Princess's from 1850 to 1859. Himself a Fellow of the Society of Antiquaries, Kean's passion for authenticity was most generously lavished on his Shakespearean productions, to which the playbills with their elaborate footnotes pay honourable if somewhat ponderous tribute; but his enthusiasm also extended to sumptuous productions of Byron's *Sardanapalus*, Boucicault's *Faust and Marguerite*, and Dumas's *Corsican Brothers*. Kean's critics have declared that his antiquarianism became an end in itself, citing his substitution in *The Winter's Tale* of Bythinia (on which information was available) for a Bohemia that existed only in Shakespeare's imagination. Doubtless, too, this antiquarianism was sometimes frustrated, as when his wife, Ellen Tree, insisted on wearing a crinoline beneath Hermione's flowing robes; and often misapplied, for there was no suggestion at the Princess's of presenting Shakespeare's plays as the author conceived them.[2] What is easily forgotten is that the Keans devoted themselves to restoring the prestige and standards of a National Theatre, such as had inter-

[1] Lady Pollock: *Macready As I Knew Him* (London, 1884), pp. 83–4.
[2] Shortly before Kean took over the Princess's, some attempt at Elizabethan staging had been introduced by Benjamin Webster in his production of *The Taming of the Shrew* at the Haymarket in 1844.

mittently flourished at the patent theatres before 1843. The unselfishness of that aim and its large measure of achievement was handsomely acknowledged when the Queen entrusted Kean with the supervision of a number of theatrical entertainments at Windsor Castle. Kean's shortcomings, his pedantry, and his mistaking over-decoration for truly imaginative staging, were characteristic of his age; so were his merits, his sense of duty, and his extreme respectability, though these were qualities less often found in the Victorian theatre.

The Interior Scene

These developments in staging were devoted to the presentation of spectacular drama, for this was the ruling taste of the Victorian audience. Yet, less obviously, such developments were preparing the way for the more modest interior scene, characteristic of the second half of the century. Probably the most valuable of the many contributions to scenic reform made by Madame Vestris and her husband, Charles Mathews the younger, was their furnishing the interior scene with the attention lavished elsewhere on spectacle and historical accuracy. Vestris had made her reputation and started a great deal of gossip as a singer and dancer. Mathews was exclusively a light comedian. Their main concern was for consistent style and taste rather than authenticity. During her management of the Olympic from 1831 to 1838 Vestris was limited both by the terms of her burletta licence and by her widely acclaimed gifts to light entertainments, the most characteristic of which were the fairy extravaganzas devised for her by Planché. She was not precluded, however, from staging short comedies, mostly from the French, to which—trivial though they were—she gave the same elegant and elaborate staging for which her extravaganzas were noted. The drawing-rooms represented on the Olympic stage were certainly not the conventional painted flats and wings of the Georgian theatre. Whether her reforms extended to a complete box-set is hard to judge. The critic of the *Examiner* noted in 1833 that their 'more perfect enclosure gives the appearance of a private chamber, infinitely better than the old contrivance of wings', but the etched frontispiece to *The Conquering Game* by W. B. Bernard, the play in question, is

3A. *The Future Prince of Wales's*

3B. *The Gaiety in* 1869

insufficient to confirm that this 'more perfect enclosure' involved flats entirely surrounding the scene and a ceiling cloth as well.[1]

Certainly the stage in such scenes was fully and handsomely furnished. Charles Mathews himself noted that the old principle of providing only essential furniture had been firmly rejected: 'Drawing-rooms were fitted up like drawing-rooms, and furnished with care and taste, two chairs no longer indicated that two persons were to be seated.'[2] Not only were chairs supplied, but also floors and walls covered with all the prerequisites of leisured and luxurious living. It has even been affirmed by the theatre's surviving stage-manager, admittedly looking back with the nostalgia of thirty years, that the stage of the Olympic was divided into six traps, so that much of its elaborate furnishing could be pre-set, thereby anticipating one of the most publicized innovations of the French actor, Charles Fechter, at the Lyceum in the 1860s.[3] The reforms introduced at the Olympic were carried on, wherever appropriate, when Vestris and Mathews transferred to Covent Garden, and their elaborate furnishing of the interiors in *London Assurance* received an acclamation proportionate to a patent theatre and to the success of the play. It was their ill-luck that they could find no Robertson to evolve a new school of comedy on which to lavish their scenic reforms.

As sponsors of Shakespeare, Vestris and Mathews inevitably suffered in their own day from comparison with Macready, whom they succeeded at Covent Garden, and in retrospect from the competition of Charles Kean, whom they preceded by a dozen years. Neither was in the least suited to Shakespearean acting and their productions of *Love's Labour's Lost*, *The Merry Wives of Windsor*, *A Midsummer Night's Dream* and *Romeo and Juliet* contributed nothing to their personal reputations. Even if these productions had been staged without taste or intelligence, Vestris and Mathews would be entitled to great credit for having restored *Love's Labour's Lost* to the London stage after two hundred years' neglect, and for observing Shakespeare's

[1] This view is put forward by Leo Waitzkin in *The Witch of Wych Street: A Study of the Theatrical Reforms of Madame Vestris* (Cambridge, Mass., 1933), p. 55.
[2] *Life of Charles James Mathews* (London, 1879), Vol. II, p. 76.
[3] See *Stage Reminiscences, by an Old Stager* (London, 1866), p. 70.

dénouement in *Romeo and Juliet* after a century of Garrick's 'happy' ending. In fact they staged Shakespeare with the same artistry and elegance, coupled with Planché's scholarship, for which all their work was notable. Their part in the development of Shakespearean production has been unduly neglected.

Stage Machinery and Lighting

The widespread changes in staging-methods effected during the Victorian period were made possible partly by the changes in theatre architecture already noted and partly by the development of theatrical machinery. The stage-traps of the Elizabethan and Georgian eras were greatly elaborated in the nineteenth century to include 'Vampire' traps, 'Corsican' traps, and 'star' traps, all of which contributed not only to the effect of spectacular drama but also to the pantomime and musical stage.[1] The elaborate scenery of the Victorian theatre also called for greatly increased flying-space above the stage, with a complex counterweight system, and this in its turn fostered one of the most popular features of Victorian staging. Divine intervention from above, so familiar a feature of the Stuart masque, had not been wholly absent from the Georgian theatre, though the ubiquitous grooves and the lack of overhead space must have presented serious obstacles. Now the new theatre presented a way round these obstacles, and flying, not only of scenery but also of actors by the dozen, became a pre-requisite of pantomime, of melodrama, and of Shakespeare. Ellen Terry, as a child of ten, took part in one of the most famous flying effects carried out by Charles Kean at the Princess's—the vision of angels before Queen Katherine in *Henry VIII*—and recorded that her ethereal appearance was largely a prelude to her ensuing sickness.[2] Equally notable was the angelic interposition after Marguerite's death in *Faust and Marguerite*, an effect described by *Punch* with the malice characteristic of its treatment of Kean:

The musical contest of the soul of Marguerite between the demons under the stage and the angels over it was somewhat bold upon a

[1] The Vampire and Corsican traps (both deriving their names from the plays in which they were introduced) gave the impression of entry through a wall and across the stage respectively. The star trap was made up of hinged segments and thus allowed the actor to be projected from below without the tell-tale withdrawal of the trap-covering.

[2] *Ellen Terry's Memoirs* (London, 1933), p. 20.

moral English public, but when the soul of Marguerite in white muslin borne by angels in satin petticoats was carried to heaven ('without wires,' cried a critic hysterical with admiration) the delight of the gods was perfect.

By far the most important mechanical development in the new theatre was the replacement of oil- and candle-light by gas-lighting, which had been adopted by the two principal London theatres by 1820, and although not adopted by the Haymarket, for instance, until 1843, was nevertheless widely installed both in London and beyond. The flexibility of gas-lighting and above all the control which its single source afforded the stage-manager, must have greatly embellished the spectacular drama. Such effects as the German Prince Pückler-Muskau saw at Covent Garden in 1826 could scarcely have been achieved with oil-lighting, however skilfully used:

At the rising of the curtain a thick mist covers the stage and gradually rolls off. This is remarkably well managed by means of fine gauze. In the dim light we distinguish a little cottage, the dwelling of a sorceress; in the background a lake surrounded by mountains, some of whose peaks are clothed with snow. All as yet is misty and indistinct; the sun then rises triumphantly, chases the morning dews, and the hut with the village in the distance now appears in perfect outline.[1]

When to this control the development of limelight (used experimentally by Macready and perfected by Charles Kean) added concentration, the powers of gas-lighting were complete. By burning a stick of lime in a gas-jet it was possible to direct a single, brilliant beam on to an individual character or feature on the stage, and to vary the limelight with a full range of coloured glass. That limelight had advantages even over the modern spotlight was maintained by later actor-managers like Henry Irving, who insisted on transporting gas-equipment to theatres already equipped with electricity, and Ellen Terry insisted that the absence with limelight of a harshly defined circle of light produced more natural effects than electricity could achieve. No doubt the full possibilities of gas-lighting were not appreciated in an auditorium which continued to be partly lit during the performance until late in the century. Doubtless, too, its advantages were gained at a high price in the loss of lives and

[1] *A Tour in England of a German Prince* (London, 1832), III, Letter 10.

buildings through fire. Nevertheless, it is above all the incandescence of gas-lighting which plays upon the Victorian theatre.

Acting Styles

All these developments brought about a general broadening and often a coarsening of acting styles. One factor working to this end was the theatre's rapid expansion and decentralization. The Georgian playhouse, a provincial Theatre Royal no less than Drury Lane or Covent Garden, was occupied by a semi-permanent company, presenting a repertory of familiar plays in rotation, interspersed with an occasional novelty. The stability of the Georgian theatre is well reflected in its 'possession of parts', a widely recognized principle that an actor had the exclusive right, so long as he remained with the company, to a part in which he had established himself. This stability, allied to formal and largely standardized methods of staging, enabled actors to give performances, both personal and collective, which adhered strictly to standards and conventions long established by tradition. The lack of adequate rehearsal and 'production', as understood in the modern theatre, and the frequency of 'guest' appearances by London actors at provincial theatres, did not upset these standards and conventions—indeed, no performance at all would have been possible without their observance.

The new theatre and the new drama, however, called for major changes in acting methods. Clearly many effects, telling in a playhouse that held 500, would be totally lost before an audience of 3,000, especially when the gradual disappearance of the apron-stage forced the actor farther and farther within the scene. The spectacular drama also demanded of its performers very different qualities from the 'old' comedies and tragedies. The long apprenticeship required in the Georgian theatre disappeared, for actors were often chosen for their acrobatic rather than histrionic gifts. It will be remembered from Dickens that Mrs. Vincent Crummles first caught the eye of her future husband by her sense of balance:

'The very first time I saw that admirable woman, Johnson,' said Mr. Crummles, drawing a little nearer, and speaking in the tone of confidential friendship, 'she stood upon her head on the butt-end of a spear, surrounded with blazing fireworks.'

22

'You astonish me!' said Nicholas.

'*She* astonished *me!*' returned Mr. Crummles with a very serious countenance. 'Such grace, coupled with such dignity! I adored her from that moment.'

In the instability and frequent bankruptcy of the early Victorian theatre, actors came and went with melancholy regularity. Though there were still outstanding performers, there can be little doubt that the general level of acting suffered. Equestrian and aquatic spectacle demanded little acting ability, and often it was not the human but the animal performer on whom the audience's attention fixed. Even with human actors, their freakish rather than their natural powers might commend them to the public, as with the numerous Infant Prodigies, amongst whom Master William Henry West Betty stands out for having caused the House of Commons to suspend a sitting in order to see him play Hamlet. With these child performances the surprising thing was not that they were done well but that they were done at all.

The back-stage staff, too, found themselves required to perform tasks far more onerous than their forebears. Edward Fitzball has left, in his autobiography, a good-tempered account of the effect on David Grove, stage-manager at the Lyceum, of the innovations for which Fitzball, as one of the most popular and prolific authors of melodrama, was responsible:

Poor Davy was one of the very old school; when actors and actresses sat around a table, and performed a whole comedy (the legitimate drama), when the actor made a hit with a twirl of *his* cane; and the actress with a twirl of *her* fan: Davy had a great horror, not of me, but of what he called my abominable introductions to the perfect upsetting of the regular business of the regular stage. In what he termed the *rational* scenes of the *rational* drama, he could sit quietly, in his stuffed chair, P.S., (something like the old Charlies, before the new police came in), and give the word, or ring up, or down, without stirring from his seat the whole evening; take a nap at intervals, and all went well. Now, thanks to my monstrous example, there was to run about the stage the whole night; to ring up this trap, to ring down that; signals to be made, with flags, as if one were working a telegraph, not a theatre.[1]

[1] *Thirty-five Years of a Dramatic Author's Life* (London, 1859), I, p. 222–3.

An account of the changes in acting styles brought about by the Victorian theatre can be safely attempted only in the most general terms; to explore further is speculation—fascinating but often fatal. A subjective account by an impressionable spectator of one of the most mercurial of human activities, an actor's performance, is open to the widest misinterpretation, and the Victorian era with its plethora of newspapers and periodicals further confuses the picture by sheer abundance of detail. The historian of acting presents his evidence but draws only the broadest conclusions. It is clear, for instance, that to their contemporaries Garrick and Mrs. Siddons, at least in her prime, conveyed more natural emotions and behaviour than their predecessors, however calculated the means they used. It is also clear that John Philip Kemble (and to some extent his numerous family) used a delivery and action formal enough to strike many spectators as declamatory and often monotonous. It is evident that Edmund Kean's most characteristic trait was the choice of certain lines to which, by abruptness of transition and intensity of expression, he gave overwhelming emphasis. 'To see him act is like reading Shakespeare by flashes of lightning,' wrote Coleridge, and it is still the most succinct account of his methods that survives.

No such clear picture exists of Macready, the first great Victorian actor. His portrait, especially in early manhood, shows a face markedly unfitted for heroic roles: large, flat, stern, even repellent. His greatest triumphs were often criticized, for audiences never surrendered to him as completely as to Garrick or Mrs. Siddons or even to Kean. Macready was physically and temperamentally incapable of playing comedy parts, save where his own temperament could be turned to comic ends, as in *Much Ado About Nothing*, or in the elder Colman's *The Jealous Wife*. But these defects were not without their compensations: his physique no less than his deeply religious, even mystical, mind contributed to that austere, even supernatural quality widely recognized in his acting and especially powerful when conveying the pathetic grandeur of his Macbeth and Lear as well as the long forgotten Virginius and Werner.

Macready's own records show that he despised the monotony of John Philip Kemble's delivery, and sought by varying his own pace and tone to give contrast and interest to his lines, an object so deliberately pursued that the 'Macready pause' remained in theatrical usage throughout the Victorian era and became in many critics' eyes a blemish in its creator. There is also ample evidence in his diaries that he sought by constant application to understand and feel his rôle, and by unflagging discipline to improve his means of conveying what he understood and felt. Few of his critics denied him consistency and lucidity in his interpretation, however much they quarrelled with the interpretation itself. Both in his intellectual approach to his parts, and in insisting on disciplined preparation, Macready was the forerunner of the dominant school of modern acting.

Beside Macready, the figure of Charles Kean is apt to seem insignificant. Handicapped by his father's shortness but denied his father's strikingly eloquent eyes, the younger Kean was further hindered by a poorly produced voice which he had no sooner mastered than another hazard beset him, in false teeth uncertainly fixed by suction. That he still contrived to hold his place in the front rank of actors is a tribute to his intelligence and discipline; nevertheless, it was only as a 'stage-manager' that Kean was outstanding. The contrast between Kean and Macready accurately reflects a transitional phase in the history of English acting. Even while Macready was thinking and feeling his way towards the modern actor's approach to his task, tragic acting could boast the triumph of traditionalists such as Charles Young or George Vandenhoff, actors in whom power of lung was substituted for subtlety of intelligence, and contemporary with the elaborate staging of Charles Kean were the successful tours of Barry Sullivan and G. V. Brooke, who required little more than three boards on which to tear their passion.

The size of the new theatres and taste of the new audiences forced on comic no less than tragic actors a broadening of style. Without exaggeration it would hardly have been possible for such favourites as Dowton or Liston to make their comic effects at all, and even Charles Lamb's idol, Joseph Munden, did not escape censure by the discerning on that score. In the disorder of the new theatre the wonder is not that 'gentlemanly comedy' almost disappeared, but that Elliston and Charles Kemble struggled so long to keep it alive. Nevertheless, those conditions tended inexorably to blunt comic acting, reducing it to a limited number of comic types, without subtlety or variation, in which the Farrens, father and son, all condemned to play old men from their youth, displayed at once the best and the worst of the system. English comic acting in the early Victorian era centred very largely on the Haymarket, of which two successive managers, Benjamin Webster and John Baldwin Buckstone, seemed to personify that acting in their own jovial personalities. Disdaining the task of interpretation, they could convulse an audience without completing a single line.

Probably Victorian acting was seen at its most characteristic not in tragedy or comedy, but in melodrama, the characteristic entertainment of the age. Melodrama demanded of its exponents a singular combination of athleticism and bravado which was instinctive rather than interpretative, but which bloomed profusely in the forcing-grounds of the minor theatres before the abolition of the Patents. T. P. Cooke, with his incomparable hornpipe, set the Jolly Jack Tar firmly amongst the gallery of theatrical types, and fathered the line of gallant heroes from which William Terriss and Fred Terry were descended. Theirs was acting to rouse the emotions without troubling the mind, and as such was admirably designed to carry the bulk of the Victorian audience into the gas-lit world of Victorian drama. Without some conception of the vigour and appeal of their acting it is impossible to account for the success of the countless threadbare melodramas, concocted by men happy in the knowledge of such methods and themselves willing victims of their magic.

Such efforts as were made in the first half of the nineteenth century to refine acting, especially the acting of comedy, are largely linked with the name of Mathews. The elder Charles Mathews was unlucky in his age, for as the contemporary of Liston and Munden he could find little support for his stand against the exaggeration of comic acting and against the comedian's timeless temptation to play his popular self, rather than interpret the untried creation of a fallible author. Thus the elder Mathews was happiest away from his fellow-actors, performing solo in his celebrated 'At Homes', which consisted of impersonations, not of prominent people as Foote had given before him, but of widely different characters of his own creation. Even though Mathews was forced by the taste of the time to draw these portraits more broadly than discriminating critics liked, the evidence that he discarded his own personality and assumed that of the character he presented is inescapable. Pückler-Muskau, for instance, noted:

Imperceptibly he passed from the narrative style to a perfectly dramatic performance in which with almost inconceivable talent and memory he placed before the eyes of his audience all that he had witnessed; while he so totally altered his face, speech, and whole exterior, with the rapidity of lightning, that one must have seen it to believe it possible.[1]

His son, Charles Mathews the younger, was luckier in his period. Even though the majority of London theatres exhibited the same exaggerated acting which had repelled his father, the younger Mathews, when deciding on a stage career in 1835, could look to one theatre at which some refinement of these excesses was already apparent. Madame Vestris had then been manager of the Olympic for four years, and her success there left the young actor in no doubt as to where his future lay:

The theatre for my *début* as an actor was chosen without a moment's hesitation. I had no passion for what was called the 'regular drama'. I had no respect for traditional acting, and had no notion of taking a 'line of business', as it is called. . . . The lighter phase of comedy, representing the more natural and less laboured school of modern life, and holding the mirror up to nature without regard to the conventionalities of the theatre, was the aim I had in view. The Olympic was then the only house where this could be achieved, and to the Olympic I at once attached myself.[2]

Having attached himself to the Olympic, he proceeded to attach himself to its manageress, marrying her in 1838, and pursuing his career by her side until her retirement shortly before her death in 1856.

[1] *A Tour in England of a German Prince*, III, Letter 4, 8 December 1826.
[2] *Life of Charles James Mathews*, Vol. II, p. 76.

The efforts of Vestris and Mathews to refine the acting of English comedy, like their reforms of staging, were subject to serious restraints. At the Olympic their choice of bill was still governed by the elusive but menacing terms of a burletta licence. Later at Covent Garden the size of the stage and house, no less than their responsibilities as Patentees, forced their hands. More serious, perhaps, was the differing scope of their respective talents, which largely precluded them from appearing in the same piece; for Vestris wisely chose to exploit in song and dance the voice and figure with which she was happily endowed, while Mathews excelled in the rôle of the engaging impostor whose presumption is matched only by his fluency.

Despite their difficulties, it is clear that both set an example to their company of delicacy and detail in their playing, which neither forced its effects nor sacrificed author to audience. Mathews, thinking understandably of his own field, recalled how this refinement of style was reflected in the costumes worn:

A claret-coloured coat, salmon-coloured trowsers with a broad black stripe, a sky-blue neck-cloth with large paste brooch, and a cut-steel eye-glass with a pink ribbon no longer marked the 'light comedy gentleman', and the public at once recognised and appreciated the change.[1]

The triumph of *London Assurance* as a 'comedy of modern life' is inexplicable, in view of the poverty of the text and the different line which Boucicault, the author, had to pursue for further success, unless Vestris and Mathews, both in their presentation and in their acting, provided the brilliance and true feeling which the play itself signally lacks. The tributes to Mathews' performance as Dazzle overwhelmingly support this view, and for the rest of his career he was acknowledged as the leading exponent of gentlemanly comedy in an age when comic acting was seldom gentlemanly. The younger Mathews never emulated his father's range, and towards the end of his life he had to answer charges of repeating himself:

It has been urged against me that I always play the same characters in the same way and that ten years hence I should play the parts

[1] *Life of Charles James Mathews*, Vol. II, p. 76.

exactly as I play them now. This I take as a compliment. It is a precision that has been aimed at by the models of my profession which I
am proud to follow, and shows, at least, that my acting is the result
of art and study and not that of mere accident.[1]

Such a limited, even mechanical, approach to acting was shown
to be outmoded when the Bancrofts at the Prince of Wales's
offered John Hare the chance of creating rôles unrecognizable
in their diversity.

The final chapter of the Mathewses' partnership—their
management of the Lyceum from 1847 to 1856—makes somewhat melancholy reading. Bowing at last to bankruptcy, they
fell back on a repertory which, save for its continuation of
Planché's fairy extravaganzas, differed little from the common
fare of the day. Their energies were chiefly spent on a series of
French melodramas, several adapted by G. H. Lewes under the
name of 'Slingsby Lawrence', which, though as scrupulously
staged as their Olympic or Covent Garden productions, seemed
a long way short of the objectives which both had set themselves. But even at this moment of triumph for the spectacular
drama, its rival was stirring in the wings at the Lyceum. There,
for a spell, sat a young actor who had been engaged as prompter, and whose modest acting talent was offset by yet unproven gifts as a playwright. No doubt he watched from the
prompt-corner the standards which Vestris and Mathews still
upheld, resolving to emulate them and, when the time came, to
profit by their mistakes. The young man's name was Tom
Robertson.

[1] *Life of Charles James Mathews*, Vol. II, p. 260.

THE NEW DRAMA

The changing face of the English theatre at the turn of the century called for a new drama. It was clearly not practicable to set within the elaborate framework of the new Drury Lane or Covent Garden many of the pieces which had held the stage of the Georgian playhouse. Hazlitt, in lamenting the passing of *The Artificial Comedies of the Last Age*, noted only one feature of a much wider transformation of taste. The rowdy, illiterate new audiences crowded into the theatres, requiring their interest to be roused by vigorous action, their emotions moved by pathos, and their troubles soothed by a happy ending. These demands had to be met as best they could. Forced to reject much of the Georgian repertory, the new theatre found itself without a drama and had too often to substitute spectacle. In these hand-to-mouth conditions manager, actor, and author were content if the fancy of their public was caught and briefly held by a new offering. There was no time or occasion to question the standards of that offering.

Inevitably that which aimed highest suffered most. Tragedy, with its demands on the spectator's intelligence and imagination, and its sense of spiritual values, made little appeal to the new public. The inspiration of tragedy had already begun to run dry in the Georgian theatre. As the Victorian era approached it became virtually extinct. Certainly classical tragedy found a die-hard practitioner in Joanna Baillie, whose *Plays of the Passions* won some literary but small theatrical success. The names of Sir Thomas Talfourd and James Sheridan Knowles are usually coupled as exponents of classical tragedy in the early years of the nineteenth century. Perhaps they better represent the last flicker of the old inspiration and the first spark of a new. Talfourd's reputation rests on *Ion*, a play which,

31

although written later than most of Knowles's work, is cast in the familiar and obsolescent mould. Knowles achieved success with *Virginius*, a play whose Roman setting hardly reflects the author's romantic temperament. The familiar story of the Roman soldier who kills his daughter to save her from the lust of the judge, Appius Claudius, is told with some pathos and a shrewd eye to theatrical effect, but without the eloquence or depth that the classical theme implies. *Virginius* is more of a piece with his later play, *William Tell*, than with a *Cataline* or *Cato*.

The Romantic Poets and the Theatre

The extinction of classical tragedy was also part of the general transformation of the literary scene brought about by the Romantic Movement. It was, however, the English theatre's loss that the leaders of that movement contributed little of value and nothing original to dramatic literature, leaving to others less gifted the creation of a new drama to fill the place of the old. It is perhaps difficult to conceive of Romantic egotists such as Shelley or Byron submitting to the discipline of the theatre; yet the history of nineteenth-century drama elsewhere in Europe suggests that the Romantic approach could find satisfactory expression on the stage. To Schiller and Hugo the theatre offered a challenge which they rejoiced to accept. To the English Romantic poets it was something they mostly preferred to ignore.

No doubt the conditions of that theatre were largely responsible for their scorn. The battleground of the nineteenth-century playhouse could only repel the sensitive writer, as it repelled the sensitive spectator. When the work of the Romantic poets took dramatic form, it was often as 'closet drama', written only for the theatre of the mind; much of it, like *Manfred* or *Prometheus Unbound*, defying adequate stage presentation. This scorn of the stage is reflected, not only in the form of the plays, but in the choice of forbidden themes, as with incest in *The Cenci*, and in unwieldy lengths. The garrulousness of English poetic drama is a tradition that lingers late in the century with Tennyson's elaborate historical surveys and the 15,000 lines of Swinburne's *Bothwell*.

But behind their aloofness most of the English Romantic poets concealed some longing for theatrical success. Coleridge condoled with Wordsworth that *The Borderers* could not follow *Remorse* on the boards of Drury Lane. Byron served on the Committee of Management of that theatre and rashly provided the Ode spoken at its reopening in 1812, after all the entries for the Public Competition had been rejected. Perhaps the disingenuousness of the Romantics' attitude to the theatre is best illustrated by the letter in which Shelley submitted *The Cenci* to the consideration of Harris at Covent Garden:

I wish to preserve a complete incognito, and can trust to you that, whatever else you do, you will at least favour me on this point. Indeed, this is essential, deeply essential, to its success. After it has been acted, and successfully (could I hope for such a thing), I would own it if I pleased, and use the celebrity it might acquire to my own purpose.[1]

Whilst unwilling to risk theatrical failure, the poet would be well content to acknowledge theatrical success.

Yet amongst the Romantic poets' excursions into the drama the supremacy of *The Cenci* remains unchallenged. Its quality survives, despite the debt which Shelley clearly owes to Elizabethan models, especially that of Webster, whose imprint appears not only in the Italian setting but in specific scenes, such as Beatrice's trial, with its echoes of *The White Devil*, and in the elaborate analysis of evil provided by the character of Cenci himself. Even more specific is the debt to *Macbeth* in much of the language of the murder scenes. Yet, derivative as it is, the play achieves a dramatic force which emphasizes Shelley's irresponsibility in choosing a forbidden theme and in finishing the story as perfunctorily as he did.

In his extended use of Elizabethan models Shelley is exceptional. Though their study of Shakespeare doubtless influenced their approach to the theatre, Wordsworth and Coleridge turned more for inspiration to the novelty of the Gothic cult. The outline of *The Borderers* is manifestly inspired by Schiller, though the play itself has little of the Gothic essence in it. Wordsworth was clearly preoccupied with the character and

---

[1] Reprinted in *The Complete Poetical Works*, edited by Thomas Hutchinson (London, 1923), p. 333.

conduct of Oswald, and his failure to give life to Oswald's attempts to extend his own guilt to the popular young leader of the Borderers, Marmaduke, is the play's great weakness. *Remorse*, on the other hand, contains most of the external features of Gothic drama: the setting in medieval Spain; the conscience-ridden brother, Osario; the concealed and complicated relationships; and even some of the stage-fireworks so popular at the time:

The incense on the altar takes fire suddenly, and an illuminated picture of ALVAR'S *assassination is discovered, and having remained a few seconds is then hidden by ascending flames.*

To its introduction of these fashionable elements the play probably owed its brief but undoubted success. Yet Coleridge conspicuously fails to penetrate beneath the surface of his models. *Remorse* possesses none of the theatrical force latent in Gothic drama. The thrills and passions are copied but not brought to life, and Coleridge could not impose any substance or originality on the tissue of absurdities which he faithfully introduced. Later Thomas Lovell Beddoes captured something of the true Gothic spirit in *Death's Jest Book*, without showing any stronger sense of stagecraft. The assimilation of German models to the English stage came from other hands, less intellectual but more certain in their theatrical touch.

Byron the dramatist stands somewhat outside the ranks of the Romantic poets. His approach to the theatre, both theoretical and practical, diverges from that of, say, Coleridge. Though no theorist, Byron accepted and in his own plays aimed at the strict discipline of neo-classical criticism. He recognized the authority of the unities, for 'with any very distant departure from them', states the Preface to *Sardanapalus*, 'there may be poetry, but can be no drama', although he is 'aware of the unpopularity of this notion in present English literature'. More significant, perhaps, was his close if brief connection with the theatrical world as a member of the Drury Lane Committee of Management from its reopening in 1812 until 1816. After he had shaken from his feet the dust of Drury Lane and of England, Byron renounced his theatrical associations, and when in his exile he turned playwright, repeatedly stated that he did not

intend his plays for performance. It is possible to take his pro-
testations too seriously. While it may well be that he did not
intend his work for performance in the contemporary London
theatre, whose struggle for existence he had witnessed at first-
hand, this does not preclude a desire for ultimate production.
His denial of theatrical ambition sounds a little over-emphatic,
and certainly he is inconsistent in claiming in the Preface to
Marino Faliero: 'Were I capable of writing a play which could
be deemed stage-worthy, success would give me no pleasure,
and failure great pain.'

At any rate his participation in the affairs of Drury Lane
seems to have endowed him with an eye to theatrical effect
which, coupled with the flexibility and force of his verse, gives
his plays qualities rarely found in English Romantic drama.
This is not to force *Manfred* or *Cain*, any more than *Prometheus
Unbound*, into the category of stage plays. Nevertheless,
Byron's four more orthodox pieces do demand fuller consideration. Of these, the two Venetian plays are the least satisfactory.
Marino Faliero certainly contains several well conceived scenes,
notably the introduction of the Doge at the Conspirators' meeting and the final execution scene. The deep introspection which
marks out Faliero as a child of the Romantic Movement is a
serious weakness in the play, obscuring, as it does, his relations
with the other characters, particularly his wife, Angiolina, and
with Israel Bertuccio, the leader of the conspiracy. In this
respect *Marino Faliero* is much inferior to *Venice Preserv'd*, with
which, by reason of its theme, the play can hardly escape comparison. *The Two Foscari* contains most of *Marino Faliero's*
weaknesses and few of its merits. The death of the younger
Foscari is entirely without dramatic significance and the character of his vengeful wife, Marina, so overdrawn as to forfeit all
sympathy for her situation.

However, *Sardanapalus* and *Werner* are more successful. Indeed, *Werner* may claim to be the only popular play which the
Romantic poets contributed to the English theatre. Although
not produced until after Byron's death, it ultimately entered
Macready's repertory, and the title part became one of his
most regular rôles. In its context *Werner* had all the requisites
of success: a fashionable Gothic setting, mysterious strangers,

unsuspected parentage, a sensational dénouement involving a secret door; above all a title rôle calling for the display of dignity and pathos in old age in which Macready excelled. Such an analysis of the play does not claim for it any great intrinsic merit, or even that merit which Byron's neglected plays possess. But a comparison of *Werner* with *Remorse* will suggest that Byron's theatrical insight enabled him to use the formula of Gothic drama with some skill, if little feeling, whereas Coleridge fell back on feeble imitation.

In *Sardanapalus* Byron again used his insight to great effect in such scenes as the deification of the living Sardanapalus and the final holocaust—scenes largely responsible for the play's success, both in Macready's production and subsequently in Charles Kean's revival. Moreover, *Sardanapalus* is not marred by the Gothic commonplaces of *Werner.* Working in a less hackneyed vein Byron was able to give the play something of the genuine emotion which *Werner* so signally lacks. In particular the devotion of the slave, Myrrha, to her king, both in triumph and in disaster, is done with conviction and feeling. Such scenes reveal Byron's power as a playwright and underline the division between him and his fellow Romantics.

After his success in *Werner* and *Sardanapalus* Macready doubtless cast an eye over the ranks of living poets to find another Byron. His choice fell upon the young Browning, already a member of his circle. 'Write me a tragedy and save me from going to America', was his appeal. But Browning's response did not spare him the journey. Macready's exertions did secure for *Strafford* a limited success, but *A Blot in the 'Scutcheon* (in which, ultimately, Macready declined to play) put an end not only to Browning's aspirations in the theatre but also to his friendship with Macready.

Browning's failure as a playwright was less predictable than that of his predecessors for he, of all the poets of this age, cast his ideas in the shape of characters. *Dramatic Lyrics, Dramatic Romances, Men and Women, Dramatis Personæ, Dramatic Idylls*— so many of his collections of poems testify by their titles to the appeal which dramatic form held for him. Unluckily he was not naturally equipped to answer that appeal and he took no steps to equip himself. Browning could portray character but not character in action. His portraits convince so long as they remain within the framework of the poems, but when in the plays he gives them the freedom of the stage, they obstinately refuse to move, to converse, or to strike the spark of life in conversing.

Though Browning's plays are free from the crude imitation of earlier Romantic drama, he introduces a scholarly precision, even pedantry, which is hardly less harmful. *Strafford* makes so many references to the detailed history of the outbreak of the Civil War that it is often unintelligible without a thorough knowledge of that period. On the other hand, the portion of the play which is Browning's invention (the devotion to Strafford of the Countess of Carlisle) is the least convincing. The unproduced *King Victor and King Charles* contains some of Browning's subtlest character-drawing; yet so complex is the motivation that no audience, least of all the early Victorian audience, could be expected to follow it in performance. And when, in *A Blot in the 'Scutcheon*, Browning tries to come to terms with that audience, the result is a feeble melodrama which scarcely rises above the rut of such pieces.

To consider Tennyson's work for the theatre in conjunction with Browning's is to anticipate but not, perhaps, to confuse; for Tennyson, like Browning, brought to his plays much of the historian's approach. Thus *Queen Mary* is so comprehensive as often to obscure the personal issues: Wyatt's rebellion and Cranmer's martyrdom are allowed to distract attention from Mary's barren love for Philip of Spain. Similarly in *Becket* Tennyson tries to combine the story of the Archbishop's struggle with the King and the love-story of Henry and Fair Rosamund: a problem which leads him to the highly unhistorical expedient of permitting Becket to save Rosamund from death at the point of Queen Eleanor's dagger.

Yet clumsy as these two plays often are, they achieved some success in the theatre. No doubt much of that success was due to the performances of Henry Irving as Philip and later as Becket, but it is to Tennyson's credit that his work proved amenable to 'arrangement for the stage', as Browning's had not. Tennyson's plays, for all their shapelessness, contain scenes written with the simple power and direct appeal of his verse.

These qualities are best seen in his two short plays, *The Falcon* and *The Cup*, both of which proved popular in performance. But this simplicity and power Tennyson, in his more ambitious plays, proved unable to sustain.

The failure of the Romantic Movement to make any lasting contribution to the theatre can be attributed largely to the refusal of the Romantic poets to come to terms with that theatre. Too often their protests that they were not writing for the stage are hard to reconcile with their disappointment at the scant success of their plays in performance. Their confusion of the functions of critic and writer led them to apply their Shakespearean studies to a theatre opposed materially and mentally to the conditions of the Elizabethan stage. Frequently their choice of an historical theme summoned up the scholar in them, rather than the creative artist. Such concessions as they made to popular taste resulted often in a crude imitation of Gothic extravagance, rather than the application of genuine theatrical insight. If Wordsworth, Shelley, or Browning desired theatrical success, they made no attempt to study the theatre in which that success must be won. The Romantic Movement in European drama can claim no English dramatist to set beside Goethe, Victor Hugo, or Pushkin. By contrast the verse-drama of the Victorian theatre was contributed by poets whose inspiration was very much smaller than their theatrical experience. The plays of Sheridan Knowles, Bulwer-Lytton, and W. G. Wills, once widely celebrated, have long been forgotten. Yet it was this measure of theatrical experience which afforded them their advantage over the Romantic poets.

The Demand for Spectacle

The insignificance of English Romantic drama laid on other shoulders the task of filling the repertory. Lacking leadership and denied adequate return for his work, the English playwright declined into a theatrical journeyman whose duty was to provide the platform on which actor, artist, and machinist could display their skill. Spectacle supplied all the distractions which the new audience craved, without making any demands on them in return. It was therefore to the provision of spectacle that the ingenuity and resources of the theatre were now directed. Soon after the opening of the new Drury Lane in 1794 the younger Colman accurately summed up the situation in a prologue he wrote for *New Hay At The Old Market*:

> Since the preference we know
> Is for pageantry and shew,
> 'Twere a pity the public to balk—
> And when people appear
> Quite unable to hear
> 'Tis undoubtedly needless to talk.
> Let your Shakspears and Jonsons go hang, go hang!
> Let your Otways and Drydens go drown!
> Give us but elephants and white bulls enough,
> And we'll take in all the town.
>   Brave boys!
>
> Or if tardily the sound
> Travels all the house around,
> 'Twixt the action and words there's a breach;
> And it seems as if Macbeth,
> Half a minute after death,
> On his back, made his last dying speech.
> Let your Shakspears and Jonsons go hang, go hang!
> Let your Otways and Drydens go drown!
> Give us but elephants and white bulls enough,
> And we'll take in all the town.
>   Brave boys!

Pantomime and opera were legacies from the Georgian theatre which could be relied on to provide pageantry and show. To them was added melodrama in which music and comedy were further subordinated to the demands of spectacle. Melodrama, in fact, became the staple fare of the new theatre.

English melodrama is generally dismissed as being of alien origin, owing much to the example of the Gothic novel and more to the example of continental playhouses. Such a verdict is substantially accurate; the Gothic frenzy certainly seized on the educated reader long before it captured the illiterate play-goer, for Horace Walpole's *The Castle of Otranto* preceded 'Monk' Lewis's *The Castle Spectre* by over thirty years. The debt of English melodrama to continental sources is also apparent from the briefest examination of its development, which was largely shaped by French and German example. Nevertheless some suggestion of melodrama had already made its appearance in Georgian drama. George Lillo's type of bourgeois tragedy, though it found more influential imitators on the Continent than in England, certainly helped to reinforce the pathetic strain creeping into English comedy. The 'joy too exquisite for laughter' which Steele had prescribed as the aim of comedy grew yet more muted with Lillo's insistence on the drama's obligation to reward virtue and punish vice: for

> . . . thoughtless youth to warn, and shame the age
> From vice destructive, well becomes the stage

declared the Prologue to *George Barnwell*. In consequence the playwright had increasingly to sacrifice character and credibility to the dictates of poetic justice. Moreover, in the last years of the century the pattern of Georgian comedy was further distorted by the increased use of rural settings and characters, introduced to point the contrast between urban sophistication and rustic innocence.

All these features reflect a drift towards melodrama, and most late Georgian comedies suggest, behind their comic façades, the strong drama and pathos of which their authors were to become exponents. Thomas Morton had established himself as a successful writer of comedies before, in 1800, *Speed the Plough* earned its audience's applause and a morsel of immortality through the unseen Mrs. Grundy, whose opinions terrorize her Hampshire village. But beside his picture of honest Farmer Ashford, Morton set the figure of the brooding baronet, Sir Philip Blandford, whose library contains the secret of his brother's fate:

SIR PHILIP. Yes, that chamber contains evidence of my shame; the fatal instrument, with other guilty proofs, lie there concealed—can you wonder I dread to visit the scene of horror—can you wonder I implore you, in mercy, to save me from the task? Oh! my friend, enter the chamber, bury in endless night those instruments of blood, and I will kneel and worship you.
HANDY, JUNIOR. I will.

SIR PHILIP (*weeps*). Will you? (*Embraces him.*) I am unused to kindness from man, and it affects me! Oh! can you press to your guiltless heart this blood-stained hand!

HANDY, JUNIOR. Sir Philip, let men without faults condemn—I must pity you.

In Thomas Holcroft, Morton found a kindred spirit, for although *The Road to Ruin* clings to its London setting, Holcroft introduces both pathos and sensation in the efforts of the prodigal son, Harry Dornton, to save his father from ruin by accepting the hand of the wealthy Widow Warren. There is certainly a suggestion in this scene of the Holcroft who, in *A Tale of Mystery*, was to provide one of the earliest nineteenth-century melodramas:

HARRY. Don't despair! I'll find relief . . . (*Aside.*) First to my friend . . . He cannot fail? But if he should! . . . Why ay, then to Megaera!—I will marry her, in such a cause, were she fifty widows, and fifty furies!

DORNTON. Calm yourself, Harry!

HARRY. I am calm! Very calm!—It shall be done!—Don't be dejected. You are my father. You were the first of men in the first of cities. Revered by the good and respected by the great. You flourished prosperously! But you had a son! I remember it!

DORNTON. Why do you roll your eyes, Harry?

HARRY. I shan't be long away!

DORNTON. Stay where you are, Harry. (*Catching his hand.*) All will be well! I am very happy!

HARRY. Tol de rol. Heaven bless you, sir! You are a worthy gentleman!—I'll not be long!

DORNTON. Hear me, Harry!—I am very happy.

(*Enter a clerk.*)

CLERK. Mr. Smith, sir, desires to know whether we may send to the Bank for a thousand pounds worth of silver.

HARRY (*furiously*). No, scoundrel! (*Breaks away and Exit.*)

DORNTON (*calling and almost sobbing*). Harry! Harry!—I am very happy!—Harry Dornton! (*In a kind of stupor.*) I am very happy!—Very happy! (*Exit following.*)

Perhaps the most representative writer of late Georgian comedy was George Colman the younger, who, as the son of the author of *The Jealous Wife* and *The Clandestine Marriage*, found

himself thrust into the life of the theatre even before he succeeded his father as manager of the Haymarket in 1789.
Colman's long and varied career illustrates well the process by
which a steady admixture of sentimentality prepared the soil of
English comedy for the young shoots of continental melodrama. In his comedies he turned from the smart London
society depicted by his father to idealized country settings, so
that *John Bull* presents not only the warm-hearted Irish inn-
keeper, Dennis Brulgruddery, but also the trusting country miss,
Mary Thornberry, pursued by a callous Honourable Tom
Shuffleton; and *The Poor Gentleman* contrasts upright but penniless Lieutenant Worthington with the wealthy and unscrupu-
lous Sir Charles Cropland, whose designs on Emily Worthington are frustrated just in time. Colman's eye for these simple
contrasts no doubt singled out William Godwin's novel, *Caleb
Williams*, as suitable for the stage. The result, shorn by
Colman of all Godwin's political and philosophic purposes,
became *The Iron Chest*, at first a failure but eventually the
hardiest of all his plays, with one of the longest-lived of the
theatre's brooding baronets as its protagonist. This Sir Edward
Mortimer is an elder brother of Morton's Sir Philip Blandford,
more elaborately drawn and atoning, in his retreat in the New
Forest, for the murder which (unlike Sir Philip Blandford) he
has actually committed. The discovery by his secretary of
written proof of his guilt provided the play with a title and a
scene dear to actors from Edmund Kean to Irving and Edwin
Booth:

WILFORD. . . . I will be mute as death;
But let me quit your service.
MORTIMER.   Never—Fool!
To buy this secret, you have sold yourself,
Your movements, eyes, and, most of all, your breath,
From this time forth, are fetter'd to my will.

Colman's position at the centre of theatrical affairs gave him
early warning of the sweeping changes afoot in the 1790s. His
early piece, *Inkle and Yarico*, had made ample use of song and
spectacle to tell its tale of an Indian princess in love with a
young English merchant. If he did not supply the 'white bulls

and elephants' of his own Prologue, he was liberal with the 'pageantry and shew' in such historical spectacles as *The Battle of Hexham* and *Feudal Times*, whose exploitation of medieval romance is another sign of the change in taste. The shrewdness of his judgement is especially evident in the striking use he makes of the elaborate mechanism of the new theatre. Thus the version of *Blue Beard* he provided for Drury Lane in 1798 must have transfixed its impressionable audience, as the heedless young wife persuades Bluebeard's servant to admit her to the forbidden Blue Chamber:

SHACABAC *puts the key into the lock; the Door instantly sinks, with a tremendous crash, and the* BLUE CHAMBER *appears streaked with vivid streams of Blood. The figures in the picture over the door change their position, and* ABOMELIQUE *is represented in the action of beheading the Beauty he was, before, supplicating. The Pictures, and Devices of Love, change to subjects of Horror and Death. The* INTERIOR APARTMENT (*which the sinking of the door discovers*) *exhibits various Tombs, in a sepulchral building—in the midst of which ghastly and supernatural forms are seen—some in motion, some fixed—in the centre is a large Skeleton, seated on a tomb (with a Dart in his hand) and, over his head, in characters of Blood, is written*
'THE PUNISHMENT OF CURIOSITY'

Gothic Drama

It was by men like Holcroft, Morton, and the younger Colman that the work of transforming eighteenth-century comedy into nineteenth-century melodrama was carried out. But the inspiration of that process came from the Continent. Indeed the word itself has a continental origin, appearing almost simultaneously in France—as a passage of mime to music—and in Germany—as dialogue spoken to music between the sung passages of opera. In spirit, however, melodrama was clearly the product of the Gothic extravagance which gripped a Europe bored by the Age of Reason, and which found architectural and antiquarian as well as literary form. In England the link between the Gothic novel and Gothic drama was established by the career of Matthew 'Monk' Lewis who published the novel which gave him his nickname in 1795 and followed it up with a Gothic melodrama, *The Castle Spectre*, in 1797. He thus established a standard of sensationalism which presented a serious challenge to his rivals. It was no light task, for instance, to cap the heroine's vision of her murdered mother:

The folding-doors unclose and the oratory is seen illuminated. In its centre stands a tall female figure, her white and flowing garments spotted with blood; her veil is thrown back, and discovers a pale and melancholy countenance: her eyes are lifted upwards, her arms extended towards heaven, and a large wound appears upon her bosom. ANGELA *sinks upon her knees, with her eyes riveted upon the figure, which for some moments remains motionless. At length the spectre advances slowly to a soft and plaintive strain: she stops opposite to* REGINALD's *picture, and gazes upon it in silence. She then turns, approaches* ANGELA, *seems to invoke a blessing upon her, points to the picture, and retires to the oratory. The music ceases.* ANGELA *rises with a wild look, and follows the vision, extending her arms towards it. The spectre waves her hand; as bidding her farewell. Instantly the organ's swell is heard; a full chorus of female voices chant 'Jubilate'. A blaze of light flashes through the oratory, and the folding-doors close with a loud noise,* ANGELA *falls motionless on the floor.*

There could be no turning-back for English melodrama after the appearance of *The Castle Spectre*, and Lewis himself had recourse to a squadron of cavalry to ensure the success of a later play, *Timour the Tartar*.

Inevitably the finest achievements of German Romantic drama made little appeal to the bloodthirsty audiences of the English theatre. But before long *Werther* and *Die Räuber* found their way on to the English stage, and more popular still were the wild outpourings of August von Kotzebue, whose career as author, diplomat, and spy itself provided a Gothic flourish, culminating in assassination at the hands of a hypercritical student. Both *Lovers' Vows*, which Mrs. Inchbald based on *Das Kind der Liebe*, and *The Stranger*, taken by Benjamin Thompson from *Menschenhass und Reue*, emphasize the pathetic rather than the sensational; but *Die Spanier in Peru*, adapted by Sheridan as *Pizarro*, became one of the mainstays of spectacular melodrama, retaining its popularity long after it had lost the topicality arising from the threat of French invasion. It was, indeed, a Gothic rather than an Indian Peru in which this play was set:

ACT III, SCENE 1: *A wild Retreat amongst stupendous rocks.* CORA *and her* CHILD, *with other* WIVES *and* CHILDREN *of the* PERUVIAN WAR-

RIORS, *discovered. They sing alternating stanzas expressive of their situation, with a Chorus in which all join.*

Moreover, Rolla, the Peruvian general who meets his death in rescuing the child of his rival, Alonso, is unmistakably the Romantic hero:

PIZARRO. . . . Their guns must reach him—he'll yet escape—holloa to those horse—the Peruvian sees them—and now he turns among the rocks—then is his retreat cut off. (ROLLA *crosses the wooden bridge over the cataract, pursued by the* SOLDIERS—*they fire at him—a shot strikes him.*) Now!—quick! quick! seize the child! (ROLLA *tears from the rock the tile which supports the bridge, and retreats by the background, bearing off the* CHILD. *Re-enter* ALMAGRO *and* DAVILLA.)

ALMAGRO. By hell! he has escaped!—and with the child unhurt.

DAVILLA. No—he bears his death with him. Believe me, I saw him struck upon the side.

The supernatural element, prominent in *The Castle Spectre*, was later exploited by many dabblers in demonic drama. James Robinson Planché, who was to devote his life to making the English theatre respectable and historically accurate, began his career by practising the blackest of magic in *The Vampyre*, which introduced a new form of trap to the stage and a new term to its vocabulary, and continued these rites by adapting *Der Freischütz*; while Edward Fitzball profited by Planché's example to write *The Flying Dutchman*, which introduced to the stage the perennially popular figure of the accursed Vanderdecken. Meanwhile, English melodrama contracted a new fever, equally delirious but of political, not supernatural, origin. French playwrights had been inspired by the gathering force of Revolution to build their melodramas round the struggles of the oppressed against the tyrant's scourge. The fall of the Bastille supplied them with an infallible dénouement in which the castle walls yield to the liberator's arms, just as the tyrant has the victim in his power. .

In René Charles Gilbert de Pixérécourt the French theatre found its supremely successful exponent of 'Bastille' drama, and the English theatre a source which it was eager to raid but reluctant to acknowledge. Pixérécourt's politics were indefensible before an English public; it was only his power to thrill that could be exported, and to extract their sting his settings were turned into a Spain, Italy, or Bohemia of wholly indeterminate period and place. When Holcroft introduced Pixérécourt's *Coelina: ou l'Enfant du Mystère* to the English public as his own *A Tale of Mystery*, he provided in the dumb hero, Francisco, a persuasive pretext for largely dispensing with dialogue in favour of musical accompaniment. The play, though presented at Covent Garden, needed little modification by the minor theatres to qualify as a 'burletta' which would not infringe the patent houses' obsolescent privileges:

(*Enter* MONTANO. *Music plays alarmingly but piano when he enters and while he says*)
MONTANO. I beg pardon, good sir, but——
(*Music loud and discordant at the moment the eye of* MONTANO *catches the figure of* ROMALDI *at which* MONTANO *starts with terror and indignation. He then assumes the eye and attitude of menace; which* ROMALDI *returns. The music ceases.*)

Indeed, Pixérécourt specialized in dumb heroes, animal as well as human, and the actors must have groaned when his *Dog of Montargis* (adapted by William Barrymore from *Le Chien de Montargis*) inspired Pocock to make a bird the centre of interest in *The Magpie or the Maid?* which he took from Caigniez' *La Pie Voleuse*. But the fickle public, raised on the horse-riding at Astley's and the Surrey, welcomed these circus-tricks on the stage of Drury Lane or Covent Garden. Pocock contrived to make some amends in *The Miller and His Men*, a melodrama of wonderful orthodoxy with an entirely human cast, in which the heroine, immured by Bohemian bandits, is rescued by her lover who joins the band in order to blow up their stronghold in a superb conflagration. Long after its popularity in the theatre had waned, *The Miller and His Men* continued to fascinate nursery audiences, by arrangement with the toy theatres of William West or Benjamin Pollock.

Native Melodrama

In the first thirty years of its life English melodrama remained resolutely an exotic—a strange, brilliant plant blooming amongst the familiar flowers of Covent Garden or on Surrey-side. Where these early melodramas reflected the English scene at all it was not a contemporary England, but a country lent enchantment by the period of the Crusades or the Armada. More often they depicted some European fastness as remote as Shakespeare's Bohemia. When eventually the appeal of Gothic ghosts and Bohemian bandits began to flag, even for this un-exacting audience, the writers were forced to turn to their own world in their own day for further subjects. Such a shift of in-terest is apparent in the many stage versions made of Pierce Egan's *Tom and Jerry* sketches, and in the work of individual authors like J. B. Buckstone and Fitzball. Early in his long career as actor, manager, and playwright Buckstone attempted in *Luke the Labourer* a melodrama with a humble, contemporary, rustic setting, which assailed its audience not with spectacle or sensation, but with simple emotions and plentiful pathos. Its power to draw tears can still be sensed behind the crudeness of its characters and action:

LUKE. . . . At last all things went cross; and at one time, when a bit hadn't been in my mouth for two days, I sat thinking, wi' my wife in my arms—she were ill, very ill—I saw her look at me wi' such a look as I shall never forget—she laid hold o' this hand, and, putting her long thin fingers all around it, said, 'Luke, would na' the farmer give you sixpence if he thought I were dying o' want?' I said I'd try once more—I got up, to put her in a chair, when she fell, stone dead, down at my feet!
CLARA. Oh, Luke! Luke!—for mercy's sake, no more—forgive him!
LUKE (*after a pause*). I were then quite ruin'd. I felt alone in the world. I stood looking on her white face near an hour, and did not move from the spot an inch; but, when I did move, it were wi' my fist clenched in the air, while my tongue, all parch'd and dry, curs'd a curse, and swore that, if I had not my revenge, I wish'd I might fall as stiff and as dead as she that lay before me.

Meanwhile, the actor T. P. Cooke, doubtless surfeited with playing Vampires and Frankensteins, had urged Fitzball to provide him with a chance to portray the breezy sailor of his own youth. As Long Tom Coffin in *The Pilot*, Fitzball's version of Fenimore Cooper's novel (drastically altered for English consumption), Cooke established himself so firmly as the hero of nautical melodrama that other managers began searching for means to show off his prowess in the hornpipe. At the Surrey, Elliston, once the monarch of Drury Lane, had as his resident playwright a young man who himself had served in the British fleet. Douglas William Jerrold found in Gay's old ballad of *Black-Ey'd Susan* a suitable subject, and as Susan's husband, William, Cooke scored a success which eclipsed even that of *The Pilot*, carried the piece triumphantly to Drury Lane, and established the pattern of English nautical melodrama.

Most of the elements in this pattern were already to hand. The Jolly Jack Tar first found a regular place on the stage in the comic operas which the elder Charles Dibdin built around his own songs of the sea. During the Napoleonic Wars the exploits of the British Fleet, and above all of the incomparable Nelson, inspired a score of naval spectacles, many of them from Dibdin's two sons, Thomas and Charles the younger. In reducing these manœuvres to the scale of melodrama Jerrold's cunning lay in his choice of Gay's ballad for his theme. Nothing in the play approaches the charm or unforced pathos of the old song:

> All in the Downs the fleet was moor'd,
>   The streamers waving on the wind.
> When black-ey'd Susan came on board,
>   Oh! where shall I my true love find?
> Tell me, ye jovial sailors, tell me true,
> Does my sweet William sail among your crew?
>
> William, who high upon the yard,
>   Rock'd with the billows to and fro;
> Soon as her well-known voice he heard,
>   He sigh'd and cast his eyes below.
> The cord slides swiftly through his glowing hands,
> And quick as lightning on the deck he stands.
>
> . . . Though battle call me from thy arms,
>   Let not my pretty Susan mourn.
> Though Cannons roar, yet free from harms,
>   William shall to his dear return.
> Love turns aside the balls that round him fly,
> Lest precious tears should drop from Susan's eye.

The boatswain gave the dreadful word,
  The sails their swelling bosom spread,
No longer must she stay on board;
  They kiss'd; she sighed; he hung his head;
Her less'ning boat, unwilling rows to land;
Adieu! she cries, and waves her lily hand.

Jerrold's own touch was a good deal heavier, but he did contrive two scenes of some theatrical force: the Court Martial at
which William is tried for striking down the Captain who
assaulted his beloved Susan, and the place of execution to which
William is brought before the inevitable reprieve arrives:

SCENE V. *The Forecastle of the ship—Procession along the starboard
gangway; minute bell tolls.*—MASTER-AT-ARMS *with a drawn sword under
his arm, point next to the prisoner;* WILLIAM *follows without his neckcloth
and jacket, a* MARINE *on each side;* OFFICER OF MARINES *next;* ADMIRAL,
CAPTAIN, LIEUTENANT, *and* MIDSHIPMEN, *following.* WILLIAM *kneels; and
all aboard appear to join in prayer with him. The procession then marches
on and halts at the gangway;* MARINE OFFICER *delivers up prisoner to the*
MASTER-AT-ARMS *and* BOATSWAIN, *a* SAILOR *standing at one of the forecastle guns, with the lock-string in his hand.—A platform extends from
the cat-head to the fore-rigging. Yellow flag flying at the fore. Colours
half-mast down.*

Moreover, Jerrold evolved for William a nautical jargon which
was to prove the stock-in-trade of the sailor-hero in countless
nautical melodramas to follow, so that William Terriss at the
close of Victoria's reign was speaking the same language that
T. P. Cooke had made his own before it began:

WILLIAM. . . . I have been three years at sea, and had never looked
    upon or heard from my wife—as sweet a little craft as was ever
    launched—I had come ashore, and I was as lively as a petrel in a
    storm; I found Susan—that's my wife, your honours—all her
    gilt taken by the land-sharks; but yet all taut, with a face as red
    and rosy as the King's head on the side of a fire bucket. Well,
    your honours, when we were as merry as a ship's crew on a pay-
    day, there comes an order to go aboard; I left Susan, and went
    with the rest of the liberty men to ax leave of the first lieutenant.
    I heard Susan giving signals of distress, I out with my cutlass,
    made all sail, and came up to my craft—I found her battling with

a pirate—I never looked at his figurehead, never stopped—would any of your honours? long live you and your wives, say I!—would any of your honours have rowed alongside as if you'd been going aboard a royal yacht?—no, you wouldn't; for the gilt swabs on the shoulders can't alter the heart that swells beneath; you would have done as I did;—and what did I? why, I cut him down like a piece of old junk; had he been the first lord of the Admiralty, I had done it!

Jerrold's success in calling English melodrama home from abroad encouraged the English theatre to depict increasingly the native scene. Jerrold himself turned from captain and crew to landlord and tenant in *The Rent Day*, and to foreman and spinner in *The Factory Girl*. His rival, Fitzball, devised in *Jonathan Bradford: or, the Murder at the Roadside Inn*, a play whose technical daring in showing four of the Inn's rooms simultaneously has somewhat obscured the impetus it provided to stories of crime in low life. It was not long before the annals of the police-court were being searched for cases as sensational as those of Maria Marten and Sweeney Todd the Demon Barber of Fleet Street.

This new appeal of the home-grown at the expense of the imported is well reflected in the tremendous popularity on the stage of adaptations from Dickens. For George IV's subjects the novels of Walter Scott had provided highly acceptable fare in the theatre: their misty Romanticism and their medieval trappings were equally attractive to a public raised on a diet of Gothic ghosts. Though Scott himself failed to come to terms with the theatre, his novels were eagerly—and unscrupulously —seized by managers blessed with a resident playwright and no copyright laws. Six different adaptations of *Ivanhoe*, for example, appeared in London in 1820 alone.[1] To the more stable Victorian audience, however, the lively picture of their own boyhood provided by Charles Dickens was more acceptable. After his early flirtation with the playwright's calling, Dickens turned understandably to the wider public and richer rewards of the novel, leaving his passion for the stage to find expression in the theatrical activities of his Devonshire House circle. But the marks of that passion remained in the framework of his

[1] See Allardyce Nicoll: *Early Nineteenth Century Drama*, pp. 93–4.

novels, so that Victorian managers seized on his strong situations and fierce contrasts of character as their predecessors had raided the romances of Scott. No less than eight different versions of *The Cricket on the Hearth* were produced in London within a year of the book's publication in 1845.[1] Shorn of much of their humour and all their original observation, Dickens's novels emerged on the Victorian stage as melodramas, crude, sensational—and tremendously successful.

Bulwer-Lytton and Boucicault

If the playwright's calling proved unattractive to Dickens, it had no appeal at all for those of his contemporaries who, like Thackeray, George Eliot, or Anthony Trollope, avoided bold emotions and broad effects. But on one at least of Dickens's contemporaries the theatre exercised a powerful fascination. Bulwer-Lytton also had the mortifying experience of seeing his novels dramatized by divers unauthorized hands. Unlike Dickens, he resolved to beat the pirates at their own game and prepared himself for the encounter by studying the methods of the French Romantic theatre. Consequently the majority of Bulwer-Lytton's plays reveal their French inspiration, the unsuccessful *Duchess de la Vallière* no less than the favourite *Lady of Lyons* and *Richelieu*. The comparison is flattering to Bulwer-Lytton, but if his verse had none of Hugo's fire, he did catch something of the elder Dumas's skill in exhibiting the attitudes of costume drama—a skill which kept these two period pieces in the repertory throughout the century.

The success of *The Lady of Lyons* is harder to understand than that of *Richelieu*. The fate of snobbish Pauline Deschappelles, married off to the gardener's son whom her rejected suitors disguise as the Prince of Como, would seem entirely satisfactory but for his gratuitous refusal to claim her until he has achieved whirlwind promotion as a Napoleonic colonel. In Macready the play must have had a most unlikely hero, and its success is perhaps best attributed to its appeal (discreetly dressed in period costume) to the radical sentiments of the decade of the Reform Bill. An audience still steeped in the *naïveté* of melodrama would doubtless relish the gentility of Claude

---

[1] Nicoll: *Early Nineteenth Century Drama*, p. 98.

Melnotte's conduct, and rejoice to see him return, full of military honours, to claim Pauline's hand and heart. *Richelieu*, on the other hand, not only provided Macready with a finely judged vehicle but is also an adroit piece of costume melodrama, often unhistorical but wholly expert in its use of sentiment, passion, colour, and, above all, declamation. Its echoes in the tones of Macready's successors were still reverberating as late as 1923 when, in *The Old Drama and the New*, a contrite William Archer recalled how Edwin Booth had stirred him as he set himself and his cloth between the heroine and her persecutors:

> Mark, where she stands!—around her form I draw
> The awful circle of our solemn church!
> Set but a foot within the holy ground,
> And on thy head—yea, though it wear a crown—
> I launch the curse of Rome!

Money, the third of his successful plays, lies outside Bulwer-Lytton's familiar field, and virtually outside the whole range of early Victorian drama. Original, contemporary, and in prose, it attempted to find some elements of comic style in the deserts of Victorian farce. That its immediate and sustained success was due to its novelty rather than to its achievement is clear enough. The misunderstandings of Alfred Evelyn and his true love, Clara Douglas, are tiresome even by the standards of stupidity established by long theatrical usage. The fun poked at the parasites who cling to Evelyn when he unexpectedly inherits a vast fortune, though crudely done, provides an interesting commentary on a materialistic age. But the Club scene, in which Evelyn tests his friends, real and feigned, by pretending to lose his fortune at cards, supplies stagecraft and atmosphere of a high order. *Richelieu* and *The Lady of Lyons* are recognizably the work of the author of *The Last Days of Pompeii*, but *Money* gives the theatre a glimpse of the world of Thackeray's novels.

The coincidence by which Bulwer-Lytton began his career as a playwright just as Victoria began her reign, underlines a change in theatrical taste. The simple thrills, whether supernatural or seafaring, of early melodrama begin to lose their power with familiarity. The surfeited Victorian audience looks increasingly for some organization of the lurid elements which make up melodrama. The evolution in France of the *pièce bien faite* of Scribe from the delirium of Romantic drama runs a slower course in the English theatre. Douglas Jerrold, trying to advance from *Black-Ey'd Susan* to polite comedy, lost his touch and retired, hurt, to the columns of *Punch,* from which he carried on a feud against the English stage. But a young Irishman of French ancestry, Dionysius Lardner Boursiquot, proved to have the adaptability which Jerrold lacked, and became Dion Boucicault, a leading practitioner of the more organized methods of mid-Victorian melodrama.

Boucicault's career reversed the pattern traced by Jerrold. Instead of moving on from melodrama to comedy Boucicault achieved success as a young man of twenty-one with *London Assurance,* hailed as a 'modern' comedy by Vestris and Mathews who presented it and by the public who kept it in the repertory throughout the century. In fact its only modern touch was its setting, to which Vestris gave her unflagging attention. In spirit, however, *London Assurance* is the palest imitation of Vanbrugh or Farquhar, lacking their vigour and drawing attention by its contemporary dress to such devices of artificial comedy as a father failing to recognize the son who is staying in the same house under an assumed name. Its liveliest characters, the horse- and husband-riding Lady Gay Spanker and the impudent Dazzle (played by Charles Mathews), are incidental to the main story, but the play's long life can only be attributed to their appeal and to the dearth of Victorian comedy.

Boucicault's efforts to continue this vein of comedy, notably in *Used Up,* another vehicle for Mathews, probably convinced him that he was losing touch with his audience. In adapting *Don Cæsar de Bazan* from Dumanoir and D'Ennery he had already turned his attention to the new school of French melodrama inspired by Scribe. He proceeded to serve an apprenticeship at the Princess's, constructing for Charles Kean English versions of the current favourites of the French stage. Much of Boucicault's work there was perfunctory, but at least two of his adaptations, *Louis XI* (from Casimir Delavigne) and *The Corsican Brothers,* brought wide acclaim not only to Kean but to many later performers. In the popularity of Kean, Phelps, and later Irving as Louis XI it is possible to see the fascination for their audiences of the superficial attributes of Richard III and King Lear, without their deeper significance. Certainly Boucicault provided Louis with the externals of both—Richard's cunning and Lear's patriarchal air—while rejecting the essence of either.

The Corsican Brothers, on the other hand, shows a certain originality of form which deserves analysis. Working, wisely, not from Dumas's novel but from the stage adaptation by Grangé and Montépin, Boucicault here presented the familiar ingredients of Romantic drama in a form sufficiently arresting for his version to hold the stage for half a century. Several of the play's incidents made theatre history, notably the first appearance of the telepathic twins:

FABIEN *folds his letter and seals it, at the same time* LOUIS DEI FRANCHI *appears, rising from R.C. without his coat or waistcoat, as his brother is, but with a blood stain upon his breast—he glides across the stage—ascending gradually at the same time.*

The long, interleaved trap-door devised to effect this entrance was christened the 'Corsican trap' and under that name remained in regular theatrical usage. Later, in the last act, the duel between Louis's murderer and the avenging Fabien established a type of single combat:

First combat of several minutes in which CHATEAU-RENAUD *exerts himself to kill or wound* FABIEN, *but is foiled by his coolness and skill. . . . Second combat in which the sword of* CHATEAU-RENAUD *is broken.*

MONTGIRON (*springing forward*). Gentlemen, gentlemen, this combat must not be continued; M. Chateau-Renaud's sword is broken— the weapons are not equal.

FABIEN. You are mistaken, sir. (*Breaking his sword beneath his heel.*) They are so now. (*To* CHATEAU-RENAUD, *pointing to the broken blade.*) Pick up that blade, sir, and let us go on.

MONTGIRON. Implacable!

FABIEN. As destiny! (*He directs* ALFRED *how to tie the broken blade to his wrist with his handkerchief.*)

. . . *A violent bodily contest—*CHATEAU-RENAUD *throws* FABIEN, *but, at the moment in which he raises his arm to strike him,* FABIEN *plunges his weapon into his heart.*

However, it was not only incidents in *The Corsican Brothers* which established precedents in the English theatre. The overall pattern of the play—the concurrence in time of the first two acts, and the two 'visions', revealing first the Forest of Fontainebleau with the dying Louis, and later Fabien's resolve to quit Corsica and revenge his brother, indicate an interest in form hitherto neglected in the rough-and-tumble methods of melodrama. Further, Boucicault was able to introduce a blend of chivalry and adventure far removed from the simple thrills of T. P. Cooke's pieces; and to this refinement of romantic appeal Charles Kean was doubtless able to give his own innate respectability and Eton education, dressed with the theatrical flourish he inherited with his name. The era of 'gentlemanly melodrama' had begun.

The lessons Boucicault learnt from the French theatre he subsequently used in putting together a series of native melodramas, owing nothing to French sources. 'Native' for Boucicault meant Ireland, and in his three popular Irish plays, *The Colleen Bawn*, *Arrah-na-Pogue*, and *The Shaughraun*, he exploited with great skill the hitherto little used backgrounds of his native country, turning on them the brilliant if deceptive limelight of his theatrical training. In so doing he was also able to exploit his acting ability, and the sly humour, touched with pathos, of his Myles in *The Colleen Bawn*, Shaun-the-Post in *Arrah-na-Pogue*, and Conn in *The Shaughraun* was loyally supported by his wife, Agnes Robertson, who, though Scots, succeeded in creating the soft Irish charm of the Colleen Bawn. Boucicault's portrayal of Irish character later enraged the literary leaders of Irish nationalism, who denounced the cheapness of his humour and sentiment, but at least his strain of pathos was a refinement on the crudely comic Teagues of so many Georgian plays. Moreover, his growing interest in America, where he ultimately settled, led him to capture for the theatre the American scene also, in *The Poor of New York*, *The Octoroon*, and in his long-lived version of Washington Irving's *Rip van Winkle*.

To his original work Boucicault brought the fully tested methods he had assimilated from the French. Both his Irish and his American plays, for all the elaboration of their plots, have a neatness of construction to which Fitzball or Jerrold never remotely aspired. His handling of the Irish idiom, too, marks an advance on the rhetoric of Romantic drama towards the authentic dialogue established by the end of the century. Of the alertness of his mind Boucicault's plays contain innumerable examples. While in no way interested in contemporary issues he lost no time in turning scientific progress to theatrical advantage. The dénouement of *The Octoroon*, for example, is brought about through the newly-invented camera, by which the villain's infamy has, unknown to him, been recorded; while *The Long Strike* achieves another topical touch by introducing the telegraph to recall from on board ship the key-witness who alone can save an innocent man accused of murder:

SLACK (*having worked apparatus*). There, sir, you see the wires are dumb. (JANE *falls on her knees.*) I am truly sorry, sir, but if you were to give me one thousand pounds I could not make them speak.

MONEYPENNY. Of course you can't. Thank you, it is not your fault, but this poor girl, sir, this poor girl—it is her sweetheart that will be tried for murder—that wire was the thread on which the lad's life was suspended and it fails her. It is hard, sir. I am a lawyer and used to hard cases, but this does appear to me a cruel one. Come, Jane.

JANE. Oh! let me pray—let me pray!

MONEYPENNY. Heaven help you, my poor girl, for we can do no more. (*To* SLACK.) You see, sir, this being assize time, his trial will come off at once. I fear it will go hard with him. (JANE's *head falls against chair.*) Why, what is the matter, Jane?

JANE. I am faint, sir. I feel very cold.

SLACK (*having come from behind counter, stands* L.). Can I assist you, sir?

MONEYPENNY. She is swooning, sir. Oh, dear—what shall I do? Jane! Jane!

(*Instrument at back begins to tap.*)

SLACK. Hark, sir! hark! There's a signal! Stop a bit. (*Runs behind counter.*) By some accident the station at the head is alive.

MONEYPENNY. Jane! Jane! do you hear? The line is open—the wire is working!

JANE (*still on knees, hands clasped*). Heaven has heard my prayer.

SLACK. Now then, sir, for your message.

MONEYPENNY (*to* JANE). Stop there. (*To* SLACK.) Ask them has the

barque *Eliza and Mary* left the Mersey. (*Pause—*JANE *sobs.*)
Hush—keep quiet.

SLACK (*who has sent message as directed by* MONEYPENNY—*receives reply.*)
Barque *Eliza and Mary* inside the bar waiting for a tide.

MONEYPENNY. Hurrah! hurrah!

SLACK. What next?

MONEYPENNY. Can you communicate with the barque? if so, how?

SLACK (*as before*). Yes—by pilot boat.

MONEYPENNY. Despatch it at once, with message from Jane Learoyd
to John Reilly, sailor—'Come back; give evidence required in
favour of James Starkee, accused of murder; case now on.
Signed Jane Learoyd.'

Perhaps the most significant feature of Boucicault's work is
the 'sensation scene'. None of his melodramas would be complete without a thrilling sequence on which the resources of the
Victorian theatre were fully extended to produce a novel and
spectacular effect. The attempted drowning in *The Colleen
Bawn*; the exploding steamboat in *The Octoroon*; the house
burnt down in *The Poor of New York*; Shaun's ascent of the
prison tower in *Arrah-na-Pogue*; the boat-race rowed in *Formosa*—all were triumphs of ingenuity, accurately aimed at their
audience's level. Moreover a detailed investigation[1] has recently disclosed how Boucicault's innovations foreshadow such
fundamentals of film-making as cross-cutting, tracking, and
panning. In short, the sensation scenes of Boucicault's plays
are not merely more ingenious than those of a Moncreiff or
Fitzball. They are expertly woven into the fabric of the play,
so that they emerge as the pivot of the story, not its *raison d'être*;
nor is the novelty of the sensation scene made the excuse for a
total lack of character, plausibility, or intelligence. Boucicault
was above all things thorough.

Taylor and Reade

Amongst the playwrights of his generation, only Tom Taylor
can claim equal influence. Unlike Boucicault, Taylor moved in
wider circles than the theatre, for he was in turn a Fellow of
Trinity College, Cambridge, Professor of English at London

[1] A. Nicholas Vardac: *Stage to Screen: Theatrical Method from Garrick to Griffith*
(Cambridge, Mass.), 1949.

University, barrister, civil servant, and editor of *Punch*, as well as playwright. Resembling Bulwer-Lytton in his linking of the literary and theatrical worlds, Taylor also followed French examples; but if Lytton's model was Hugo, Taylor kept more closely to Scribe. Thus he shared Scribe's fondness for historical plays in which both persons and places bore only nominal resemblance to their originals. *Two Loves and a Life* (written with Charles Reade) embroiders an elaborate romantic pattern on the background of the 1745 Rebellion, and *The King's Rival* (also with Reade), being set at the Court of Charles II, had, of necessity as well as choice, to touch-up the picture. Taylor's debt to Scribe emerges most clearly in *Plot and Passion* (written with John Lang), for its preposterous story of spy and counter-spy in the era of Napoleon and Fouché is worked out with all Scribe's recognized devices, down to sliding panels and secret documents in such improbable containers as a cane-head and a chocolate-box.

In Taylor's defence it should be said that the prejudices of the Victorian public largely restricted him to such fatuous themes. A Dumas *fils* or an Augier could take Scribe's formula of the *pièce bien faite* and apply it to subjects with a claim to serious attention. But the English audience which cheerfully swallowed murder and assault pronounced itself shocked at any suggestion of plain-speaking. Only a lifetime of tearful contrition could bring the English public to forgive Mrs. Haller, the erring wife in *The Stranger*. There could be no justification of Marguerite Gautier, however, and *La Dame aux Camélias* was proscribed in any recognizable English version, although by a combination of sophistry and snobbery the Lord Chamberlain allowed it to be spoken—or sung—in French.

Taylor's efforts to widen the appeal of his plays were hampered by both official and public prejudice. Some of his later pieces do contain the germ of a serious theme. *Settling Day*, for example, introduces not only a carefully drawn picture of the banking world, with its precariously balanced order, but also a personal relationship of some interest: the devotion of the elderly banker, Markland, to a young wife whose extravagance precipitates a financial crisis which, however, brings them both to their senses. Much the most popular of Taylor's plays on a more adult theme was the long-lived *Still Waters Run Deep*, in which, however warily, the subject of infidelity is raised, for Captain Hawksley's efforts to seduce Mrs. Mildmay are only baulked by the interposition of her domineering aunt, Mrs. Sternhold, once Hawksley's lover, who spurs on the self-effacing Mildmay to decisive action.

Still Waters Run Deep held the stage long after Taylor's death, and certain of its scenes still retain their theatrical force: notably the midnight encounter between Hawksley and Mrs. Sternhold and Mildmay's effective methods of outwitting Hawksley. But the prudery of the Victorian theatre forced Taylor to neglect the heart of his play for its externals. The French source (*Le Gendre*, a novel by Charles Bernard) made the older woman the wife's mother. Taylor felt himself obliged to alter their relationship to aunt and niece, and to develop the action of the play rather than the people and passions involved. Mrs. Mildmay is a particularly negative character, and her response to Hawksley's advances is mere skittishness. Far from providing the dénouement, her reaction to Mildmay's newly-exercised authority is one of tame submission:

MILDMAY. . . . Trust to me, henceforth, to make you what a wife should be. I should prefer to win you by a lover's tenderness, but, if I cannot do that, I know how to make a husband's rights respected.

MRS. MILDMAY. Oh, thank you, dearest, thank you—tell me of my faults—I will try to correct them. I will honour and obey you as a wife should.

It was not in this fashionable field of intrigue and passion that Taylor's most popular achievement lay, but in the humbler sphere of petty larceny. *The Ticket-of-Leave Man*, a direct descendant of Fitzball's *Jonathan Bradford*, brought two touches of originality to its story of an innocent man first convicted of passing counterfeit notes and then hounded by the real criminals. One was the introduction of a stage detective, the protean Hawkshaw, whose facility for make-up fired a string of successors to more and more impenetrable disguises. The second was the scrupulous detail with which Taylor established his settings—whether the colour and life of the Bellevue Tea

Gardens and the Coffee Room of the Bridgwater Arms, or the staid routine of Mr. Gibson's bill-broking office in the City. The same thoroughness is apparent in the jargon of the gang who ensnare the hero, Bob Brierly, and their richly idiomatic dialogue now lies strangely beside the threadbare sentiments of Bob and his faithful sweetheart, May. Thus, when the gang disclose to Mr. Gibson that his trusted employee is a discharged prisoner or ticket-of-leave man:

MAY. Am I dreaming? Robert, what does this mean?

BRIERLY. It's hard to bear. Keep up your heart—I'm discharged. He knows all.

MAY (*to* GIBSON). Oh, sir, you couldn't have the heart—say it is not true.

MR. GIBSON. Sorry for it. You have both deceived me—you must both leave the place.

BRIERLY. You hear—come, May.

MAY. I'll go, sir. It was I deceived you, not he. Only give him a chance—— (*Music—piano, till end.*)

BRIERLY. Never heed her, sir. She'd have told you long ago, but I hadn't the heart—my poor lass—let her bide here, sir—I'll leave the country—I'll 'list.

MAY. Hush, hush, Robert! We were wrong to hide the truth—we are sorely punished—if *you've* courage to face what's before us, *I* have.

BRIERLY. My brave wench! Thank you for all your kindness, sir. Good-bye, friends. Come, May, we'll go together.

It cannot be too strongly emphasized that in their context such sentiments called forth from the Victorian audience the identical response on which a well-made melodrama can rely from the modern cinema audience. Then as now the visual impact of a spectacle sufficiently striking in conception and efficient in execution covered up its intellectual poverty, making superfluous all but the most functional dialogue. The clichés of the modern film differ from the commonplaces of the Victorian melodrama only in their phrasing—the responses at which they aim do not change. Standard characters, strong passions, and vigorous action were the essence of melodrama then and filmmaking now, but in the Victorian theatre the actor had to supply the degree of enlargement provided in the cinema by the camera.

Besides its technical advances, *The Ticket-of-Leave Man*

shows some originality of theme. There is at least implied criticism of a society which allows Bob Brierly to be wrongly convicted and, when he has served his sentence, refuses him the right to an honest living. In this respect the play foreshadows Galsworthy's treatment of the subject fifty years later in *Justice*. The difference of approach is equally instructive, for whereas Galsworthy lays the blame for his victim's suicide squarely on popular prejudice, which sets its face against the convicted criminal, Taylor finds another scapegoat. It is the villainy of the counterfeiters that brings Brierly to the brink of ruin, and—no less typical—it is Brierly's superhuman courage, assisted by Hawkshaw's wizardry, that brings about the gang's downfall and a happy ending. Victorian melodrama remained unshakably moral.

Tom Taylor's name was regularly coupled in the Victorian theatre with that of Charles Reade, like Taylor an influential figure in the theatrical world, and also one of the few Victorian novelists who troubled to adapt his own work for the stage. That Reade had a certain gift for broad theatrical effects is apparent from the success of many of his plays, from *The Courier of Lyons*, which he adapted for Charles Kean from the French of Moreau, Siraudin, and Delacour, to *Drink*, his sensational version of Zola's *L'Assommoir*. Yet the very boldness of his methods was often a source of weakness, especially when abridging his elaborately planned novels for the stage. *It Is Never Too Late To Mend* appears to be, in its stage version, an extraordinarily crude and disjointed production in which the convincingly-drawn prison scenes (the harshness of which provoked a first night demonstration) are set in a shoddy framework of true love in rustic England and deepest villainy in the Australian goldfields.

Reade's happiest collaboration with Taylor was in the comedy, *Masks and Faces*, in which his characteristic roughness of outline was softened by Taylor's command of the sentimental strain then so popular. The appeal of *Masks and Faces* not only kept it regularly on the stage for half a century but also inspired Reade to turn it into a novel, *Peg Woffington*—a curious reversal of the standard Victorian practice. With its Georgian setting and the introduction of such characters as Kitty Clive, James

Quin, and Colley Cibber, as well as Woffington herself, the play would seem to adhere to the same vein of historical romance as *Two Loves and a Life* or *The King's Rival*. Certainly the main story of Mabel Vane, the country wife who follows her husband to London only to find him infatuated with Peg Woffington, while she attracts the notice of the wicked Sir Charles Pomander, is firmly rooted in the truisms of the Victorian theatre.

Yet the character of Woffington herself is given the saving grace of humour, and her enterprise in foiling Pomander's designs on Mabel and reconciling husband and wife indicates both vigour and originality. There is originality, too, in the picture of James Triplet, equally unlucky as painter, poet, and playwright, whose starving family are rescued by Woffington in a scene written with some delicacy and much dexterity:

WOFFINGTON (*in* MRS. TRIPLET'S *ear*). Shake hands with distress, for it shall never enter your door again. (MRS. TRIPLET *clasps her hands.* WOFFINGTON *meets the children with the cloth, which she lays.*) Twelve plates, quick! twenty-four knives, quicker! forty-eight forks, quickest.
(*Enter* POMPEY, *door L.2.E., who sets pie on table, and exit, looking wistfully at it.*
Mr. Triplet—your coat, if you please—and carve.
TRIPLET. My coat, madam!
WOFFINGTON. Yes; off with it, there's a hole in it. (TRIPLET, *with signs of astonishment, gives her his coat, then carves pie—they eat.* WOFFINGTON *seats herself.*) Be pleased to cast your eye on that, ma'am. (BOY *passes housewife to* MRS. TRIPLET.) Woffington's housewife, made by herself, homely to the eye, but holds everything in the world, and has a small space left for everything else; to be returned by the bearer. Thank you, sir! (*Stitches away very rapidly.*) Eat away; children, when once I begin the pie will soon end; (GIRL *takes plate to her mother.*) I do everything so quick.
GIRL. The lady sews faster than you, mother.
WOFFINGTON. Bless the child, don't come near my sword-arm, the needle will go into your eye, and out at the back of your head. (*Children laugh.*) The needle will be lost, the child will be no more, enter undertaker, house turned topsy-turvy, father shows Woffington the door, off she goes, with a face as long and as dull as papa's comedy, crying 'Fine Chaney o-ran-ges!' (*The children laugh heartily.*)

GIRL. Mother! the lady is very funny!

WOFFINGTON. You'll be as funny when you're as well paid for it.

(TRIPLET *chokes with laughing, and lays down knife and fork.*

MRS. TRIPLET. James, take care!

WOFFINGTON. There's the man's coat, (*aside*) with a ten pound note in it.

Though its setting is Georgian and its sentiment Victorian, there is a keen air of anticipation in the whimsical humour of *Masks and Faces*. In this scene, at least, Peg Woffington proves herself the forerunner of Barrie's Painted Lady.

The Eclipse of Comedy

This slight but unmistakably original strain in *Masks and Faces* shows up the dull and derivative character of Victorian comedy as a whole. The success of another comedy with some claim to originality, *Money*, has already been noted. The sustained popularity of a piece with as little to recommend it as Boucicault's *London Assurance* may be compared with that of Tom Taylor's other famous comedy, *Our American Cousin*, originally a feeble melodrama in which the comic relief supplied by Lord Dundreary was, through a familiar stage process, worked up by Edward Sothern into the leading rôle and ensured the play's success. A theatre which must offer *Money* and *Masks and Faces* as evidence of its comic spirit, and *London Assurance* and *Our American Cousin* as its popular choices, is clearly starved of comic inspiration.

In fact the conditions of the Victorian theatre were almost uniformly unfavourable to comedy. The theatres themselves were too big, the audiences' understanding too small. The repertory of comedies from Dryden to Sheridan, many of which had retained their popularity for a hundred years, therefore disappeared from the bills. Several of Shakespeare's comedies continued in favour, largely for the chances they afforded of spectacular staging. The comedies of Shakespeare's contemporaries and successors, however, were virtually ignored by the Victorian theatre.

Few old comedies were revived; few new comedies were written. The strain of late Georgian comedy represented by Morton or the younger Colman was readily absorbed in the vogue for melodrama. The mission of Romantic criticism was to restore Elizabethan tragedy to the favour which neo-classic theory had bestowed on Elizabethan comedy. Romantic critics, therefore, could not be expected to resuscitate either old or newer comedy. That a measure of their Elizabethan enthusiasm did in fact spill over into the field of comedy is apparent. John Tobin's long-lived comedy, *The Honey Moon*, is a successful re-working of *The Taming of the Shrew*, and Sheridan Knowles showed in his comedies something of the same feeling for colourful and effective situations that commended his tragedies to the public. *The Hunchback*, *The Wife*, and *The Love Chase* used period settings and inflated language; but their popularity, like that of *Caius Gracchus* and *Virginius*, derived from situations consciously designed to appeal to a contemporary audience. Moreover, Tobin and Knowles remained outside the charmed circle of the Romantic movement in England, none of whose poets contemplated writing comedy. The Romantic imagination was too preoccupied with inner conflict and the supernatural to tackle the natural conflicts which give birth to comedy.

The Victorian theatre witnessed the complete subordination of comedy to spectacle, signs of which were apparent in the last years of the Georgian theatre. In general, melodrama was given pride of place on the evening's bill, with a comic afterpiece tacked on to satisfy the half-price customers who had missed much of the melodrama. Alternatively a comedy might be played as the curtain-raiser. In either case the comedy was limited to two or three acts, in which neither character nor intrigue had sufficient space for development. Thus farcical incident took the place of comic impetus and character-building was discarded for the crude opposition of stock types or virtuoso playing by the leading actor.

The popular writers of English comedy in the early nineteenth century were theatrical journeymen, trained to run up an afterpiece to an actor's or manager's order. *Raising the Wind* by James Kenney, one of the most persistent of such pieces, shows all the limitations of their work. The play exists to provide Jeremy Diddler with a series of impostures, carried off with an engaging swagger. Neither plot, dialogue, nor subsidiary characters have any substance, but W. T. Lewis, the original Jeremy Diddler, secured the audience's approval, and Charles Mathews and Henry Irving were only two of his successors in the same part with the same popularity.

Play-collections of this period are therefore full of such sketches, designed solely as a vehicle for some popular favourite. Probably the younger Mathews was the most influential of these, and in *Cool as a Cucumber*, perhaps his most successful piece, W. B. Jerrold slavishly applied the formula of *Raising the Wind* to enable Mathews as Horatio Plumper to inflict on the Barkins household the same impostures as Jeremy Diddler, with much the same material result. The most that can be said for these Victorian farces is that before their own audience they did quicken into life, whereas the more ambitious efforts of Douglas Jerrold or Boucicault remained still-born.

Amongst scores of such after-pieces possibly only *Box and Cox* by John Maddison Morton retains an individual flavour. Morton's piece is modest in scope, but its humour derives neither from a single character, nor from absurd disguises. There is an attractive symmetry in the efforts of Box, the Journeyman Printer, and Cox, the Journeyman Hatter, to disentangle themselves first from the room they share, then from the wife they appear to share. Their exchanges are gaily antiphonal, and at the end Morton is not afraid to laugh at the conventions of his own drama:

MRS. BOUNCER (*putting her head in at the door*). The little second floor back room is quite ready.

COX. I don't want it!

BOX. No more do I!

COX. What shall part us?

BOX. What shall tear us asunder?

COX. Box!

BOX. Cox! (*About to embrace*—BOX *stops, seizes* COX's *hand, and looks eagerly in his face.*) You'll excuse the apparent insanity of the remark, but the more I gaze on your features, the more I'm convinced that you're my long-lost brother.

COX. The very observation I was going to make to you!

BOX. Ah—tell me—in mercy tell me—have you such a thing as a strawberry mark on your left arm?

cox. No!

box. Then it is he! (*They rush into each other's arms.*)

The popularity of the adaptation, *Cox and Box*, which Francis Burnand later made for Sullivan, has perhaps obscured the merits of Morton's original.

Burlesque

For any continuous evidence of a thriving comic tradition in the nineteenth-century theatre it is necessary to look, not to Drury Lane nor even the Haymarket, but to the new, upstart, often illicit minor theatres. Just as the minor theatres gave birth to a native strain of melodrama, which touched the emotions of the Victorian audience when tragedy left them largely unmoved, so these same minor theatres fostered in burlesque the only truly spontaneous form of Victorian comedy.

The emergence of the word 'burletta' as a theatrical term in both legal and general use naturally led to a confusion between 'burletta' and 'burlesque'. They were in fact two quite separate things, for the essential characteristic of the burletta was its form, whilst that of the burlesque was its subject and the spirit in which that subject was treated. But the confusion was inevitable, for the interpolation of music and song which established the burletta form lent itself very easily to the purposes of burlesque. Moreover, at the minor theatres, obliged by law to confine themselves to the burletta, the audiences welcomed the exuberance and exaggeration of burlesque no less heartily than the thrills of spectacle and melodrama. A high proportion of burlettas, therefore, were in fact burlesques, and the burlesque-writer becomes a prominent figure in the Victorian theatre, with a clearly established pedigree, descending from Planché to Robert and William Brough, Francis Talfourd, Burnand, H. J. Byron, and, most interesting of all, W. S. Gilbert.

Burlesque in the English theatre had been severely limited when in 1737 the Licensing Act virtually excluded political matters from the stage, for politics and personalities had provided Fielding with material for the great majority of his plays, even though the best-known, *Tom Thumb*, was, like Buckingham's *Rehearsal* before it, aimed largely at theatrical targets. Baulked of his political platform, Fielding had quitted the

66

theatre, and English burlesque fell back on the absurdities of its own stage until, in *The Critic*, Sheridan capped all the comments on theatrical usage made by his predecessors. But with the gradual disappearance from the boards of the heroic tragedy at which Buckingham, Fielding, and Sheridan laughed in turn, the scope for burlesque of theatrical convention was seriously curtailed. Perhaps this curtailment fostered the development of mock-classical burlesques, in which the figures and fables of ancient Greece and Rome were turned to up-to-date and usually ludicrous ends. Such devices had been employed in the English theatre from Elizabethan times, but their use became increasingly popular towards the end of the eighteenth century, when such titles as *Midas* (by Kane O'Hara), *The Court of Alexander*, and *Poor Vulcan* (by Charles Dibdin) recur frequently.

Such mock-classical burlesques earned their laughs simply— with the audience at the minor theatres there was probably no choice. The joke derived from the grandeur of the figure represented—Greek hero or Roman god—and the bathos of his lines and antics. No doubt the acting of such pieces was often as crude as the writing. When Planché turned his attention to burlesque, the cheapness of its presentation, even by leading comedians, repelled him. As he put it:

Liston thought to the last that Prometheus, instead of the Phrygian cap, tunic and trousers, should have been dressed like a great lubberly boy, in a red jacket and nankeens, with a pinafore all besmeared with lollipops; others that, as in *Midas*, the costume should be an incongruous mixture of the classical and the farcical.[1]

Planché was lucky enough to find in Madame Vestris a manager who shared his aim of refining both the style and the staging of classical burlesque. This aim they achieved in *Olympic Revels; or, Prometheus and Pandora* (written in collaboration with Charles Dance), the first production which Madame Vestris staged at the Olympic; and Planché and Dance explored the same vein in *Olympic Devils; or, Orpheus and Eurydice; The Paphian Bower; or, Venus and Adonis; The Deep, Deep Sea; or, Perseus and Andromeda;* and *Telemachus; or, The Island of*

---

[1] *The Extravaganzas of J. R. Planché* (London, 1879), Vol. I, p. 40–1.

Calypso. Later, for other theatres, Planché alone wrote *The Golden Fleece*; *Theseus and Ariadne*; *Cymon and Iphigenia*; and *Orpheus in the Haymarket.*

In these classical burlesques Planché, like his colleagues, relied mainly on putting irreverent sentiments into revered mouths. Yet his dexterity in matching the two gives his work a grace lacking in the clumsy humour of lesser burlesques. So, in *The Paphian Bower*, Venus sings to her early Victorian Adonis:

> Quit the chase, my dear Adonis,
>   Cut the turf and kennel clean.
> Sell your hunters, racers, ponies,
>   Burn your Sporting Magazine.
> Broken hearts we hear of
>   But we seldom see the wrecks.
> There is much more fear of
>   Broken arms or necks.

His audience's taste insisted on punning as a principal source of laughter: yet in meeting that taste Planché displayed a neatness of phrase and idea which suggests not only the dexterity of his own mind, but also that, on familiar ground, his audience could reveal a sharpness with which they are rarely credited. The well-known exchange from *The Golden Fleece*, for example, moves almost too fast for the modern reader, and would surely leave the modern spectator far behind:

JASON.   Now, madam, you talk sense.
         I'm vexed you gave my friend, the King, offence.
         And as to Glauce——
MEDEA.   —Oh, don't name that creature!
         I heard her say: If your wife bores you, beat her.
JASON.   You quite mistook her—the reverse meant she—
         Beta, in Greek, you know, is 'Letter B'.

Despite his success in refining the burlesque, something of a note of discontent with the form began to creep into Planché's work. His urge to break away from the classical framework resulted in a series of commentaries on the theatrical scene. The first of these, *The Drama's Levée*, was produced by Vestris at the Olympic, but it was to Buckstone at the Haymarket that the majority of these entertainments owed their appearance, and Planché acknowledged the debt in such titles as *Mr. Buckstone's Ascent of Mount Parnassus*, *Mr. Buckstone's Voyage Round the Globe*, and *The New Haymarket Spring Meeting*. In these pieces Planché did not bring out the absurdities of a particular style of play, as Fielding or Sheridan had done; nor did he hold up a current favourite for ridicule, in the increasingly popular 'travesty' form. His aim was to take a quick look at the whole theatrical scene, before and behind the curtain, within and without the theatre. Often his findings sum up some paradox or anomaly, for example the burletta rule in this extract from *The Drama's Levée*:

DRAMA. The Drama's proper place is on the stage.
PRAISE. Yes, at a patent house! But here you know,
It's quite against the law. I'll tell you, though,
How you can manage. Sing some arietta!
And if they question you, say, you're burletta!

Several of these running commentaries were styled 'a dramatick review', and in the speed and range of their comments they certainly suggest the modern revue.

But Planché wished to go further, and in *The Seven Champions of Christendom* extended the scope of his 'dramatick review' to the whole European scene. The result was unimpressive, for Planché's arrows, which had earlier found the theatrical bull, fell wide of the mark on the larger target. Encouraged by the success of his burlesques, he had felt himself drawn on 'to lay the foundations of an Aristophanic drama, which the greatest minds would not consider it derogatory to contribute to' (as he put it), and to this end had already brought *The Birds* up to date at the Haymarket. Neither his powers nor his period were apt for the purpose. He could scarcely hope to achieve at the end of his career a change in theatrical taste to which W. S. Gilbert subsequently devoted the greater part of his life-work.

Yet Planché did bring about another important development in the English theatre. After his early classical burlesques for Vestris at the Olympic, he began to turn to the French fairy tales of Perrault and Madame D'Aulnoy as another source of material. The first, *Riquet with the Tuft*, was followed by *Puss in Boots* and *Blue Beard*. Then, when Vestris moved from the miniature Olympic to the vast Covent Garden stage, Planché elaborated his new style in *The Sleeping Beauty in the Wood*. That this departure was already regarded as important is suggested by Planché's own note: 'The Sleeping Beauty was therefore announced as an extravaganza, distinguishing the whimsical treatment of a poetical subject from the broad caricature of a tragedy or a serious opera, which was correctly termed a "Burlesque".'[1] In placing the emphasis of extravaganza on fantasy and of burlesque on caricature Planché provided a distinction which still serves a useful purpose, though it is not a definition which has been consistently acknowledged or observed.

The Sleeping Beauty was followed by *Beauty and the Beast* and *The White Cat*, and later by other extravaganzas on fairy themes for other theatres. The influence which Planché's work thus exercised on the changing face of English pantomime was far-reaching. One factor, immediately apparent, was the impetus given to the casting of an actress as hero (not yet 'principal boy'). Vestris, already unequalled as a male impersonator in burlesque, was now able to use these gifts as Ralph in *Puss in Boots* at the Olympic, as Prince Paragon in *The White Cat* at Covent Garden, and in the title rôle in *King Charming; or, The Blue Bird of Paradise* at the Lyceum later. Equally far-reaching was Planché's widening of the range of pantomime by the use in his extravaganzas of French fairy tales, and by his emphasis on fantasy and romantic spectacle. This feature of his work, when taken over by the 'opening' of the pantomime, conflicted strongly with the simpler humour and cruder colours of the surviving Harlequinade elements, handed down by John Rich and his successors to the great Grimaldi—a conflict in which the romantic and spectacular elements gradually gained the upper hand.[2] In fact Planché's extravaganzas sometimes suggest a style far removed from his own burlesques—nearer, indeed, to his opera librettos, such as *Oberon*. In *The Yellow Dwarf*, one of Planché's

---

[1] *Extravaganzas*, Vol. II, p. 66.
[2] In *Conquest: The Story of a Theatre Family* (London, 1953), Miss Frances Fleetwood notes that the Conquest family introduced into their famous pantomimes at the Grecian and Surrey Theatres many strange and sinister creatures: the Flying Dutchman, Herne the Hunter, the Demon Dwarf, the Spider Crab, Grim Goblin and the Rock Fiend amongst them.

last extravaganzas, the name part was taken by Frederick Robson, perhaps the outstanding burlesque-actor of the Victorian theatre. Robson brought to his part pathetic and even sinister qualities which, in effect, raised Planché's work to the level of Romantic drama. That his lasting contribution to the pantomime form fell short of this level was largely due to the infusion of fresh comic elements from the Music Hall later in the century. But a major change had been effected, and in the upheaval which followed the Harlequinade gradually dwindled and disappeared.

None of Planché's immediate successors in the field of burlesque inherited his pioneering spirit. Possibly recognizing that Planché had been once bitten by the Aristophanic wasp, they were twice shy of it. At any rate Talfourd and the brothers Brough aimed little higher than the popular theatrical fare of the day, and were content to make the pun their principal weapon. That did not preclude their using it with a great deal of skill and variety. In his essay, *Exit Planché—Enter Gilbert*, in the Royal Society of Literature volume, *The Eighteen-Sixties* (1932), Granville Barker singled out a passage from William Brough's *The Field of the Cloth of Gold* to illustrate this variety:

KING FRANCIS. These fine old trees my view on all sides border;
They're Foresters of the most Ancient Order.
Still, for their king thus trapping there's no reason;
And so *high trees*, I charge you with *high treason*.
My royalty at least there's no mistaking;
I've walked till every bone tells me I'm *a king*.
I'll lie down 'neath these boughs, for I protest,
Walking this *forest long*, I *long for rest*.
Francis, full length extended 'neath these branches
Will be what's called '*extension of the Franchis*'.

Here eight lines provide examples of the pun direct ('high trees', 'high treason'), the pun implied ('I'm a king'), the pun reversed ('forest long', 'long for rest'), and the pun topical ('extension of the Franchis'), since in 1868 the Reform Bill of the previous year would be very much in the audience's mind.

Nevertheless, the calibre of that audience must seriously have cramped the burlesque-writers' style. Their efforts to 'take-off' the popular plays of the day, for instance, become wilder and wilder, until the achievement of bathos by the use of the incongruous is often their sole aim. There is little in mid-Victorian burlesque to match Fielding's or Sheridan's skill in raising a recognizable theatrical style or convention to the level of inspired absurdity. Had it been done, the Victorian audience might well have failed to recognize the original, for the popularity of melodrama had largely driven the traditional repertory from the stage. Even Shakespearean references could prove elusive, so that the Shakespearean burlesque became no more than a facetious re-working of a cherished plot in the 'travestie', as most of Talfourd's burlesques were styled. At least Talfourd never descended to the level of the *Othello Travestie* cited by Granville Barker, in which Desdemona was made to sing to the tune of 'Bonnie Laddie':

> I'll tell you why I loved the Black;
> > *Too ral, etc.*
> 'Cause ev'ry night I had a knack,
> > *Too ral, etc.*
> Of list'ning to his tales bewitchin',
> My hair while curling in the kitchen.
> > *Too ral, etc.*[1]

A new impetus to burlesque was provided by the gradual return to the theatre of those classes which had abandoned it to the masses at the turn of the century. The original strain of Gilbert's librettos for the Savoy Operas provided one line of development, by relegating the parody of popular stage fare to a subordinate place. At the same time the emphasis of traditional burlesque turned increasingly from the 'travestie' of the title to incidental song and dance. With Planché's pioneering spirit gone, burlesque, like pantomime, was shaped increasingly by artists rather than authors. The burlesque-writer was required to cut his text to the measure of his actors. It was in this limited capacity that H. J. Byron served; but if his task was modest, its results, though indirect, were momentous, for one of his duties whilst serving the Strand Theatre in this capacity was to provide a vehicle for a little-known burlesque actress, Marie

---

[1] *Exit Planché—Enter Gilbert*, pp. 107–8.

Wilton. He chose *The Maid and the Magpie* as his subject, and designed the part of the boy, Pippo, for Marie Wilton. Of the effect she made on her audience in this part a letter from Charles Dickens to John Forster gives a vivid impression:

I escaped at half-past seven and went to the Strand Theatre; having taken a stall before-hand for it is always crammed. I really wish you would go, between this and next Thursday, to see the *Maid and the Magpie* burlesque there. There is the strangest thing in it that ever I have seen on the stage. The boy, Pippo, by Miss Wilton. While it is astonishingly impudent (must be, or it couldn't be done at all) it is so stupendously like a boy, and unlike a woman, that it is perfectly free from offence. I never have seen such a thing. Priscilla Horton as a boy, not to be thought of beside it. She does an imitation of the dancing of the Christy Minstrels—wonderfully clever—which in the audacity of its thorough-going is surprising. A thing that you *can not* imagine a woman's doing at all; and yet the manner, the appearance, the levity, impulse and spirits of it, are so exactly like a boy, that you cannot think of anything like her sex in association with it. It begins at eight, and is over by a quarter-past nine.[1]

It was understandable that when, seven years later, Marie Wilton was offered a chance to run her own theatre, even though it was the despised Queen's or 'Dusthole', to be re-named the Prince of Wales's, she should turn again to Byron for help. He provided her with the burlesque on the opening night (15 April 1865), *La! Sonnambula! or, The Supper, the Sleeper, and the Merry Swiss Boy*, and another, *Lucia di' Lammermoor; or, The Laird, the Lady and the Lover*, when the autumn season opened. But neither the public, nor, probably, Marie Wilton herself found in such traditional stuff the new departure which her entry into management had promised. There seemed a better chance of novelty from the pen of Byron's close friend and colleague, T. W. Robertson, to whom the production a year earlier of *David Garrick* had brought the first taste of material success after twenty years' continuous labour. Robertson's comedy, *Society*, had recently been rejected by Buckstone at the Haymarket, but a trial performance at Liverpool suggested that Buckstone had miscalculated. Marie Wilton and

[1] Printed by A. Filon in *The English Stage* (London, 1897), pp. 102–3.

her leading man, Sydney Bancroft (soon to be Squire Bancroft as she was to be Mrs. Bancroft), decided to put it on at the Prince of Wales's. The production there of *Society* on 11 November 1865 not only ensured the fame of both the Bancrofts and Robertson, but marked the eclipse of burlesque by comedy. The new drama had found a new exponent.

5. *Macready's* Henry V, *Covent Garden,* 1839
ABOVE: *Before Harfleur.* BELOW: *Back-cloth for Agincourt*

6 *Kean's The Winter's Tale, Princess's, 1856*

7. *Irving's* Much Ado About Nothing, *Lyceum*, 1882

8. *Tree's King John, Her Majesty's, 1899. The Fight near Angiers.*

9. *Granville Barker's* A Midsummer Night's Dream, *Savoy*, 1914

10. *Pantomime: Behind the Scenes*

11. *Pantomime: In the Wings*

12 The 'Star Trap' at the Princess's Theatre

3

THE RETURN OF RESPECTABILITY

From the immense output of a hundred years of English drama only *Caste* retains a hold on the modern repertory. Robertson is now generally recognized as the first modern English dramatist, and his work for the Bancrofts as inaugurating a new era in the English theatre. Yet Robertson was very much the child of the traditional Victorian theatre. His parents, managers of the Lincolnshire Circuit, lived to see the first and the last of their twenty-two children famous, for Tom Robertson was their eldest, and Madge Robertson, later to be Dame Madge Kendal, their youngest child. Tom Robertson's apprenticeship in the theatre was long and bitter; early pressed into service by family necessity, he never achieved much success as an actor, even after wide experience. Nor, for many years, did he achieve recognition as a dramatist. Although his first piece was presented in London in 1851, it was not until Edward Sothern staged *David Garrick* in 1864 that his ability was acknowledged. With the Bancrofts' production of *Society* in the following year, Robertson found his true centre, and the six comedies for the Prince of Wales's Theatre by which his fame was assured were written and produced in the six years before his death in 1871, at the age of forty-two.

Robertson's Plays

Robertson's entire training was therefore provided by the early Victorian theatre, and much of his work faithfully reflects the commonplace standards of that theatre. Before the production of *David Garrick* his style had scarcely been distinguishable from that of dozens of his fellow-dramatists. He adapted *The Ladies' Battle* from Scribe, had an indeterminate share in the spectacular version of *Faust and Marguerite* staged by

75

Charles Kean at the Princess's, and put together a series of melodramas of which the titles (e.g. *The Battle of Life*, and *The Half-Caste; or, the Poison'd Pearl*) speak for themselves. Even after his position was assured his work for theatres other than the Prince of Wales's hardly rose above the feeble level of his contemporaries. Without the Bancroft company for his inspiration, a serious theme could only draw from him sensational treatment.

For instance *Progress* (based on *Les Ganaches* by Sardou) presents an interesting and strictly topical conflict between the young railway engineer, Ferne, and the ancient Mompesson family, through whose estates Ferne proposes to build his line. But Robertson soon dismisses the wider issue for a romance between Ferne and Eva, Lord Mompesson's ailing niece, so that when their marriage is forbidden the dramatist can drag in a favourite device of melodrama:

EVA. . . . Oh! air! air! (*Approaches window.*) I cannot breathe! No! (*Returning.*) I must not. The cold will kill me! (*Raising her head.*) Well, why not? Life is tasteless! Let me die!
Music—piano till end of Act. She opens window and steps out into the balcony amid the thick falling snow. Noise of wind heard as the casement is opened. EVA *throws off the wrappings from her neck and shoulders so that she stands exposed to the snow in her petticoat body. She coughs frequently and places her hands on her chest.* FERNE *appears on balcony, and as she faints catches her, and brings her into the room again.*

Even those moments of insight and genuine feeling which still give interest to his Prince of Wales's comedies tend at the same time to draw attention to their general contrivance. Robertson, no less than his contemporaries, uses stark coincidence to keep his plot spinning and simple contrast as the basis of his character-drawing. He is content, in *Society*, to let his heroine renounce her lover because on hearing the child he has befriended call herself 'Mr. Daryl's little girl' she at once believes him her father. As the dénouement of *Caste* he presents his hero's return, unheralded, from death on the Indian battlefield. In *Ours* he allowed Marie Wilton to make rolypoly pudding on the stage while the Crimean War raged all around her. He is capable of such crude character-drawing as the upstart Chodds in *Society* or the patrician Marquise de St. Maur in *Caste*, with her verbatim reports from Froissart.

Yet originality—in both purpose and performance—is apparent in Robertson's best work. His titles alone: *Society, Caste, Home, Progress, Birth, War*—show him stretching towards wider themes than the simple story-telling which satisfied his predecessors. That his conclusions should prove commonplace was the consequence of his training and temperament:

Oh, Caste's all right. Caste is a good thing if it's not carried too far. It shuts the door on the pretentious and the vulgar; but it should open the door very wide for exceptional merit. Let brains break through its barriers, and what brains can break through love may leap over.

This is typical of his findings. When, in *School*, he briefly considers the movement for women's emancipation then gathering momentum, his view is that of the well-meaning but slow-thinking traditionalist:

LORD BEAUFOY. Some women would kill gallantry and chivalry by something called equality with men. What is equality with men? Having their clothes made by a he-tailor instead of a she-milliner. How pleasant for man and wife to be measured together; or, at an election, for him to walk arm-in-arm to the hustings with a wretched, half-mad, whole-mannish creature, who votes for the candidate you wish to exclude.

JACK. I agree with you there. If women were admitted to electoral privileges they'd sell them for the price of a new chignon. Man, as the nobler animal, has the exclusive right to sell his vote for beer.

Robertson could not evolve a play of ideas because his own ideas were largely superficial. But he did suggest how more forceful ideas could be given dramatic form. In *Caste* his portrait of old Eccles, the drunken father, whom not even the final curtain can reform, marks a break with one of the most popular conventions of melodrama. Even more interesting is his handling of Gerridge, the good-hearted plumber, and his adored Polly, through whom he illuminates class distinctions far more effectively than by his haughty Marquise or swaggering Captain

Hawtree. There is genuine understanding and affection for their sturdy self-reliance in the scene in which they plan their home together:

SAM. . . . I'll new-paper it, and new-furnish it, and it shall all be bran-new. . . .

POLLY. But won't it cost a lot of money?

SAM (*bravely*). I can work for it. With customers in the shop, and you in the back-parlour, I can work like fifty men. (*Sits on table R., beckons* POLLY *to him. She comes L. of table.* SAM *puts his arm round* POLLY *sentimentally.*) Only fancy, at night, when the shop's closed, and the shutters are up, counting out the till together! (*Changing his manner.*) Besides, that isn't all I've been doin'. I've been writin', and what I've written I've got printed.

POLLY. No!

SAM. True.

POLLY. You've been writing—about me? (*Delighted.*)

SAM. No—about the shop. (POLLY *disgusted.*) Here it is. (*Takes roll of circulars from pocket of his canvas-slop.*) Yer mustn't laugh—you know—it's my first attempt. I wrote it the night before last; and when I thought of you the words seemed to flow like—red-hot solder.

By capturing the authentic accents and conduct of Gerridge and Polly, Robertson gives substance to their situation, although incapable of tackling his theme with any depth or force.

How far he contrived to modify the system of stock characterization which he inherited can be illustrated from the sequence of parts which John Hare undertook for the Prince of Wales plays. As a young man of twenty-one he played the doddering old Lord Ptarmigant in *Society*; then the suave Russian diplomat, Prince Petrovsky, in *Ours*; honest Sam Gerridge in *Caste*; the crafty gambler, Bruce Fanquhere, in *Play*; the desiccated Beau Farintosh in *School*; and Dunscombe Dunscombe, bankrupt but debonair, in *M.P.* That Robertson could write such a diversity of parts for a single actor suggests a real advance in technique.

Robertson's 'Stage-Management'

Indeed it is on his handling of the technical resources of the stage that Robertson's reputation now rests. That reputation is perhaps too closely linked with the provision of real door-knobs for the stage-doors. Pinero embodied this conception in his affectionate portrait of Robertson as the struggling actor-dramatist, Tom Wrench, in *Trelawny of the 'Wells'*:

I tell you, I won't have doors stuck here, there, and everywhere; no, nor windows in all sorts of impossible places! . . . (*Pointing to the left.*) Windows on the one side, (*pointing to the right*) doors on the other—just where they should be architecturally. And locks on the doors, *real locks*, to work; and handles—to turn! (*Rubbing his hands together gleefully.*) Ha, ha! you wait! wait——!

In fact most of the individual features of Robertson's stage had been introduced by Vestris and Mathews twenty years earlier, as their apologists have since asserted. If the evidence for their introduction of the box-set is not conclusive, the Vestris management clearly employed ceiling cloths, carpets, and elaborate furnishings, although these features had not come into general use. Robertson's particular achievement was to apply the skill and resource widely employed in the staging of spectacular drama to the miniature canvas of drawing-room drama. The attention he gave to the details of stage management are still reflected in the exactness of his stage directions, which mark a final break with the formal presentation of the Georgian theatre. That he was resolutely opposed to antiquated methods of staging is suggested by this stage direction from *Birth*:

ACT III, SCENE 1: Ivy-covered Ruins and grass plot, supposed to have formed the old courtyard of the castle; the chapel at the back. The tower, L.H.1 E., to be new (i.e., restored), and to look habitable. The door practicable. No moon in the cloth. The moonlight to be on the grass. The ivy to be real ivy, and the grass to be grass matting—not painted.

Not only does he give the most precise details of each setting, but the use of tiny effects to establish the atmosphere and further the action of the play is regularly required. In *Society* the scene in a London square calls for 'the effect of setting sun in windows of houses'. In *Ours* a stage direction runs: 'Throughout the Act the autumn leaves fall from the trees'; while it was chiefly on account of the kitchen tea-party in *Caste* that Robertson's work was named 'cup-and-saucer comedy':

SAM *cuts enormous slice of bread, and hands it on point of knife to* HAWTREE. *Cuts small lump of butter, and hands it on point of knife to* HAWTREE, *who looks at it through eye-glass, then takes it.* SAM *then helps himself.* POLLY *meantime has poured out tea in two cups, and one saucer for* SAM, *sugars them, and then hands cup and saucer to* HAWTREE, *who has both hands full. He takes it awkwardly, and places it on table.* POLLY, *having only one spoon, tastes* SAM's *tea, then stirs* HAWTREE's, *attracting his attention by so doing. He looks into his tea-cup.* POLLY *stirs her own tea, and drops spoon into* HAWTREE's *cup, causing it to spurt in his eye. He drops eye-glass and wipes his eyes.*

It was this attention to detail which led William Archer to call Robertson 'a pre-Raphaelite of the theatre'.[1] But this detail is not introduced merely for its own sake, nor solely to enhance the appearance of the play. Robertson regularly employs a piece of stage business to catch and hold a delicate emotion which dialogue alone could not convey. In *School* the flexibility of limelight is deftly used in the love-scene between Bella, the Cinderella of the story, and Lord Beaufoy:

LORD BEAUFOY. What long shadows the moonlight flings. See—there I am.
BELLA. But so tall—so high.
LORD BEAUFOY. And there you are.
BELLA. But not so tall as you are.
LORD BEAUFOY. And yet you're nearer the skies—see! (*Moving.*) Now we're far apart.
(*The moonlight throws shadows from R. to L.*)
BELLA. And now—— (*Moving.*) We're joined together.

Robertson's insistence on precise detail in performance was possible because of the authority with which the Bancrofts invested him in the preparation of his own plays. In the field of spectacular drama Boucicault had already asserted the claim of the author to control the rehearsals of his own play. Now Robertson applied that control to the rehearsal of drawing-room drama, and since, unlike Boucicault, he did not appear in his own plays, he was able to give greater attention to ensemble and balance. This appearance of an artistic director who was neither actor nor prompter marks a definite stage in the

[1] *The Old Drama and the New* (London, 1923), p. 260.

evolution of the modern producer or director. W. S. Gilbert's testimony to Robertson's importance in this evolution is well known. Robertson, he declared:

> . . . invented stage-management. It was an unknown art before his time. Formerly, in a conversation scene, for instance, you simply brought down two or three chairs from the flat and placed them in a row in the middle of the stage, and then people sat down and talked, and when the conversation was ended the chairs were replaced. Robertson showed how to give life and variety and nature to the scene by breaking it up with all sorts of little incidents and delicate by-play. I have been at many of his rehearsals and learnt a great deal from them.[1]

Such a tribute is all the more valuable since it comes from a dramatist whose absolute rule over his own rehearsals was universally acknowledged. The dramatist-director is an influential factor in the late Victorian theatre, the succession passing from Robertson to Gilbert, to Pinero, and ultimately to Shaw. But these men exercised their powers by virtue of their pre-eminence as dramatists. Lesser men were less respected, and in general the actor continued to rule the Victorian stage. The emergence of an artistic director who was neither actor nor dramatist but an independent mind, shaping the entire performance, belongs to the next century.

Meanwhile Robertson's authority at the Prince of Wales's extended over the actors themselves, no less than the management of the stage. Plainly his aim was to refine the exaggeration of mid-Victorian acting, along with the commonplaces of character-drawing. The variety of rôles with which he provided Hare has already been noted. But even when providing familiar material he protests against a crude or ludicrous handling of it. In *M.P.*, when the bankrupt nobleman witnesses the sale of his mother's portrait, the author gives this explicit instruction:

> The actor playing Dunscombe is requested not to make too much of this situation. All that is required is a momentary memory of childhood—succeeded by the external phlegm of the man of the world. No tragedy, no tears, or pocket-handkerchief.

[1] Sydney Dark and Rowland Grey: *W. S. Gilbert* (London, 1923), p. 59.

And in *War*, the last play Robertson wrote, there is an admonition against caricature in the part of the Frenchman:

The author requests this part may be played with a slight French accent. He is not to pronounce the words absurdly or duck his head toward his stomach like the conventional stage Frenchman.

This sustained demand of Robertson's for subtler interpretation and more subdued effects must greatly have influenced the distinguished company at the Prince of Wales's who interpreted his plays. It was, moreover, an influence which gradually permeated late Victorian acting. Not only did Squire and Marie Bancroft demonstrate it when they moved to the Haymarket, but Hare carried the style to the Court Theatre, where he worked with Ellen Terry, and to the St. James's, which he ran in partnership with the Kendals. On his debt to Robertson, Hare was explicit:

My opinion of Robertson as a stage-manager is of the very highest. He had a gift peculiar to himself, and which I have never seen in any other author, of conveying by some rapid and almost electrical suggestion to the actor an insight into the character assigned to him. As nature was the basis of his own work, so he sought to make actors understand it should be theirs. He thus founded a school of natural acting which completely revolutionized the then existing methods, and by so doing did incalculable good to the stage.[1]

Even actors like Wyndham and Alexander, who had never worked under Robertson, reflected some of his precepts in their acting. That these muted methods did not displace the big, colourful style of the Romantic school of Irving and Tree is evident. But the gradual assimilation of Robertson's teaching must powerfully have assisted the new school of acting which the new century inaugurated.

Auditorium and Audience

At the Prince of Wales's under the Bancrofts the auditorium as well as the stage invited comment. No doubt the elegance of its fittings—the rosebud chintz in the circle, and the carpet

[1] See T. Edgar Pemberton: *Society* and *Caste* (Belles Lettres Series: Cambridge, Mass., 1905), Introduction, p. xxxi.

in the stalls—was enhanced by the squalor of the surroundings. What seemed so daring at the former 'Dusthole' off the Tottenham Court Road might not have startled the patrons of the Haymarket or the St. James's. But the Bancrofts' feat in coaxing back polite society into an unfashionable playhouse was substantial. The stigma which had marked playgoing since the era of the O.P. Riots clung tenaciously. The Opera was respectable and Shakespeare, when performed by Macready or Charles Kean, might become so, but melodrama was not polite, and Queen Victoria was severely criticized for attending *The Corsican Brothers* at the Princess's. For this distrust the behaviour of the mid-Victorian audience often gave grounds. But the Bancrofts were lucky in their era. In particular the evolution of the Music Hall at this time began to draw off the violent element in the audience. By its transformation from the semi-secret haunt of the raffish man-about-town into the popular resort of the working man, providing both drink and entertainment, the Music Hall took over one of the chief functions of the mid-Victorian theatre. The way was thus cleared in the 1860s for the building of new, smaller playhouses for a smaller, more discriminating audience—the first spate of theatre-building since the passing of the Act of 1843.

There is a direct link, too, between Robertson and the Bancrofts and the transformation which took place in the provincial theatre during the 1860s and 1870s, for *Caste* was one of the first plays in which a London company was sent out on a national tour, and thereafter the practice gradually became general. Such touring companies represented a serious threat to the old stock companies whose survival since their heyday at the end of the eighteenth century had been protracted but precarious. The favourites of the early Victorian theatre, London stars like Macready as well as provincial idols like G. V. Brooke and Barry Sullivan, had undertaken their tours alone, or with two or three supporting actors. The remainder of the company and the mounting of the play were provided by the theatres they visited.

The transportation of a complete and often elaborate production—scenery, costumes, and properties as well as the entire cast—was made possible by the rapid advance of the railways.

To house these touring productions there grew up from about 1870 a chain of large, well-equipped provincial theatres, often without a resident company. The change clearly entailed a loss of local loyalties towards local favourites and of local colour in the drama itself, as the provincial theatre became increasingly a mirror of the London theatre. On the other hand the standard achieved by the touring company must generally have outdone that of the stock company, both in acting and particularly in presentation and ensemble, born of long practice. It is also an accurate reflection of an expanding public that an audience could be found for the six or more performances of a single play given by the touring company, whereas even with a nightly change of bill the stock company had often played to half-empty houses.

The Bancrofts' achievement in reducing the bill to a single piece was no less influential than their coaxing of polite Society out to the Tottenham Court Road. It marked the replacement of a lengthy, ill-assorted menu, from which the customer could pick and choose, by a single carefully prepared dish, for which his attention and judgement were requested. Admittedly the Bancrofts did not finish the battle. The prejudice in polite Society against the playhouse, though diminished, still persisted, and the well-established pittite did not willingly surrender his privileges to the fashionable playgoer. This the Bancrofts discovered for themselves when in 1880 they took over the Haymarket and replaced the remaining pit-benches by stalls. But they were able to ride out the opening-night storm, and it was on their foundations that the brilliantly fashionable audiences at the Lyceum and the Savoy were built up.

Robertson's Successors

The effects of the Bancroft-Robertson régime on production and on playgoing continued to make themselves felt. On the writing of plays that influence was at first much less obvious. Robertson's style was too distinct to affect the established practitioner of melodrama. Only Tom Taylor seems seriously to have studied his methods. In *New Men and Old Acres* Taylor essayed a theme closely akin to *Society* or *Birth*: the replacement at Cleve Abbey of the impoverished Vavasours by the self-made Samuel Brown. Morover, the treatment of this theme has

84

a good deal of Robertson's delicacy, especially the gradual growth of Lilian Vavasour's love for the intruder:

LILIAN. . . . I hope you'll keep up the old garden, and the maze, and the old sun-dial with the broken nose, and the fish-pond—it's full of duckweed and there are no fish in it, but please don't have it filled up.

BROWN. Certainly not. I'll have the duckweed kept in and the fish kept out—religiously. I'll change nothing you wish left as it is.

LILIAN. Thank you so much! And there's the schools—you'll look particularly after them?

BROWN. Oh, that'll be a job after my own heart! I'll have a thoroughly efficient master and mistress——

LILIAN. Oh, but you must keep the old ones!

BROWN. Are they up to the mark?

LILIAN. I don't know; but they've been there ever since I can remember. And there's the old women in the Vavasour Almshouses. How they'll miss me on Wednesdays!

BROWN. I'm afraid I can't make up for that disappointment.

LILIAN. Well, I think tobacco would go a long way—or tea.

BROWN. I'll try both—— Anything else?

LILIAN. The old thoroughbred brood mare, and Nep, my black retriever—they are past moving. And then there's the old lame peacock, with one eye. I shouldn't mind leaving them, if you'd promise to take great care of them all.

BROWN. I'll be as good as a father to them. I promise you that.

LILIAN. I think—what you promise, you mean.

But *New Men and Old Acres* belongs to the last phase of Taylor's work—a phase dominated by a series of elaborate historical dramas of little theatrical significance. Nor did the generation of dramatists succeeding Robertson study him closely, and the Bancrofts themselves could find no successor to him. Their repertory after Robertson's death was therefore largely made up of revivals of his plays, and their greatest success during these years was with *Diplomacy*, an adaptation by Clement Scott and B. C. Stephenson of Sardou's *Dora*. Thus the French *pièce bien faite*, of which Robertson had striven to make English drama independent, reasserted itself as soon as he died. His work for the writing of English drama was not fruitless, but it needed twenty years before it was harvested.

The only dramatist who could be regarded as his immediate successor was James Albery, whose talents unhappily were only fully displayed at the outset of his career. In *Two Roses* Albery caught some of the delicacy of feeling and all the dexterity of stage-management which mark Robertson's best work. Both qualities are present in the first appearance of the heroine, Lotty, and her sister, Ida, the two roses of the title:

(*They are heard counting*, 1, 2, 3, 4, *etc.*, IDA *getting ahead.*)

GRANT. What on earth are they counting ? Not money!

IDA (*outside*). 37, 38, 39, 40. (*Her head gradually appears at L. of window, and her finger passes along the rose branch as she counts the roses.*) 42, 43, 44—45—46!

LOTTY. 41, 42, 43, 44. (*She appears in like manner at R., same business.*) 45, 46, 47, 48—49—50! (*Triumphantly.*)

IDA (*disappointed*). But I like the perfume of mine better, Lotty.

LOTTY. I don't know, I think mine's as good. *I* like it—let me smell yours.

(*They smell first one, then the other, till at last they run their faces together, when they both laugh, throw their arms round each other's necks and kiss, then leave the window.*)

Furthermore, Albery achieved in Digby Grant a character as shrewdly observed and perhaps more forcefully drawn than any Robertson himself had provided. In the hands of the young Henry Irving this engaging and resourceful impostor caught and held the imagination of the London public. The climax of the first act, when Grant, learning that he has inherited a title and a fortune, snubs all his former friends, still has a fine theatrical verve:

GRANT. . . . Our Mr. Jenkins, a much esteemed though humble friend, has a good heart. I have on various occasions noticed that he has, under the disguise of disburdening his sample case, left various things for my daughters, such as—as—shall be nameless. He cannot be expected to possess that refinement that would have made it clear to him that even if we required such aid our pride would not have allowed us to accept it; but he meant well, and I ask him to accept—a little cheque. Mr. Deecie, with whom I deeply sympathise, lent my daughters a piano; he did not mean to offend. I thank him—a little cheque. . . . As for that young man Wyatt, though a plebeian, I would, had I found him worthy, have formed an alliance with him, but he is not; only a few minutes back, to test him, I asked him to lend me ten pounds—he would have been repaid in thousands—but he has the worst vice of the vulgar—no faith, no confidence—I will have no more to do with him. (LOTTY *goes to* WYATT. GRANT *takes her hand and crosses her in front of table L., where she sinks in grief.* IDA *goes behind and consoles her.*) I am indebted to him in some small sums—twenty, perhaps thirty pounds. I wish never to see him again. I clear the score—a little cheque. (*Takes out cheque and offers it.*)

The development of the play, in which Grant finds his claim to the title rejected in favour of Deecie, Ida's blind suitor, though faithful to Robertson in spirit, is much less effective. But Albery provided Irving with an opportunity from which he never looked back. Unluckily the dramatist himself never again looked forward. Dispersing his energies on trivial farces, like the once notorious *Pink Dominos*, on commonplace adaptations from the French and uneasy musical pieces, he repeated in his own life the premature climax of *Two Roses*.

Yet in catching and refining Robertson's style, however briefly, Albery stands alone. It seems that English drama, having taken this step forward, needed a twenty years' pause to recover its breath before the next advance. It is perhaps possible to detect something of Robertson's influence in the later plays of H. J. Byron, his constant companion, who added to his vast output of burlesques and farces a number of more seriously conceived pieces. In particular he seems to have been interested in the conflict of domestic and professional ties. This theme appears in *Cyril's Success*—a play of which Byron was plainly very proud, for his Dedication admits to being 'somewhat tired of being termed a "droll", a "punster", and so on; and, as a mere piece of self-justification—self-assertion, it may be termed—beg to remind any one who may care to recollect the fact that *Cyril's Success* is original, and a comedy—and, even in these vicious dramatic days—in five acts! There!' The hero of this play is a writer who loses his inspiration when his wife leaves him. In a later play, *Married in Haste*, both husband and wife are artists, and an undercurrent of professional rivalry

87

contributes to their estrangement. In selecting such a theme Byron does at least suggest that Robertson's example had induced him to look further than the burlesque and knockabout fun of his earlier plays.

But that example extended no further than the subject-matter. In approaching his theme Byron grows painfully cautious, and his conclusion is as superficial as it is sentimental. In *Cyril's Success* the wife is so feebly drawn that the domestic issue is never properly put, for, as she tells her old school-mistress:

MRS. CUTHBERT.   No neglect, no cruelty, could ever make me leave Cyril, Miss Grannett. There is no excuse for a woman leaving her husband—except perhaps one.

MISS GRANNETT. And what may that be, my dear?

MRS. CUTHBERT. If I thought another held my place in his heart, nay, if I found out that I only possessed a share in his affection, I should leave him at once. I would not hesitate one moment, but would quit for ever the roof of a man who had dared to offer me a divided love.

In due course her mistaken belief that her husband is paying attention to the 'fascinating widow', Mrs. Singleton Bliss, prompts her to leave him, and a prodigious series of mis-understandings keeps them apart until they are reconciled on a suitably sententious note:

MRS. CUTHBERT. . . . You shall grow well and strong and hopeful soon again—happier and more hopeful, dear, than in the old days when you told me that my love was more precious in your eyes than anything the world might call "Success".

The heroine of *Married in Haste* has at least material grounds for leaving her husband, but it is hard to accept the ease with which by her painting she then supports both herself and her parents, and harder still to swallow the glib reconciliation be-tween husband and wife effected by a wealthy uncle:

. . . *you*——
With all your work to be attended to,
The art you love to be pursued with pleasure:
Married in haste you *were*; "Repent at leisure"!

Pooh! On fresh fields and pastures new intent,
You'll find that you've *no* leisure to repent.

Moreover Byron shows none of Robertson's skill in using the technical resources of the stage. His methods are painfully traditional, and in his character-drawing there is no attempt to break away from the accepted divisions, as Robertson had broken away in drawing Sam Gerridge or old Eccles. The *dramatis personæ* of *Cyril's Success*, for instance, are listed as follows:

> Cyril Cuthbert (Walking Gentleman)
> Major Treherne (Comedy Lead)
> Viscount Glycerine (Walking Gentleman)
> Matthew Pincher (Character Comedy)
> Fitzpelham (Walking Gentleman)
> Jonas Grimley (Old Man)
> Colonel Hawker (Old Man)
> Bingo (Utility)
> Pepper (Utility)
> Fred Titeboy (Juvenile Comedy)
> Mrs. Cuthbert (Comedy)
> Mrs. Bliss (Walking Lady)
> Miss Grannett (1st Old Woman)
> Perkins (Chambermaid)

—a list which suggests how completely Byron accepted the stock characterization of his day. He was much more at home with the farcical complications of *Our Boys*, a wholly commonplace piece whose unprecedented run of 1,362 performances throws more light on the increased popularity of playgoing than on the increased powers of the playwright.

Robertson's aims were in some measure carried on by Sir Charles Young, another successful dramatist of this generation who, however, made very little use of Robertson's methods. A baronet in the rôle of popular dramatist was itself a sign of the times, and Young's particular achievement was to reinforce the ties between fashionable Society and the theatre, not only in himself but in his work. Thus his most successful play, *Jim the Penman*, attracted notice by setting a sensational story of forgery and larceny against a carefully drawn background of

London's fashionable and financial worlds. Here Young owes more to Tom Taylor than to Robertson, but in certain of his lesser-known pieces there is something of Robertson's seriousness of purpose, particularly in *Gilded Youth*, with its definite though moderate criticism of leisured luxury; and the introduction in *Shadows* of a parallel plot, worked out first in Cavalier, then in contemporary, terms. It may well be that Young's 'comediettas', though insubstantial in themselves, proved more influential than his longer pieces, for they depict the fashionable world with a real sense of style and humour. *Petticoat Perfidy*, for instance, in which Mrs. Mountrevor tries to outwit Mrs. Jones by introducing her maid as the Princess Borodinski, gives more than a hint of the society comedies of R. C. Carton and Henry Arthur Jones.

Perhaps the most significant dramatist in the twenty years which followed Robertson's death was Sydney Grundy, a prolific and popular writer whose preference for 'strong' drama did not preclude his writing several comedies, a musical play with Sullivan, *Haddon Hall*, and an Adelphi melodrama, *The Bells of Haslemere*, for William Terriss. The interest of Grundy's work arises not only from its range and popularity, but also from a curious combination of technical facility and poverty of theme that clearly reflects a period of stagnation in the drama.

At its best Grundy's dialogue commands an idiom which, like Robertson's, suggests the authentic accents of general speech. But Grundy totally lacked Robertson's interest in broadening the subject matter of his plays, and also his gift of directing the resources of the stage towards a more convincing presentation of his subject. Grundy's preference was for outworn themes, presented as a series of sensational and highly artificial situations. He did not hesitate in *The Silver Shield*, for example, to make a husband leave his wife because a single detached page from her letter suggested wrongly that she loved another; or in the same play to make a wife leave her husband because she mistakes an extract from his new tragedy for a declaration of love to his leading lady.

This use of mechanically contrived situations Grundy drew from the French dramatists whom he adapted and copied. The traffic in misunderstanding and mystery they practised on the

French stage might serve a *farceur* like Labiche, but it robbed the more serious play of any genuine emotion or effect. Grundy regularly employed the climax of contrivance well illustrated in *A Wife's Sacrifice* which, with Sutherland Edwards, he adapted from a French play, *Martyre*, by D'Ennery and Tarbe. The misunderstanding here arises between Julien and his wife, Isabelle, who has omitted to tell him of the existence of her illegitimate half-brother, Robert. The sensational climax can therefore be foreseen from the start:

ISABELLE. Stay—Robert—brother! (*He turns.*) You are poor—wretched! I am happy—rich. Take these from me. (*Offering the notes.*) Not as a price, but as a gift from one who loves you. (*Pause.*)

ROBERT. You love me? (ISABELLE *opens her arms.*) Sister! (*Embraces her.*)

(*Re-enter* JULIEN.)

ISABELLE. Yes, I love you! I love you!

JULIEN. Ah!

ISABELLE. My husband!

ROBERT. Heavens!

Since Isabelle's loyalty to her mother prevents her from allaying Julien's suspicions, it is only after she has been divorced, demented and harried generally for three more acts that she is allowed to disclose the truth. Yet this material proved acceptable to the Hare-Kendal management and to the St. James's audience of 1886.

The narrowness of Grundy's intellectual sympathies placed him firmly among the opponents of the 'New Drama' which from the 1880s looked increasingly to Ibsen for inspiration. Thus in *The New Woman* Grundy restates the familiar arguments against emancipation, and puts up a homely lady's maid, Margery, to refute the Feminists of the play:

You call yourselves New Women—you're not New at all. You're just as old as Eve, and just as hungry for the fruit she plucked. You only want one thing—the one thing every woman wants—the one thing no woman's life's worth living without! A true man's love! Ah, if we all had that, there'd be no problem of the sexes then.

So much for John Stuart Mill on the Subjection of Women! Yet, when his prejudices were not aroused, Grundy could explore a genial vein of humour, best illustrated by *A Pair of Spectacles* to which, although also of French origin (*Les Petits Oiseaux* by Labiche and Delacour), he succeeded in giving a convincingly English atmosphere. The story of kindly Benjamin Goldfinch who sees life quite differently through a borrowed pair of spectacles but recovers his benevolence with his own glasses, allowed Grundy to exercise his technical dexterity without obtruding his opinions:

CHARLOTTE. Your spectacles—just come, sir. . . .
GOLDFINCH. Ah, my old spectacles! (*Puts them on.*) I'm glad to have them back! (*Beams through them.*)
MRS. GOLDFINCH. You look yourself again! . . .
GOLDFINCH. I *feel* myself. (*Rises, produces* GREGORY's *spectacles and returns them.*) Gregory, there are yours. . . . I'm obliged for the loan; but they don't suit me. (*Turns to* LUCY.) I will go on feeding the sparrows. If there *are* some impostors in the world, I'd rather trust and be deceived than suspect and be mistaken.

The play charmed audiences when Hare played Goldfinch, and it will continue to charm. But Grundy was unrepentant. In the year of his death he wrote his own Apology: *The Play of the Future; by a Playwright of the Past*—a violent attack on the 'New Drama' which he himself had opposed but could no longer withstand.

Gilbert and Sullivan

In the period following Robertson's death, therefore, it is the public rather than the plays which advance the theatre's status. This return of polite Society to the playhouse was a gradual process, stretching over a quarter of a century, and encouraged by each manager in his own way. Thus the Bancrofts' lead was followed by Irving at the Lyceum, when he completely darkened the auditorium to give dignity to the stage; by Gilbert when he popularized the *matinée* at the Savoy; by Hare at the Court, when in place of the stronger drinks of the early Victorian theatre, he provided coffee and tea during the intervals; by Wyndham at the Criterion, when he supplied his patrons with a detailed programme in place of a cut-down playbill. But perhaps the series of Gilbert and Sullivan Operas provide the best evidence of the new air of respectability slowly pervading the Victorian theatre.

In both form and content the Savoy Operas asserted their independence. Gilbert's librettos, after the unsuccessful *Thespis*, steer entirely clear of the mythical element characteristic of Victorian extravaganza, and are largely free of the parody essential to Victorian burlesque; while Sullivan's scores firmly rejected the selection of popular airs which had regularly served the English musical stage since John Gay's time. In tone their work reflected clearly the growing refinement and respectability of the Victorian audience. Gilbert saluted his public's intelligence by recalling political satire to the English stage after more than a century's exile at the sentence of Sir Robert Walpole's Licensing Act. But it was a satire carefully trimmed to the taste of a conservative public. Of individuals Gilbert could make pointed, though good-humoured, fun; of institutions his criticisms were invariably circumspect. If, in *Iolanthe*, he declared that

> The House of Peers throughout the War
> Did nothing in particular

he was quick to add that it 'did it very well'. Towards the end of the series, in *Utopia (Limited)*, he assured his largely female audience

> Go search the world and search the sea,
> Then come you home and sing with me
> There's no such gold and no such pearl
> As a bright and beautiful English girl!

Thus encouraged, English ladies ventured to attend performances at the Savoy unescorted, and in so doing opened a new era in English theatre history.

Gilbert's evolution of Savoy Opera followed an apprenticeship in the traditional forms of mid-Victorian drama. Two of his earliest essays in the theatre, *Dulcamara; or, The Little Duck and the Great Quack* and *The Merry Zingara; or, The Tipsy*

Gipsy and the Pipsy Wipsy, suggest by their titles how closely the young Gilbert imitated H. J. Byron's methods in burlesque; while both *Pygmalion and Galatea* and *Thespis; or, The Gods Grown Old* clearly owe something to Planché's handling of mythology. At the same time Gilbert set himself to study Robertson's brand of realistic drama, following Robertson's interest in social themes in *Charity* and his handling of sentiment in *Sweethearts*. But although often imitative, these early plays of Gilbert also show traces of his struggle to find an individual style which would commend itself to the new theatre public. Thus *Pygmalion* curiously combines an arch Victorian humour with an undertone of genuine passion and despair; and the unsuccessful *Engaged* conducts its farcical complications with an air of ludicrous logic which, as has been pointed out,[1] anticipates not only the style but many of the incidents of *The Importance of Being Earnest*. In this play Gilbert developed and polished his particular brand of irony well beyond the level which Victorian comedy had yet attained:

SYMPERSON. . . . And I am to lose my pet at last; my little dickey-bird is to be married to-day! Well, well, it's for her good. I must try and bear it.

MINNIE. And as my dear old papa comes into £1,000 a year by it, I hope he won't allow it to distress him too much. He must try and bear up. He mustn't fret.

SYMPERSON. My child, I will not deny that £1,000 a year is a consolation. . . . And my darling has not done badly either, has she?

MINNIE. No, dear papa, only fancy! Cheviot has £2,000 a year, from shares in the Royal Indestructible Bank.

SYMPERSON. And don't spend £200. By-the-bye I'm sorry that my little bird has not contrived to induce him to settle anything on her; that, I think, was remiss in my tom-tit. . . . I can't help feeling that if my robin had worked him judiciously——

MINNIE. Papa, dear, Cheviot is an all but perfect character, the very type of knightly chivalry; but he *has* faults, and amongst other things he's one of the worst tempered men I ever met in all my little life. Poor, simple, little Minnie thought the matter over very carefully in her silly childish way, and she came to the

---

[1] See Lynton Hudson: *The English Stage*, 1850–1950 (London, 1951), pp. 102–5.

conclusion, in her foolish little noddle, that on the whole, perhaps she could work it better after marriage, than before.

SYMPERSON. Well, well, perhaps my wren is right. (*Rises.*)

MINNIE. Don't laugh at my silly little thoughts, dear papa, when I say I'm sure she is.

In 1877, however, the public was unprepared for such thoroughgoing methods, and *Engaged* was condemned as heartless. Later in the same year Gilbert hit on an acceptable compromise with *The Sorcerer*, in which his successful collaboration with Sullivan in *Trial by Jury* was extended, and the series now known as the Savoy Operas firmly launched by D'Oyly Carte.

In this series Gilbert contrived to blend his individual vein of humour with a sentimental strain owing something to his own lyrics and a great deal to Sullivan's fund of melody and soothing harmony. By such blending was a suspicious public won back to the musical stage. Nor was their achievement limited to the English public. While legitimate drama marked time, the popularity of Savoy Opera raised the prestige of the English stage on the Continent, and above all in North America. Furthermore, its popularity has withstood the test of time so stoutly that for modern audiences Savoy Opera and the Victorian theatre have largely become synonymous.

Irving at the Lyceum

In 1882, when the Savoy Theatre was opened as material proof of the partnership's success, Henry Irving had already been four years in command of the Lyceum, where he had been acting, at first under the management of the Bateman family, for eleven years. Within their respective fields Irving and Gilbert shared both aims and methods, above all in the discipline they imposed on their subordinates. But whereas Gilbert was sometimes accused of treating the theatre as a seminary, Irving clearly conceived it as a temple of the arts. The reverence which he himself felt for the art of the theatre set the tone of his rule at the Lyceum for a quarter of a century. Although both scholarship and money were freely expended on his productions, Irving practised neither the antiquarianism of Charles Kean, nor the prodigality of Herbert Tree. The outstanding quality of his productions lay in their unity of style: in the harmony of their different elements, conceived by Irving and brought about by the discipline demanded of his company and the loyalty he inspired in them.

It was towards achieving this artistic unity that Irving directed the technical advances he evolved. To focus attention on the action of the play he not only insisted on the regular lowering of the auditorium lights, but increased the illusion by equipping the stage with a black false proscenium which finally disposed of the imperfect masking of the wings, inherited from the Georgian theatre. Clearly his handling of stage-lighting, particularly of limelight, was at once more elaborate and more subtle than his predecessors', blinded as they were by the brilliance of gas-lighting. In her memoirs Ellen Terry declares that even after the introduction of electric lighting, Irving preferred the subtler, softer effects of gas-lighting, and restored the gas-equipment at the Lyceum[1]. The precision of his judgement extended to the smallest of rôles, and embraced the advances in ensemble effects achieved by his predecessors, just as his artists, especially Hawes Craven and Joseph Harker, and his carpenters profited from the notable technical advances of the Victorian theatre. Irving's assimilation of existing methods and evolution of new methods were alike directed towards sustaining the magical atmosphere of the Lyceum stage, which so many witnesses corroborate.

The confidence which Irving's leadership inspired backstage soon began to communicate itself to his audience. Their trust in him expressed itself partly in the widening classes from which the Lyceum audience came to be drawn and partly in the social and intellectual brilliance of his first-night assemblies and of the dinners he gave on great occasions in the Beefsteak Room of his theatre. As a result of this growing trust Irving gradually emerged as a leading figure in public life, not merely as a leader in the private and often bizarre world of the theatre. The dignity with which he occupied this unprecedented position led, as early as 1883, to a tentative offer from Gladstone of a knighthood—an offer then declined but ultimately accepted in 1895, when his profession was generally acknowledged to have been

[1] *Ellen Terry's Memoirs*, p. 134.

rightly honoured. His work in restoring the actor's prestige reinforced the work of Gilbert and Sullivan in re-establishing the prestige of the musical stage.

Irving the actor clearly made little use of the restraint practised by the Bancrofts and their disciples. His chief concern was with strong passions achieved by means of bold effects, though these effects were always artistically conceived and painstakingly executed. Irving's achievements as an actor were all the more remarkable in view of his serious physical limitations: a voice lacking in flexibility, a highly individual delivery, and a bearing which remained unmistakable even when cured of its awkwardness. These limitations were minimized by scrupulous self-discipline and turned to advantage by a skilful choice of plays and parts. It was natural that for his Shakespearean productions Irving should choose those characters to which his strongly personal style could give most force; and that his planning, both of his own performance and of the whole production, should bring out those features he could best express. It was to this end that he employed the cuts and transpositions of which, like his predecessors, he made liberal use.

Undoubtedly the caution which Irving had to observe in his choice of play sometimes bore hard on his leading lady. Ellen Terry was herself an actress of unusual physique and personality, who could not easily be fitted with a part. Especially in the last years of the partnership her rôles too often made little use of her particular talents, and her autobiography reveals how she was forced to modify her performance as Portia to harmonize with Irving's Shylock,[1] and, for lack of a suitable part for him in *As You Like It*, to abandon her hopes of playing Rosalind.[2] Against this must be set the enormous advantage which her successful performances at the Lyceum gained from Irving's collaboration. At any other theatre her Ophelia, her Lady Macbeth, her Beatrice, her Imogen, could not have achieved the same popularity. The care which Irving lavished on his company's as well as on his own performance is evident from their record: under his guidance Terriss and Forbes Robertson achieved maturity, Alexander, Martin Harvey, and Benson served their

[1] *Ellen Terry's Memoirs*, p. 128.
[2] *Ibid.*, p. 231.

apprenticeship; while veterans like Bancroft, Mrs. Stirling, and Genevieve Ward also contributed to the general rising standard.

Irving's Repertory

However, it was not only in his choice of Shakespeare that Irving had to consider his own powers. An even more striking feature of his repertory was its reliance on melodramas, usually of French origin, which Charles Kean, another actor of marked though very different physical limitations, had made popular during his management of the Princess's in the 1850s. The stagecraft of Boucicault, which had served Kean well in versions of *The Corsican Brothers* and *Louis XI*, now answered Irving's purpose. Charles Reade's version of *The Courier of Lyons* had also been made for Kean; refurbished as *The Lyons Mail* it gave Irving a chance to follow up his dual rôle in *The Corsican Brothers* with the stronger contrast of the saintly Lesurques and the villainous Dubosc. Irving's first great success at the Lyceum, *The Bells* by Leopold Lewis, was also an adaptation from the French (*Le Juif Polonais* by Erckmann and Chatrian), and though its bold outline and crude characterization recall the methods of Dumas and Delavigne, there is a certain subtlety in the presentation of the haunted Burgomaster, Mathias, on which Irving seized and to which he gave overpowering life. In particular the two 'sensation' scenes—the re-enactment of the murder to which Mathias owes his fortune and the hallucination in which he undergoes his trial—explore the technical resources of the theatre with discretion and real force. Throughout there is imaginative use of the sleigh-bells, which remind Mathias of his crime, and when, in the trial scene, he gives himself away under the spell of a mesmerist, his confession is all the more telling for being implicit, rather than circumstantial:

MATHIAS. . . . Quick, quick! The girdle! I have it. Ha! (*He performs the action in saying this of taking it from the Jew's body and buckling it round his own.*) It is full of gold, quite full. Be quick, Mathias, be quick! Carry him away.
(*He bends low down and appears to lift the body upon his back; then he walks across the stage, body bent, his step slow as a man who carries a heavy load.*)

MESMERIST. Where are you going?

MATHIAS (*stopping*). To the lime-kiln. I am there. (*He appears to throw the body upon the kiln.*) How heavy he was! (*He breathes with force, then he again bends down to take up a pole—in a hoarse voice.*) Go into the fire, Jew, go into the fire! (*He appears to push the body with the pole, using his whole force, suddenly he utters a cry of horror and staggers away, his face covered with his hands.*) Those eyes, oh, those eyes! How he glares at me. (*He sinks on to stool, and takes the same attitude as when first thrown into sleep.*)

PRESIDENT (*with a sign to the* MESMERIST). It is well. (*To the* CLERK OF THE COURT.) You have written all?

CLERK. All!

PRESIDENT (*to* MESMERIST). It is well—awake him now, and let him read himself.

The effect of this scene, and of the whole of the play, depends on the completeness of the illusion. If the attention is distracted from the action being played out within the proscenium arch, then the spell is broken. In this respect, *The Bells* is true to the species of spectacular melodrama which the realistic staging of the Victorian theatre made possible. Where it excels is in its use of 'sensation' to illustrate the workings of Mathias's mind and not purely as shock tactics. Perhaps for this reason *The Bells* remained Irving's most enduringly popular play, and survived most of the earlier melodramas in his repertory.

In his first years at the Lyceum Irving turned to melodramas still earlier than Charles Kean's: to *The Iron Chest* and to two of Bulwer-Lytton's costume pieces: *The Lady of Lyons* and *Richelieu*. At the same time he was introduced to an Irish painter-poet with a gift for putting together costume plays in much the same vein. William Gorman Wills soon became something of a dramatist-in-residence at the Lyceum, and his contribution to the Lyceum repertory was a substantial one, for it included *Charles I, Eugene Aram, Vanderdecken,* and *Faust,* the most successful financially of all Irving's productions. In addition Wills made versions for Irving of *King René's Daughter* (produced as *Iolanthe*) and of *Don Quixote,* whilst *Olivia,* his adaptation of *The Vicar of Wakefield,* was revived by Irving so that Ellen Terry might repeat her earlier success in the title-rôle at the Court, under Hare.

Wills, like Bulwer-Lytton (whose *Eugene Aram* he adapted), provided the Victorian theatre with a form of verse-drama serviceable to the actors and shrewdly designed for theatrical effect. In this respect he belonged to the small circle of nineteenth-century dramatists who, like Sheridan Knowles, could manipulate verse in a form acceptable to the contemporary audience. Wills's long and profitable connection with the Lyceum may usefully be contrasted with Tennyson's work for that theatre. Although Tennyson's intermittent power, especially in *The Cup*, should not be overlooked, not even Irving's performance as Philip of Spain could give theatrical life to *Queen Mary*, while the undoubted success of *Becket* was achieved only by a ruthless re-shaping of the poet's material to the actor's needs.

In the last phase of the Victorian theatre a number of poets appeared who shared Wills's theatrical flair, allied to powers of imagination and expression he never approached. Although Stephen Phillips in *Faust* and *Paolo and Francesca*, Rudolf Besier in *The Virgin Goddess*, and James Elroy Flecker in *Don Juan* and *Hassan* handled verse in the theatre far more sensitively and skilfully than the Victorian poets, their miscalculation lay in the expression of the Romantic spirit when outside the theatre the Romantic movement was a spent force. Theatre audiences, starved of genuine Romantic drama, greeted them with extravagant praise, Phillips in particular being acclaimed as a second Shakespeare, but once the anti-Romantic spirit had penetrated the theatre, their work lost its appeal. The problem of English poetic drama to-day, as fifty years ago, is to find an acceptable form of non-Romantic verse.

Wills's death in 1891 added to the difficulties which the Shakespearean repertory had begun to present to Irving and Ellen Terry, with their choice of parts already limited by their years. Out of sympathy with the English dramatists of the new generation, Irving turned once more to French melodrama in the work of Victorien Sardou whose *Madame Sans-Gêne*, *Robespierre*, and *Dante* he staged in the last ten years of his life. This dependence on a veteran French dramatist provoked much criticism of Irving, especially from a young Irish dramatist, Bernard Shaw. In fact Irving had little freedom of choice. If he lacked sympathy with the school of Robertson, he was directly opposed to the school of Ibsen, the intellectual discipline of whose plays would have afforded no scope whatever for his particular gift of theatrical illusion. Irving's tenure of the Lyceum belatedly endowed England with a Romantic Theatre, and his powers, both as actor and director, magically concealed the lack of a Hugo or a Pushkin. If in his last years he could no longer work the miracle, its former magic remained undisputed.

The twenty years which followed Robertson's death were years of prosperity and expansion in the English theatre. The Bancrofts' lead in restoring the prestige of playgoing had been followed triumphantly by Irving and by the Savoy Opera series; and, on a more modest scale, by Hare, the Kendals, and Wyndham. Moreover, it was in these twenty years that the final evolution of the realistic stage took place. The disappearance of the surviving remnant of the apron stage was marked by the Bancrofts when, on taking over the Haymarket in 1880, they decorated the proscenium opening with a gilt picture frame which bounded the action of the play and established the frontier between stage and auditorium. The introduction of electric light in the theatre in the 1880s did not immediately change the principles of stage-lighting evolved by the development of gas and limelight, although electricity was to prove the basis of radical changes in stage-lighting with the turn of the century. What the use of electricity in the theatre did immediately achieve was a great economy in manpower and, above all, a far higher degree of safety after the heavy toll of life and buildings in the gas-lit theatre. With the new decade the prestige of the playhouse was firmly established.

Where the English theatre of these twenty years flagged was in following up Robertson's efforts to evolve a strain of native English drama which would serve the new theatre audiences in place of the farce and melodrama of an earlier generation. Instead the English repertory remained very largely repetitive or derivative. Only in the field of comic opera had tradition been discarded in favour of independence and originality. It was the feebleness of English dramatic writing that stirred Henry James's scorn when he settled in London in 1877.[1] After the

[1] See his article 'The London Theatres', published in *The Galaxy* in May 1877 and reprinted in *The Scenic Art* (London, 1949), pp. 93–111.

ferment of new ideas he had witnessed in continental theatres the repertory of the Lyceum or the St. James's must have struck him as strangely outmoded.

Nevertheless, help was at hand. Among Irving's company in his early years at the Lyceum was a young man in whom, as with Robertson, the actor was no more than the dramatist in the making. Arthur Pinero had some of his earliest sketches produced at the Lyceum, and then moved on to the St. James's where he supplied Hare and the Kendals with adaptations from the French and with original work. At the same time Wilson Barrett kept the flag of melodrama flying at the Princess's by employing another new dramatist, Henry Arthur Jones, to provide him with a series of colourful and sensational pieces. In these traditional schools were trained the new dramatists who were to supply the late Victorian theatre with a drama worthy of its new position.

4

THE ERA OF SOCIETY DRAMA

The thirty years which followed the opening of the Bancrofts'
management at the Prince of Wales's witnessed the theatre's
gradual achievement of respectability. The next twenty years,
the era separating the first performance of *The Second Mrs.
Tanqueray* from the outbreak of the Great War, mark the full
flowering of the fashionable theatre. It was during this period
that the earlier exertions of Irving, the Bancrofts, Gilbert, and
Hare earned a rich reward for their successors. Irving's first
nights at the Lyceum had attracted the leaders of the fashionable
and intellectual world. Now those leaders were obliged to keep
up, not with a single theatre but with the entire theatrical
scene.

The changes in theatrical ritual brought about by the return
of fashionable Society were widely apparent. A later dinner-
hour meant a later curtain-rise. The disappearance of the 'half
price' public substantially reduced the length of the bill. The
absorption of the pit by the orchestra-stalls continued, and at the
same time the old division of the various tiers into private and
public boxes gave way to open balconies, decorously conducted
and plainly classified as Dress Circle, Upper Circle, and Gallery.
The popularity of playgoing with the leisured classes also fostered the matinée performance, both of regular productions and
of untried plays. These changes in the audience's habits entailed a big increase in bookable seats at the expense of un-
reserved accommodation, a change which in its turn encouraged
the growth of the long run, and put further difficulties in the
path of the old 'stock' system. The picture of a theatre smoothly
organized and securely established which all these changes suggest is usually labelled 'the Edwardian Theatre'. In fact 1901,
the year of Edward VII's accession, marked no development

in theatrical conditions which had not already obtained for a decade, and it was not his death in 1910 but the outbreak of war in 1914 which altered the conditions of the English theatre beyond recognition. Thus it is perhaps permissible to treat the whole period 1893–1914 as the last chapter in the history of the Victorian theatre.

That the patronage of fashionable Society put its stamp on the theatre of that period is clear enough; but the glory thus reflected should not obscure the fact that the late Victorian audience, unlike the Restoration audience, was not a côterie of courtiers and courtesans. The prestige and popularity of the theatre during these years was firmly based on its general appeal. Diamonds and white ties might sparkle in the stalls, but the pit and the gallery were filled with loyal supporters from the old Victorian audience. It was for these seats that the patient queues waited to approve some particular idol in his latest success, and to these seats that the occasional curtain-raiser was still played before the late diners took their places in the stalls. Their loyalty to their own favourites, being longer established, was longer lived. Many such favourites, when the patronage of society was withdrawn from them, found that in the provinces the seasoned playgoer still welcomed familiar faces in familiar rôles. It was a distinguished procession that trod the provincial circuit or followed the North American trail blazed by Irving and Ellen Terry.

An Age of Actor-Managers

The pattern of this chapter in English theatrical history was woven around the actor-manager. The leaders of the previous epoch now found themselves challenged on all sides. Irving, handicapped by ill-health and out of sympathy with the drama of the day, had to surrender control of the Lyceum in 1898 and quitted it altogether in 1902, spending most of the last years of his life before the loyal provincial public. John Hare, more resilient, established himself at the new Garrick Theatre, specially built for him in 1889, but after six years left it in favour of touring, and quietly withdrew from the stage in 1911. Of the earlier actor-managers only Charles Wyndham at the Criterion braved the competition of younger men, to such good effect that he was able to open the theatre named after himself in 1899, and to complete his triumph by building the New Theatre in 1903.

Meanwhile two younger men had found themselves permanent homes in the London theatre world. Herbert Beerbohm Tree, established at the Haymarket in 1887, was able out of the profits of *Trilby* to build himself a palatial new home across the street on the site that Vanbrugh had chosen in 1705 for the Queen's Theatre. Tree called his theatre Her Majesty's and Her Majesty's it has become once more. In 1891 the St. James's, to which the aura of Hare and the Kendals had restored its long-lost respectability, was taken over by the young George Alexander, fresh from apprenticeship to Irving at the Lyceum. In Oscar Wilde he found a playwright who could draw a fashionable audience, and in Pinero's *The Second Mrs. Tanqueray*, a play bold enough to mark the beginning of an era. That era is perhaps better epitomized by Alexander's discreet and distinguished tenancy of the St. James's than by any other feature of its crowded history.

Other, shorter, tenancies made their contribution to the pattern of the actor-managers' theatre. Arthur Bourchier took over the Garrick and Cyril Maude succeeded Tree at the Haymarket. The transformation of theatrical taste was well illustrated at the Adelphi, where almost a century of melodrama gave place in 1904 to the Shakespearean and new verse drama offered by Oscar Asche and Lily Brayton. At least two actor-managers left an imprint on the age much deeper than their occupancy of any one theatre might suggest. Johnston Forbes Robertson, with his noble bearing and saintly character, could not be said to belong to the same calling as George Frederick Cooke or Edmund Kean. Nor could Lewis Waller, whose powers were more considerable than the frenzied applause of his admirers implied. The ladies whose K.O.W. badges revealed that they had enrolled in the Keen-on-Waller brigade seem more than a century removed from the O.P. Rioters.

The material evidence of this refinement of theatrical conditions lay in the success of the actor-managers and the stability of their theatres. Its official recognition was regularly gazetted. After Irving's knighthood had been acclaimed in 1895, public opinion was prepared for further recognition of services to the theatre. Squire Bancroft received his knighthood—very appropriately—in the Diamond Jubilee Honours of 1897; and Wyndham, Hare, Tree, Alexander, and Forbes Robertson were all similarly honoured before 1914. More striking still were the knighthoods conferred on Gilbert and Pinero, for in achieving this distinction the playwrights had started even later and so had risen faster than the actors.

In the stability of this era the audience counted on and the actor-managers guaranteed the style and standards of the entertainment. The burden of their critics, then and now, was that their interest lay in the manner of presentation, not in the material presented. Above all, the Shakespearean productions at Her Majesty's under Tree were attacked for exploiting Shakespeare, just as Irving's productions at the Lyceum had been attacked. Indeed, there is an unusually close parallel between their two careers. Both were severely limited actors, physically and vocally; yet if Tree did not exert Irving's personal magic, he was capable of performances as diverse as the flamboyant Svengali and the genial, gentlemanly Colonel Newcome. In addition, both actors avoided modern dress parts in their later years, and there is a curious affinity between Mathias in *The Bells*, the part that proved the turning-point of Irving's career, and Svengali in *Trilby*, to which Tree owed much of his success. By a final coincidence Irving was forced to surrender control of the Lyceum to a Board of Directors within a year of Tree's opening Her Majesty's in 1897.

It scarcely seems just to Tree's achievement that the elaborate scale on which he mounted his productions should now be remembered chiefly for his partiality for real livestock in Shakespeare. That he often outdid Irving in the sumptuousness of his Shakespearean productions is well attested, and by commissioning a new version of *Faust* from Stephen Phillips and tapping the steam from the kitchens of the Carlton Hotel for the Brocken scene he even challenged Irving on ground hitherto undisputed. He had a particular weakness for interpolating scenes not required by the author, such as the entry of Richard and Bolingbroke into London in *Richard II*, a Magna Carta tableau in *King John*, an elaborate chorus of birds in Leonato's garden in *Much Ado About Nothing,* and a vision of the Sphinx in *Antony and Cleopatra.* For these he exacted a higher price even than Irving or Charles Kean before him in long intervals and savage cutting. Tree appears to have lacked Irving's monumental devotion to detail, relying more on brilliant flashes of intuition for guidance. In his disregard of inessentials he was inclined to leave his supporting cast to their own devices (though he never relaxed his control of crowd effects, for which he was justly famous), and even his own rôle suffered, once its challenge had been met and overcome. But his instinct was sound and shrewd enough to retain the services of a highly accomplished supporting company, among them Constance Collier, Marie Löhr, Lewis Waller, Lyn Harding, and Basil Gill.

Moreover, like Irving, Tree was largely contemptuous of financial reward and regularly withdrew productions which were still playing to capacity. From 1905 his annual summer season of Shakespeare provided London with a repertory of full-scale Shakespearean productions offered in a quite uneconomic variety and splendour. The years before 1914 witnessed much discussion of the idea of a National Theatre and Theatre School. Tree took unofficial but characteristic action by making Her Majesty's serve some of the functions of a National Theatre and by founding the future Royal Academy of Dramatic Art. It was his withdrawal from theatrical affairs, and the withdrawal of his fellow actor-managers, which threw on the Old Vic, hitherto more of an opera house, the responsibility of keeping Shakespeare before the public in the competitive conditions of the first World War and the post-war theatre.

The Playwright's Progress

What distinguishes the era of Tree and Alexander from that of Irving and Hare is, however, the emergence of a native drama largely independent of foreign sources and able to stand comparison with the favourites of continental playhouses. The English playwright's rising status found legal recognition in the International Copyright Act of 1887 and the American Copyright Act of 1890, which put an end to the shameless theatrical piracy from which Gilbert and Sullivan in particular had suffered severely. It was on this statutory protection that the prosperity of playwrights famous and less famous was now established. More tangible evidence of their prestige can be found in the greatly improved editions of plays which began to appear in the 1890s. 'Note: throughout, "Right" and "Left" are the spectators' Right and Left, not the actor's' is prefaced to many of Pinero's printed plays. Clearly a reading public had arisen for the stage play, as opposed to the closet drama, and Henry Arthur Jones regularly arranged for private publication by the Chiswick Press to coincide with the first production of his plays. There was a complete reaction from ephemeral acting editions and manuscripts withheld from publication for fear of piracy. When George Bernard Shaw turned from writing unheeded novels to the publication in 1898 of *Plays Pleasant and Unpleasant*, they stood very little chance of production by the actor-managers. Yet Shaw justifiably believed that there was a potential reading audience who, having read his plays, would press for their performance. Meanwhile his Prefaces and stage-directions would give them plentiful food for thought!

The characteristic offering of this fashionable era was understandably the Society drama. Managers and playwrights recognized the need to make the occupants of the orchestra stalls feel at home, without becoming so exclusive as to alienate the pit and gallery. Their solution was to lay their scenes in 'our little parish of St. James's' (to use Pinero's own phrase), but to build the play around a handful of themes and situations easily recognizable to the humblest patron, whose knowledge of High Life did not extend beyond standing room in the upper circle on a Saturday night. In this way the Society drama could come to terms with its audience at every level. The use of the term 'problem play' to cover such narrowly defined themes was, however, unacceptable to one section of the English public who, with their eyes firmly fixed on Ibsen, conceived the word 'problem' to cover a far wider field than Society drama.

The efforts of parvenus or the déclassés to penetrate the magic circle of London society by marriage, the accolade, or more dubious means, and the efforts of those so admitted to stay there, were among the favourite themes. Both subjects usually had recourse to the 'woman with a past', a lady whose previous conduct, rightly or wrongly, disqualified her from any position of rank or respect. The exposition of this fatal failing regularly lent itself to the gradual uncovering of a buried secret in the best traditions of the *pièce bien faite*: the official secret stolen or sold, the compromising document, or the still more compromising love-letter. The weapons already sharpened by long usage in the French theatre from Scribe to Sardou were now turned by English playwrights to their own purposes. Certain situations of proven worth were elaborated and exploited to the full. Any reference on the programme to bachelor chambers was enough to whet the spectator's appetite for the moment when the heroine would be trapped there in incriminating circumstances. No experienced playgoer put any trust in the family relationships indicated by the list of characters, when all his training told him that by the end of Act III one or more would certainly have changed partners or parents in mid-play. Nor, after the stirring *coup-de-théâtre* of this Act, need he fear further nervous strain. The final act of a problem play could be relied on to dispatch the awkward characters to the grave or to the Colonies, and the others to church, with equal speed and skill.

The ubiquity in these pieces of the 'woman with a past' has often provoked the comment: 'Why not a play about a man with a past?' The answer lies in the habitual discretion which Victorian society exercised in favour of male adultery. The idea that a man was 'fast' added salt to Victorian gossip and provided Charles Hawtrey with the theme for a long series of highly successful farces, wholly acceptable to his fashionable public. Any slur on a woman's conduct, however, was sufficient to imperil her position in society and to qualify her for the rôle of tragedienne on the stage. By embodying this prejudice in their plays Victorian dramatists were faithfully reflecting English law, which until 1923 accepted a wife's adultery as ground for divorce but required proof of a husband's cruelty or desertion as well as adultery before it would grant a wife's petition.

The Plays of Oscar Wilde

Such was the stuff of Society drama, and there can be no more compelling evidence of its supremacy during this era than the plays of Oscar Wilde. Three of the plays by which, between 1892 and 1895, he added fortune to fame adhere strictly, even slavishly, to the established formula of the problem play. Wilde wanted a medium for his epigrams, and lazily chose the model most readily to hand. The 'strong' drama taken by Grundy from the French provided him with his framework; a High Society setting added novelty and glamour; and the polished dialogue was all that Wilde could really call his own. It is for the sake of the dialogue that these three plays still receive a hearing to-day, but for the most part the wit gleams fitfully in its tarnished setting, and designers, costumiers, and adapters are called in to add a new polish.

Each of Wilde's plays is built round a shameful secret. In the first, *Lady Windermere's Fan*, it is the conduct of the heroine's mother who, after deserting her husband and child for a lover, returns twenty years later to find her daughter about to make the same mistake. In *A Woman of No Importance* it is the seduction of Mrs. Arbuthnot by Lord Illingworth, and her dilemma when their son, Gerald, is offered employment by the father he has never known. In *An Ideal Husband* it is the youthful lapse of Sir Robert Chiltern in selling state secrets and the attempt of the adventuress, Mrs. Cheveley, to blackmail him on that score.

Nor is it merely Wilde's plots that are commonplace. His characters, almost without exception, conform to the popular types. Each play has its woman with a past (Mrs. Erlynne, Mrs. Arbuthnot, Mrs. Cheveley), and there are distressed wives (Lady Windermere, Lady Chiltern) and distraught husbands (Lord Windermere, Sir Robert Chiltern). Wilde certainly showed originality in the witty commentaries of the Duchess of Berwick, Lady Hunstanton, or Lord Goring, but these are rather creatures of the dinner table than of the drama. Moreover, the action with which Wilde felt obliged to break up their epigrams is an anthology of stage clichés. It includes the young wife trapped in a bachelor's rooms (*Lady Windermere's Fan*), the compromising letter which the heroine's faithful friend wrests from the scheming adventuress (*An Ideal Husband*), and a shameless piece of sensationalism to bring down the curtain on Act III of *A Woman of No Importance*:

GERALD (*he is quite beside himself with rage and indignation*). Lord Illingworth, you have insulted the purest thing on God's earth, a thing as pure as my own mother. You have insulted the woman I love most in the world with my own mother. As there is a God in Heaven, I will kill you!

MRS. ARBUTHNOT (*rushing across and catching hold of him*). No! no!

GERALD (*thrusting her back*). Don't hold me, mother. Don't hold me— I'll kill him!

MRS. ARBUTHNOT. Gerald!

GERALD. Let me go, I say!.

MRS. ARBUTHNOT. Stop, Gerald, stop! He is your own father!

Then, having demonstrated his orthodoxy in these three plays, Wilde showed himself a joyous rebel in a fourth. *The Importance of Being Earnest* is his exuberant parody of the 'trivial comedies' (his own amongst them) which the 'serious people' had established in the English theatre. It contains all the features of Wilde's earlier plays—the shameful secret (Worthing's origin in a handbag), the mistaken and assumed identities (Bunburying), and the sensational dénouement in which Worthing turns out to be Lady Bracknell's long-lost nephew. It even contains a sally against the dual morality which distinguished between male and female infidelity:

MISS PRISM. . . . The bag is undoubtedly mine. I am delighted to have it so unexpectedly restored to me. It has been a great inconvenience being without it all these years.

JACK (*in a pathetic voice*). Miss Prism, more is restored to you than this hand-bag. I was the baby you placed in it.

MISS PRISM (*amazed*). You?

JACK (*embracing her*). Yes . . . mother!

MISS PRISM (*recoiling in indignant astonishment*). Mr. Worthing, I am unmarried!

JACK. Unmarried! I do not deny that is a serious blow. But after all, who has the right to cast a stone against one who has suffered? Cannot repentance wipe out an act of folly? Why should there be one law for men, and another for women? Mother, I forgive you. (*Tries to embrace her again.*)

In tone *The Importance of Being Earnest* also owes a good deal to W. S. Gilbert's exploitation of ludicrous logic, and for several incidents it borrows freely from his *Engaged*. Yet with all these debts the play remains triumphantly alive. It has some of Wilde's best lines, but more than that, it solemnly expounds an argument ridiculous but irresistible, which never fails to convulse its audience.

Three years before the production of *The Importance of Being Earnest*, London first saw another Victorian play which has since maintained a firm hold on the stage. *Charley's Aunt*, by Brandon Thomas, treads the tight-rope of absurdity and alights safely at the end without tumbling into the fatuous. But the frankly farcical characters and treatment of *Charley's Aunt* suggest that *The Importance of Being Earnest* had further to fall, and make Wilde's achievement in keeping his balance all the finer.

Arthur Wing Pinero

Lady Windermere's Fan gave George Alexander one of his first successes on assuming management of the St. James's, and *The Importance of Being Earnest*, though its initial run was cut short by Wilde's disgrace, proved in revival to be amongst Alexander's most popular pieces. But Wilde's career as a playwright was soon over and it was not his plays but Pinero's that became most closely associated with Alexander's theatre. Unlike Wilde, Arthur Wing Pinero had to serve a long and arduous apprenticeship in the theatre before winning recognition. Inevitably much of that apprenticeship took the form of adapting from the French, and one such adaptation, *The Iron Master* (from Ohnet's *Le Maître des Forges*), ranked amongst the Kendals' favourites. The lessons in construction which Pinero thus acquired were put to excellent use in the series of farces which he provided for the Court Theatre in the 1880s. The best of these, *The Magistrate*, *The Schoolmistress*, and *Dandy Dick*, went far towards restoring the self-respect of English comedy after its long eclipse. Pinero's skill in developing a novel farcical situation and his feeling for characters who remain recognizable and likeable, however ridiculous, established him firmly as an entertainer before he began to aspire to Society drama.

Yet even in these early, light-hearted pieces, a note of

seriousness was often detectable. Pinero was one of the very few playwrights of his generation who acknowledged a debt to T. W. Robertson, and *The Squire*, his first play for the Kendals, presented a heroine, Kate Verity, 'Squire' of Market-Sinfield, with many of the boyish, self-reliant qualities Robertson had exploited so successfully through Marie Wilton. There is, too, a marked return to Robertsonian atmosphere in a stage direction such as: 'The lights are getting duller, the faint glow of the setting sun is seen outside the windows.' Pinero's most deliberate exploitation of bygone sentiment was in the enormously popular *Sweet Lavender*, which would have no greater claim to consideration than a hundred other such pieces, equally contrived, were it not for the figure of Dick Phenyl, the broken-down barrister whose unanswerable 'If you don't take weak drop whiskey an' wa'er after the labours of the day, when do you take weak drop whiskey an' wa'er?' excuses his many failings, both to the audience and to his fellow-characters.

More striking is the note of comment which begins to creep into Pinero's comedies. *The Hobby-Horse* unexpectedly adds an undertone of genuine feeling to its story of two impractical philanthropists, and later *The Times*, with its upstart Bumpuses bribing their way into London's smart set, clearly owes something to Robertson's handling of the Chodds in *Society* and of Isaac Skoome in *M.P.* But experiments of this kind can hardly have prepared his audience for the reversal of style which Pinero displayed in *The Profligate*, the piece he supplied for the opening of the Garrick Theatre under Hare's management. Here his new seriousness of purpose is uncompromisingly displayed in the career of a philanderer who believes he has found happiness in marriage, only to be confronted by one of the several women from his past. So uncompromising was Pinero's purpose that the husband's suicide, after his wife had left him, proved too much for Hare, and a reconciliation was extorted from the author before the play was produced. Yet Pinero's contempt for compromise had been aroused and with *The Second Mrs. Tanqueray* he was able to satisfy his craving for serious drama and at the same time to achieve general recognition.

Besides making a reputation for Mrs. Patrick Campbell and confirming Alexander's position at the St. James's, this play placed Pinero firmly in the ranks of the Society dramatists. Henceforth life and love in fashionable Society was to be his theme, with only an occasional backward glance at the modest settings of his early comedies. *The Second Mrs. Tanqueray* uses most of the ingredients employed by Wilde: Paula is the familiar woman with a past, struggling for a foothold in polite Society; there is the usual recourse to coincidence in the attachment of her stepdaughter, Ellean, to one of Paula's lovers, and unabashed melodrama in such exchanges as

ELLEAN. . . . From the first moment I saw you I knew you were altogether unlike the good women I'd left; directly I saw you I knew what my father had done. You've wondered why I've turned from you! There—that's the reason! Oh, but this is a horrible way for the truth to come home to everyone! Oh. . . !

PAULA (*madly*). It's a lie! It's all a lie! (*Forcing* ELLEAN *down upon her knees.*) You shall beg my pardon for it. (ELLEAN *utters a loud shriek of terror.*) Ellean, I'm a good woman! I swear I am! I've always been a good woman! You dare to say I've ever been anything else! (*Throwing her off violently.*) It's a lie!

On the other hand Pinero manipulated familiar material with a finesse to which Wilde did not aspire, as when Paula rashly rejects the sincere if belated overtures of Mrs. Cortelyon, and in placing beside the Tanquerays another ill-assorted couple in the acidly-drawn Orreyeds. It is this finesse which has fired Pinero's apologists to extol his craftsmanship—a service doubly dangerous since it exposes him to charges of clumsiness in, for instance, the laboured exposition of the opening scenes, and at the same time obscures the much rarer gift of sympathy. The play may be conventionally conceived and too often mechanically executed, but Paula's moments of self-knowledge lift it above this level. Such insight is evident at her first appearance when she gives Aubrey a chance to change his mind about marrying her:

AUBREY. . . . What *is* the matter?

PAULA (*pouting*). Well, I think you might have said, 'You're very generous, Paula,' or at least, 'Thank you, dear', when I offered to set you free.

AUBREY (*catching her in his arms*), Ah!
PAULA. Ah! ah! Ha, ha! It's all very well but you don't know what it cost me to make such an offer. I do so want to be married.

And at the end, while Aubrey still clings to any shred of hope, Paula will no longer deceive herself or him:

AUBREY. We'll make our calculations solely for the future, talk about the future, think about the future.
PAULA. I believe the future is only the past again, entered through another gate.

Much of Pinero's later work reflects this struggle between a spontaneous sympathy and a strictly disciplined technique. It was the latter which assured him his contemporary success. By calculating precisely the quantities required for a big theatrical climax he contrived the bedroom scene in *The Gay Lord Quex*, in which the humble manicurist sacrifices her own good name to save her foster-sister from the designs of the disreputable Quex. Pinero's capacity for taking pains often led him to overlay his original inspiration by too much attention to detail. The heroine of *Iris*, for example, is a young widow so steeped in luxury as to be incapable of rousing herself or her audience. She cannot sacrifice this luxury to marry for love on the Canadian prairies:

LAURENCE. Within a few years there would be comforts, pretty walls to gaze at, servants to wait on you——!
IRIS (*looking up piteously*). Two Chinamen—or three? An extra boy to maid me? Oh, Laurie!

and so she falls back on the protection of the wealthy Frederick Maldonado. It is difficult to feel pity for such self-indulgence when at the end Maldonado discovers her again communicating with her suitor and drives her out of the house. Pinero is constantly in danger of sacrificing sympathy and credibility by such calculated contrivance. Both these gifts desert him at the end of *His House in Order*, when he forces the ill-used heroine to give up her chance of revenge and accept reconciliation with her unlikeable husband and his unspeakable relatives.

Yet Pinero should not be denied credit for his measure of honesty and humanity of purpose. He is at his happiest in the theatrical world of *Trelawny of the 'Wells'*, where the characters share his own limited vision. It is not only the portrait of Tom Robertson in Tom Wrench that engages sympathy, but the whole company of penniless, irresponsible players. They scandalize Cavendish Square by visiting their former leading lady late at night during a thunderstorm, yet at the end find dignity even in their displacement by another generation:

TELFER. Let us both go home.

MRS. TELFER (*restraining him*). No, let us remain. We've been idle six months, and I can't bear to see you without your watch and all your comforts about you.

TELFER (*pointing towards the green room*). And so this new-fangled stuff, and these dandified people, are to push us, and such as us, from our stools!

MRS. TELFER. Yes, James, just as some other new fashion will, in course of time, push *them* from their stools.

Even within the confines of Society drama Pinero was brave enough to criticize the principles of his audience by blaming Paula's fate on the injustice of their dual morality: Ardale, her former lover, is made the whipping boy for his class.

AUBREY. . . . Curse him! Yes, I do curse him—him and his class! Perhaps I curse myself too in doing it. He has only led 'a man's life'—just as I, how many of us, have done! The misery he has brought on me and mine it's likely enough we, in our time, have helped to bring on others by this leading 'a man's life'.

A much bolder bid was the portrait, in *The Notorious Mrs. Ebbsmith*, of a free-thinking Feminist and natural leader whose courage and strength have won her the devotion of a young politician, Lucas Cleeve. But at the last moment Pinero's own courage deserted him and he denies Agnes Ebbsmith both her courage and her self-respect. Fearing to lose Lucas, she sets herself to seduce him; defeated, she first spurns the Bible offered for her solace and throws it into the fire, then plunges her hands into the flames to retrieve it. Finally, when Lucas will not break with her, she gives in to his wife's appeal:

SYBIL. . . . I despise him, he hates me. (*Walking away, her voice breaking.*) Only—I did love him once. . . . I don't want to see him utterly thrown away—wasted. . . . I don't quite want to see that. . . .

(AGNES *rises and approaches* SYBIL *fearfully.*)

AGNES (*in a whisper*). Lift your veil for a moment. (SYBIL *raises her veil.*) Tears—tears—(*with a deep groan*). Oh—(SYBIL *turns away*) I—I'll do it . . . I'll go back to the Palazzo . . . at once. (SYBIL *draws herself up suddenly.*) I've wronged you! wronged you! O God! O God!

Pinero's portrait of Agnes Ebbsmith ends in the failure of a gallant attempt to explore beyond the confines of the Victorian problem play, in which he found himself beyond the confines of his own understanding.

His later career was largely made up of such experiments. In *The Thunderbolt* he turned from the London drawing-room to a middle-class living-room in a provincial town, to people it with the grasping family of a rich brewer who has died, apparently intestate. Their expectations are checked when the existence is disclosed, first of a natural daughter, then of a will in her favour which a needy sister-in-law, overcome by temptation, has destroyed. The family portraits and the story itself, if somewhat laboured, have more substance than many of Pinero's Society dramas; but the drab setting and, above all, the spectacle of George Alexander as a shabby music-teacher were abhorrent to the audience at the St. James's. Consequently Pinero returned to Belgravia for *Mid-Channel*, probably the most sensitive of his Society plays, with its touching portrait of childless Zoe Blundell, who is driven by her husband's neglect into a brief affair with a younger man; then, finding that neither he nor her husband wants her, to suicide. There is a deliberate rejection here of the over-statement of *The Second Mrs. Tanqueray*, but the softer colours and quieter tones did not appeal to Pinero's public and the play's setting was altogether too rich and rare to commend it to an exclusively intellectual audience.

Out of sympathy with the old world and out of touch with the new, Pinero continued to write almost until his death in 1934, venturing with *The Enchanted Cottage* into the untried field of fantasy, but failing to catch the ear of the post-war public. His success had been achieved by gauging accurately the temper of the Victorian public and the scope of his own talents. His eclipse was due to his efforts to extend those talents. There is a lack of balance between manner and matter in Pinero's work, well reflected in the increasing flatulence of his dialogue. His understanding of life was smaller than his understanding of the stage, and his style grew ponderous as he struggled to be profound. Yet it is for the courage which inspired those struggles that he is assured of respect.

Henry Arthur Jones

Courage was always evident in the character and career of Henry Arthur Jones, the playwright who with Pinero did most to establish the pattern of Society drama. Nevertheless, any analysis of his work must conclude that his courage is now more apparent in his public pronouncements than in his plays. Jones, like Pinero, served a long apprenticeship in the traditional forms of Victorian drama before reaching the vanguard of the new movement. Much of that time he was playwright-in-residence at the Princess's, where Wilson Barrett persevered with melodrama. It was for him that Jones (with some help from Henry Herman) devised in *The Silver King* the part of Wilfred Denver, the gambler who escapes to America, believing he has killed his persecutor in a drunken stupor, but returns from the silver-mines a rich man, intent on tracking down the gang who have planted their guilt on him. In his use of up-to-date touches, such as the skittle-alley of the first act or the scene in a railway station, Jones continued the documentation of melodrama begun by Tom Taylor; but *The Silver King* owed its success largely to Wilson Barrett's exploitation of its vigorous expression of remorse ('Oh, God, put back thy universe and give me yesterday') and revenge.

This success bound Jones to the yoke of melodrama for another ten years. Yet he was already feeling his way towards a higher purpose. In an address delivered in 1884 and reprinted ten years later in his *Renascence of the English Drama*, Jones declared: 'Our great need is, then, for a school of plays of serious intention, plays that implicitly assert the value and dignity of human life, that it has great passions and great aims, and is full of meaning and importance.'[1] He had the same year made some attempt to practise what he preached with *Saints and Sinners*, a largely commonplace story of a young girl, seduced by the local squire, who dies in her sweetheart's arms after expiating her shame with good works. Yet Jones's boldness in making the girl's father a Dissenting minister and in attacking his canting congregation, who drove father and daughter from their home, was sufficient to provoke an outcry in 1884. Before long, however, Jones's plea for a more ambitious drama and a more discriminating audience was answered, and by the time he published *The Renascence of the English Drama* in 1894 he could confidently assert in the Preface: 'Had the playgoing public of 1882 been the playgoing public of 1894, that is, if there had been in 1882 a body of cultivated playgoers sufficiently numerous to understand and welcome such plays as have recently been successful in some of our West-End theatres, not a single word of the following papers would have been written or spoken.'[2]

The fact remains that, though evidently conscious of the opportunity which this revolution in theatrical affairs offered the playwright, Jones himself never rose to it. Hampered in his approach by a narrow though vigorous intellect, he was further hampered by habits of thought and style acquired during his long apprenticeship in melodrama. Such limitations are especially noticeable in his own 'plays of serious intention'. Save for his single, somewhat pedestrian essay in verse drama, *The Tempter*, there is not one of his more ambitious pieces that does not fall seriously short of its purpose through sensationalism and a ludicrous lack of genuine humour. Conversely, it was Jones's command of melodrama that supplied the spectacular scenes in his plays which largely commended them to his public.

Thus the promising theme of faith-healing dwindles in *Judah* to a somewhat naïve portrait of a Welsh minister, consumed with passion for a charlatan's daughter and accomplice. More characteristic still is *The Dancing Girl*, which, produced by Tree at the Haymarket, brought Jones into the ranks of Society playwrights. This hugely successful piece is little more than a succession of brightly coloured pictures, lacking coherent argument

[1] *The Renascence of the English Drama* (London, 1894), p. 171.
[2] Preface, p. vi.

or analysis. The dissolute Duke of Guisebury and Drusilla Ives, the Quaker girl with whom he is infatuated, are set first against an idealized Cornish seascape, then in a whirl of London dissipation, with Drusilla established as a famous dancer and the bankrupt Duke about to take poison:

One word more, old love—Adieu. One word more, old world— Adieu. Ten minutes to twelve. About another two hours' consciousness, and then perhaps another hour more—without consciousness! Strange! I shan't drop off to sleep to-night—I shall drop off to death. But really one drops off to death every night for eight hours. Except when one has insomnia. Life's nothing more than insomnia after all— and I've had it badly.

The totally unconvincing conclusion sees Drusilla dead in America and the Duke recovering in the sunshine of his tenants' smiles and the tender care of the crippled girl who has always loved him.

There is more to respect in *The Masqueraders*, which Jones designed for Alexander and Mrs. Patrick Campbell to follow up their triumph in *The Second Mrs. Tanqueray*, thereby measuring his talent against Pinero's. Here the infatuation of a mystic astronomer for the ill-used wife of the vicious Sir Bryce Skene does command some sympathy, though there is neither mystery nor passion in its presentation, and the dénouement whereby the lovers renounce happiness at the dictates of convention sounds an ominous note of cant:

HELEN. I know the woman who gives herself to another man while her husband is alive betrays her sex and is a bad woman.
DAVID. I love her. I love her. (*Going towards door.*)
HELEN (*stopping him*). Then make your love the best thing in her life, and the best thing in yours. You have loved her so well. You have made so many sacrifices for her. Make this one last sacrifice. Keep her pure for her child.

It is much the same lack of true imagination that offsets the courage of *Michael and His Lost Angel*, with its brave attempt to portray a young priest, seduced by a rich and unhappily married parishioner. The priest's public confession in church displays unusual dignity and feeling, but the conclusion drops sharply into bathos, with the priest a recluse in an Italian monastery, to which the wife, now mysteriously consumptive, comes to die:

MICHAEL. She is dying?
(*She has gained the room, just enters, leaning back against the post.* MICHAEL's *back is toward her.*)
AUDRIE. I'm afraid I am. . . . Sir Lyolf, pay—coachman—(*taking out purse feebly*) outside—— No, perhaps—better—wait—or bring another sort—of—carriage. But no mutes—no feathers—no mummery. . . .
MICHAEL. You're suffering?
AUDRIE. No—that's past. (*Shuts her eyes. He watches her.*) Very comfortable—very happy—just like going into a delicious faint.

A serious theme was never strong enough in appeal for Jones to resist the temptation of sensational treatment. That he sometimes achieved, in succumbing, some striking moments of melodrama is now cold comfort. 'The pity is,' as William Archer noted, 'that the world of his imagination is not sunlit but limelit.'[1]

Disappointed by the failure of *Michael and His Lost Angel*, Jones turned increasingly to Society comedy, choosing often a flimsy and repetitive pattern of intrigue as his theme, but tracing its course with a sure feeling for climax and a shrewd sense of the atmosphere and accents of fashionable society. That he had no gift for satire is apparent from his clumsy handling of philanthropy in *The Crusaders* and greedy materialism in *The Triumph of the Philistines*. But in *The Case of Rebellious Susan* he found a much happier vein; and this story of Lady Susan Harrabin, stung by her husband's infidelity into encouraging the attentions of a romantic young diplomat under the Egyptian stars, is told with a nice control of irony and suspense. The intrusion of some painfully broad comedy is a legacy from Jones's early days; more serious is the note of resignation on which the play ends. Lady Susan is persuaded into reconciliation with her loutish husband because, she is assured by her uncle, her attempt to pay him out in kind won't work:

LADY SUSAN. I want somebody to show me some way of paying him back without—without——

[1] *The Old Drama and the New*, p. 297.

SIR RICHARD. Without losing your place in Society and your self-respect. Ah! that's the difficulty. There is an immense reputation to be made as a moralist by any man who will show you ladies the way to break the seventh commandment, without leaving any ill-effects upon society.

LADY SUSAN. Well he'd better make haste, or we shall find out the way ourselves.

SIR RICHARD (*shakes his head*). My dear Sue, believe me, what is sauce for the goose will never be sauce for the gander. In fact there is no gander sauce.

Sir Richard's smug acceptance of the unjust ways of the world, though doubtless convincing in Charles Wyndham's persuasive tones, is a trait that increasingly marked out Jones as a convert to the established order of things. There was no marital misunderstanding, he seemed to believe, that a shopping expedition to Bond Street could not clear up. This was Sir Richard's advice in *The Case of Rebellious Susan*:

. . . If I were Sue, I would accept the villa at Cannes and a diamond ring and bracelet from Hunt and Roskell's, not in the least as any reparation of your fault—nothing can repair that—but as a sign of belief in the genuineness of your—your remorse.

And it was Sir Christopher Deering's advice (again proffered by Wyndham) in *The Liars*. In this, the most successful of all Jones's comedies, the third act provides a handsome example of his gift for scene-building, as one by one all Lady Jessica Nepean's friends are involved in a frenzy of lying, to conceal from her jealous husband her assignation with the young explorer, Edward Falkner. But Jones, the spokesman of Society, could not allow their association to prosper, and at the end Sir Christopher must convince Falkner and Lady Jessica that their proposed elopement, also, 'wont work'. It would be easier to swallow his advice if it did not spring from avowedly false values:

SIR CHRISTOPHER. Now! I've nothing to say in the abstract against running away with another man's wife. There may be planets where it is not only the highest ideal morality, but where it has the further advantage of being a practical way of carrying on society. But it has this one fatal defect in our country to-day—it won't work! You know what we English are, Ned. We're not a bit better than our neighbours, but thank God! we do pretend we are, and we do make it hot for anybody who disturbs that holy pretence.

That, after sending Falkner to Africa still a bachelor, Sir Christopher should himself gain the hand of a companionable widow, Beatrice Ebenoe, seems preferential treatment even for an actor-manager.

While it is possible to accept Jones's treatment of the frivolous Lady Jessica, it is much harder to endorse his sentence on the heroine of *Mrs. Dane's Defence*. Her story, which strikes a more serious note than most of Jones's Society plays, shows the playwright at his most skilful. The investigations of Sir Daniel Carteret into the past of the woman whom his adopted son wishes to marry, gather momentum until, in the justly famous cross-examination scene, he breaks down her defence and establishes that she is, after all, the governess who was once involved in a scandal in Vienna. But is her concealment of this fact sufficient to ostracize her? On the sketchy information that Jones supplies this is highly dubious, and even Sir Daniel's old friend has her doubts:

LADY EASTNEY. Oh aren't you Pharisees and tyrants, all of you? And don't you make cowards and hypocrites of all of us? Don't you lead us into sin, and then condemn us for it? Aren't you first our partners, and then our judges?

But Sir Daniel is inexorable:

The rules of the game are severe. If you don't like them, leave the sport alone. They will never be altered.

So Mrs. Dane is exiled to Devonshire, Lionel supplied with a homely Scots lassie as substitute, and all Jones's honest work in building up his climax is dissipated by the dishonesty of his conclusion.

His assimilation of the conventional code of his audience gave Jones's more serious work an increasingly narrow outlook. For this reason it is often his least ambitious pieces that now seem most entertaining. *Whitewashing Julia* tackles a theme closely akin to that of *Mrs. Dane's Defence*, for scandal has linked Julia Wren's name with that of the Duke of Savona and the cathedral town of Shanctonbury is agog to probe the affair. But here Jones is content to forswear moral judgements and keep his audience guessing, while Julia is busy fascinating the Hon. Bill Stillingfleet. He is happier still when he can break away from gossip and gossips. An early play, *The Rogue's Comedy*, suggests what he might have achieved in a picaresque vein, for it presents an engaging rascal, Bailey Prothero, and a magnificently managed party scene, in which Prothero performs his tricks as a soothsayer, with the audience as his accomplice. Before the end sentimentality threatens to break in, but Jones resists the temptation and the extraordinary precision with which he draws the world of sharpers and speculators is evident from a single speech by the old reprobate, Lord John Bucklow:

My dear Bicester and gentlemen (*splutters*), I wish to add my testimony (*whistles a few notes*) to that of my enthusiastic young friend who has just sat down (*smacks his lips*)—to the merits of our worthy host—dammy—I have arrived at—time of life (*grimace*) when having exhausted all other delights (*whistles a few notes*) I have nothing before me—dammy—but an old age of sincere repentance (*whistles*) for having enjoyed myself to the best of my powers every day—dammy—and all day long for the last seventy-two years. (*Smack of lips.*) Providence, having blessed me (*spluttering*) with wonderful constitution (*grimace*) and having given me—dammy—most expensive and exclusive tastes in wine—(*grimace*) in food—in cigars—in clothes—and in love—(*whistles a few notes*)—forgot—dammy—to provide me with any solid and visible means of indulging those tastes. (*Splutters and whistles.*) I was therefore compelled either to live—(*smack of lips*) life of most offensive virtue and industry—(*whistles*) or to gratify those tastes—dammy—at other people's expense. (*Grimace.*) I took latter alternative. But just as other people were (*smack*)—were getting tired of this arrangement, I had good fortune (*whistles*) to meet with our worthy host, Mr.—Mr.—Mr. (*grimace*)—— He obligingly made use of my name, and in return gave me most useful advice—(*spluttering*) with regard to certain—dammy—mines. I have not the remotest idea where those mines are situated—(*whistles*)—I do not know how our worthy host obtained his information—I only wish to express my implicit confidence in Mr.——
PROTHERO. Bailey Prothero.

Something of the same hitting power is apparent in *Mary Goes First*, an ironic account of the traffic in titles among the leaders of provincial society. But the most satisfying of these entertainments is probably *Dolly Reforming Herself*, for in this play Jones had neither convention to uphold nor abuse to attack. The argument of *Dolly Reforming Herself* is nothing more than an indulgent husband's vain efforts to curb the extravagance of his spendthrift wife. Yet so skilfully are the phases of his campaign planned and conducted that the thinness of the material is rarely apparent, and the single combat in which the two engage is sustained with extraordinary ease and variety. Here practised playwriting is seen at its best.

Jones's long and prolific career accurately reflects this era of Society drama. He grew up just at the time that the Victorian theatre was growing up, and he was therefore keenly aware of the greatness within its grasp. In the event that greatness had to be grasped by others and his own contribution was limited to a reform of the mechanics of playwriting. His emergence as a Society dramatist led to his adoption of the ideas of that Society, and thereafter a creeping paralysis of outlook gradually cut him off from new ideas and the new audience. His last successful play, *The Lie*, which, though written before 1914, was not produced in England until 1923, completed his identification with a vanished era. This story of a girl who steals her sister's fiancé, by allowing him to believe her sister the mother of her own child, is built up to a tremendous climax of recrimination, with the slighted Elinor screaming, 'She blew me a kiss! Judas sister! Judas sister! Judas sister!' But the characters live only in the heat of their theatrical moment. They have little power to stir or satisfy a modern audience. Jones survived until 1929, fighting to the last the encroachments on the established order, of which he had become (especially since the Great War) an outspoken champion. To-day his plays are seen only as a training exercise for young actors, to whom a firmly articulated framework offers a welcome basis for interpretation. His public has passed away with the society for which he wrote.

Society Dramatists

The prestige and prolific output of Jones and Pinero inevitably obscured other Society dramatists who catered successfully for the tastes of their audience. Much of their work was lightweight: the high spirits in High Society which R. C. Carton distilled in *Lord and Lady Algy* and *Lady Huntsworth's Experiment* made small demands on the digestion. The plays of Charles Haddon Chambers, however, reflect more keenly the development of theatrical taste during his time. Himself an Australian, he provided Tree in *Captain Swift* with the rôle of a bushranger who blunders on the secret of his birth in London society, and disarmed criticism by presenting it with the term, 'the long arm of coincidence'. In *The Idler* and *John-a-Dreams* he followed—a long way behind—the formula of Pinero and Jones. But *The Tyranny of Tears* cannot be dismissed as mere imitation, for in turning from high society to the modest though comfortable home of the Parburys, Chambers found a style of his own. The uninflated dialogue and the economy of means employed are more significant than the story of a wife who has recourse to tears once too often. There is individuality of both style and theme in a later play, *Passers By*, with its sympathetic and convincing portrait of an unmarried mother. The contrast between Mrs. Seabrook in *Captain Swift*, with her shameful secret, and Margaret Summers in *Passers By* is the measure of Chambers's maturity. Margaret declares:

'You needn't be embarrassed for me, Peter. I'm not ashamed and I've no remorse. He's my child. I've won him and he's mine only.'

And a little later:

'Peter, I have two priceless things in the world—my child and my independence. I shall cling desperately to them both.'

Mrs. Seabrook belongs wholly to the world of melodrama. Margaret Summers is on the threshold of the modern naturalistic play.

A similar development can be traced in the career of Hubert Henry Davies, who provided Charles Wyndham and Mary Moore with the well-bred comedy expected of them in *Mrs.*

Gorringe's Necklace, Captain Drew on Leave, and, later, *Lady Epping's Lawsuit.* Davies's approach to the theatre, however, was always more restrained than that adopted by most Society dramatists, and in *The Mollusc* he produced a miniature comedy whose tiny but perfect proportions have not lost their charm. There are resemblances between this play and *Dolly Reforming Herself,* though Davies's heroine is cursed not by extravagance but by laziness. Like Jones, Davies constructs his story largely round the efforts of a good-natured husband to cure his obstinate though delightful wife; but *The Mollusc* achieves its end with only four characters and can cheerfully throw aside the elaborate contrivance of Society drama. All that Davies lacked was deeper understanding to quicken the easy rhythms of his plays. But the war put an end to his career and he died as a result of his war service, so that it was left to younger writers to carry on his work.

To set J. M. Barrie among the Society dramatists may seem curious. Yet Barrie's early apprenticeship in the theatre followed most of the phases through which Pinero had passed ten years earlier. In *Walker, London,* Barrie provided Toole with a cleverly contrived farce, not unworthy of Pinero's series for the Court, and in *The Wedding Guest* he contributed his woman-with-a-past to that crowded gallery in the person of Kate Ommaney, who returns to reproach her former lover on his wedding-day. More relevant are his adaptation of his novel *The Little Minister* and his first important play, *Quality Street.* A comparison between *Quality Street* and Pinero's *Sweet Lavender* will suggest where Barrie's originality lies; both plays appeal frankly to the emotions, but while Pinero exploits the sentimental, Barrie explores it, finding his own vein of smiles and tears to draw on. From his models he learnt so well how to put his story before an audience that the process continually defies detection, but it was his particular achievement to refine the sentimentality of the Victorian theatre into a style which not only satisfied his own generation but still captivates a large section of the modern public, however much it upsets the rest.

Barrie was at his weakest when tilting at the absurdities of his own theatre in *Alice-Sit-By-The-Fire,* and for long it was

127

only in *Peter Pan*, an avowedly children's play, that he could
allow his imagination full play. Yet he succeeded by transcend-
ing realism, and it is the imaginative quality of his treatment
that lifts *The Admirable Crichton* out of the rut of Society drama,
for all its titles and tiaras; and in *What Every Woman Knows*
transforms the conventional triangle into a figment of Barrie's
own world. The summit of his achievement was to be reached
only after 1914, when in *Dear Brutus* and *Mary Rose* he ventured beyond the realistic in his themes, as well as in their treatment, so that subject and style were attuned and his particular
magic doubly potent. But there is still magic enough in the
plays he wrote for the Society audience of the pre-war period.

Intellectual Drama: Shaw

An unmixed diet of Society drama did not satisfy every
section of the Victorian audience. As the prestige of the theatre
rose, so the discriminating playgoer began to deplore the limitations of the drama, and to point out that the manifest refinement of playgoing habits had not been matched by a corresponding rebirth of the drama. In the 1870s and 1880s the
growing popularity of the matinée was fostered by the demand
of a small but influential section of the public for plays outside
the established repertory. By 1890 this demand had crystallized
into a movement to familiarize the English audience with the
plays of Henrik Ibsen. The first complete English translation
of Ibsen's plays (including in many instances the first translation
at all) appeared under William Archer's editorship between
1889 and 1890. Yet Ibsen had been writing for the theatre
since 1850, and *Peer Gynt* had appeared in 1867, the same year
as Robertson's *Caste*. Ibsen's first English editor was not
merely a Scandinavian enthusiast. First and foremost he had a
mission to perform in the English theatre. Quitting his native
Edinburgh for London in 1878, Archer published four years
later *English Dramatists of To-day*, a survey which is as shrewd
in its recognition of undeveloped talent in Jones and Pinero as
in its rejection of the popular playwrights of the day. Before
long Archer discovered in an adjacent seat at the British
Museum Reading Room a kindred spirit in George Bernard
Shaw, whom he was presently able to introduce to the risks and

rewards of journalism. Thus Shaw, too, was enrolled in the Ibsenite ranks, and in 1890 was able to combine his loyalty to Archer and Ibsen with his political and social enthusiasms by delivering to the Fabian Society the lectures later published as *The Quintessence of Ibsenism*. But lectures on Ibsen without performances of Ibsen were as smoke without fire. In 1891, therefore, the Independent Theatre was founded, largely through the efforts of a fellow critic, J. T. Grein. 'To give special performances of plays which have a literary and artistic rather than a commercial value' was their declared object, and *Ghosts*, chosen as their first production, was performed on 13 March 1891 and denounced by the doyen of dramatic critics, Clement Scott of the *Daily Telegraph*, as 'an open drain', 'a loathsome sore unbandaged', 'a dirty act done publicly', and 'a lazar-house with all its doors and windows open'.

Such a challenge to a man of Shaw's temperament was irresistible. He had beside him the unfinished script of a play started as far back as 1885, his treatment of which had long outrun the sober inspiration supplied by William Archer. The play, hastily polished off and titled *Widowers' Houses*, was produced by the Independent Theatre on 9 December 1892. If its reception was a shade less hysterical than that of *Ghosts*, it was only because the critics had already exhausted the fiercest of their pejoratives. Shaw's career as a playwright had been appropriately launched.

The connection between this début and the Ibsenite cause in England was more apparent than real. Shaw could not fairly be termed a disciple of Ibsen, for the greater part of *Widowers' Houses* had been written before he came to share Archer's enthusiasm for Ibsen's plays, and in *The Quintessence of Ibsenism* he inevitably fixed on those features of Ibsen's work which corresponded to his own concept of the playwright's purpose. Of the exposure of romantic cant and selfish obscurantism Shaw found ample evidence in Ibsen; but his own Fabian conception of 'blue-book drama' (as he called *Widowers' Houses*) was less obvious in his predecessor. Most of Ibsen's social plays from *A Doll's House* to *Hedda Gabler* could somehow be squeezed into this category, but the vast dramatic poems proved less tractable, and Shaw's interpretation of *Peer Gynt* and *Emperor and*

Galilean was as confused and confusing as his analysis, in a later edition of *The Quintessence*, of Ibsen's last plays from *Little Eyolf* to *When We Dead Awaken.*

Shaw, in fact, had set out to plough his own theatrical furrow and no amount of studies in Ibsenism could make up for lack of theatrical experience. He knew what sort of play he wanted to write but not, as yet, how to write it: 'It is a propagandist play— a didactic play—a play with a purpose,' stated the Preface to *Widowers' Houses* in 1893, but in the event long passages of the play were neither technically good nor particularly holding. Shaw accurately defined his purpose as 'playing off your laughter at the scandal of the exposure against your shudder at its blackness'; but in *Widowers' Houses* he provided too many shudders at the iniquity of rack-renting, and only Lickcheese to laugh at. Even clumsier was its successor, *The Philanderer*, in which much of the fun poked at Ibsenite poseurs is dull and disagreeable where it has not become unintelligible.

Yet Shaw was shrewd enough to profit by his mistakes. His appointment as dramatic critic to the *Saturday Review* from 1895 to 1898 enabled him to study at first hand the methods of showmanship exhibited by the leaders of the London theatre. These methods, acutely analysed in the series of weekly articles later collected as *Our Theatres in the 'Nineties*, he began to put to his own finely conceived purpose.

. . . My stories are the old stories; my characters are the familiar harlequin and columbine, clown and pantaloon (note the harlequin's leap in the third act of *Cæsar and Cleopatra*); my stage tricks and suspenses and thrills and jests are the ones in vogue when I was a boy. . . .

was his own admission in the Preface to *Three Plays for Puritans.*

Even before taking up his post on the *Saturday Review* Shaw had begun to use the models of the commercial theatre by writing *Mrs. Warren's Profession*, his play about a woman with a past. Mrs. Warren, however, is no candidate for High Society struggling to conceal her one false step, but a woman whose present as proprietor of a string of continental brothels is no less lurid than her past as a prostitute. Such outspokenness set St.

130

13. *Interior Scene*: The Minister and the Mercer, *Drury Lane, 1834*

14. *Vestris and Mathews*: Court Favour, *Olympic*, 1836

James's Palace by the ears, and it was not until thirty years later that the Lord Chamberlain licensed the play for public performance. Beside his woman with a past Shaw sets his woman with a future: Mrs. Warren's daughter, Vivie, the Cambridge Wrangler whose talent for actuarial work leaves her independent both of her mother's tainted allowance and of her self-seeking suitor. The play's exposure of the sweated labour conditions which drove women on the streets is 'blue-book drama' with a vengeance, but *Mrs. Warren's Profession* is more than 'blue-book drama', for Shaw reveals the details of Mrs. Warren's past and indicates the direction of Vivie's future with a command of suspense which preserves the play as a human drama long after its statistics have become valueless.

From the Victorian problem play Shaw turned to the stage romance, and in *Arms and the Man* deftly upset the standards of cloak-and-dagger drama by drawing a hero who fought for pay and stuffed his holster with reserves of chocolate. *The Man of Destiny*, though written in the same vein, falls short of the same success, for here Shaw came near to imitating those tricks of Sardou which he himself had denounced as 'Sardoodledom'. In attempting a vehicle for Irving and Ellen Terry he had fallen back on those devices—concealed identities, compromising letters and stolen despatches—which had long outstayed their welcome. *The Devil's Disciple*, however, marked a return to the level of *Arms and the Man* by taking over the basic plot of an Adelphi melodrama, even to the scaffold scene and last-minute reprieve, and *Cæsar and Cleopatra* provided an anti-toxin to the theatre's overdose of historical romance.

Meanwhile Shaw was feeling his way towards a single unifying theme: the accurate definition of the relationship between the sexes. In *Candida* he supplied the obverse of Nora's portrait in *A Doll's House*. The Reverend James Morell is as much a child under his wife's guardianship as Nora was a child under Torvald's guardianship, and Morell moreover has the grace to accept the situation. *Candida* is a miniature work, but on its own limited scale it is well-nigh perfect, save perhaps for Shaw's failure in Marchbanks to draw a character he could not understand. It is certainly more successful than the more ambitious *Captain Brassbound's Conversion*, which Shaw conceived as Ellen Terry playing a Candida-with-a-title in the middle of Morocco. Lady Cicely Waynflete is no less delightful than Mrs. James Morell, but Shaw was much less happy in the world of Ouida or P. C. Wren than in a Hackney parsonage. *You Never Can Tell*, however, makes a significant addition to his analysis of male and female: here Valentine, the dentist-hero, styles himself the Duellist of Sex, but finds himself out-fought at every point by his intended victim, Gloria Clandon. It is a theme ripe for development, although in *You Never Can Tell* it provides probably the least pleasing part of the play, which sparkles far more gaily in the bright chatter of the twins and the wisdom and humanity of William the Waiter.

In *Man and Superman* Shaw developed this theme fully, working it out with much of the brilliance and elegance of Restoration comedy. To have demonstrated the woman's pursuit of her chosen mate with good taste and good humour was a major achievement, brought about by the infinite dexterity with which Ann Whitefield is presented in the play. 'Not at all, if you please, an oversexed person: that is a vital defect, not a true excess. She is a perfectly respectable, perfectly self-controlled woman, and looks it', runs the first description of her, and Ann's pursuit and final capture of John Tanner, the amiable anarchist, stimulates the intellect and satisfies the sensibility of the audience in equal measure. When, to this splendidly managed central theme, are added such incidental excellences as 'Enery Straker, Tanner's straight-speaking chauffeur and a sturdy example of the New Man with his Polytechnic training, the level of Shaw's achievement in *Man and Superman* may be gauged.

But this play established another precedent. Satisfying as its acting version remains, the full text contains in Act III the 'Don Juan in Hell' scene in which the main characters, disguised as their Mozartian counterparts, expound the philosophy of the play, and in defining the Life Force and its aim of self-knowledge through selective breeding of the Superman, provide both the motive force and the goal for which Ann pursues Tanner. The performance of this act is therefore essential to a full understanding of the play; yet by adding over an hour to the running time it strains the stamina of both audience and actors.

132

Here Shaw has thrown off the discipline which his earlier plays accepted and mastered. The precedence of argument before form grows ever larger in Shaw's work after *Man and Superman*.

This does not mean that he would no longer accept discipline. In *Fanny's First Play* he brings out a skeleton from the family cupboard and breathes a great deal of life into it. The delectable ironies of *Pygmalion* arise very largely from its stagecraft and much less from its argument, though even here the argument is given the last inconclusive word over the stagecraft. But *Getting Married* and *Misalliance* are all argument, and though from the first Shaw had recognized the discussion scene as the feature of Ibsen's technique which appealed most strongly to him, he does not always recognize in these later plays that the discussion needs to be both relevant and trenchant.

Even in the major works which followed *Man and Superman*, therefore, in *The Doctor's Dilemma*, in *Major Barbara*, in *Androcles and the Lion* and in *Heartbreak House*, the listener must be prepared to swallow draughts of somewhat diffuse argument, as well as the strong, sharp taste of the true Shavian dialectic. He must stomach the last act of *The Doctor's Dilemma* for the sake of its predecessors, and see *Heartbreak House* from a vantage point which reveals the grandeur of the whole design and softens some of the redundant detail. Indeed *Heartbreak House* (begun on the eve of the Great War, though not performed in England until 1921) seems intended to mark the end of a phase in Shaw's history, as well as marking the end of an era in theatrical and world history, with Captain Shotover's cry of 'Breakers ahead!' Certainly the vast pentateuch of *Back to Methuselah* reveals Shaw as a philosopher rather than a playwright, and afterwards it was only in *St. Joan* that he permitted the playwright to display his magnificent powers to the full, mellowed now by the compassion of old age.

The Court Theatre Seasons, 1904–7

Shaw's ultimate recognition as a great playwright should not obscure the precariousness of his position in the English theatre before 1914. However controversial, even notorious, a figure he became after the appearance of *Widowers' Houses*, his name was to be found everywhere but on the playbills. In fact of the eleven plays he wrote before *Man and Superman*, only *Arms and the Man* was publicly produced in the West End of London until the inauguration of the Vedrenne-Barker management at the Court Theatre in 1904. The remainder were given occasional private performances by the Independent Theatre and its heir, the Stage Society, or put on for a few matinées. The greatest of the Vedrenne-Barker management's many achievements at the Court was making known Shaw's plays in performance to an influential if restricted audience. In all, eleven of his plays were staged there, and of the 988 performances given at the theatre by this management, 701 were of plays by Shaw. After *Man and Superman*, whose total of 178 performances made it by far the most popular of the plays offered, five further plays by Shaw head the list before the first non-Shavian piece (*Prunella*, by Laurence Housman and Granville Barker with forty-eight performances). Clearly it was Shaw's work which won recognition for the management's enterprise, above all by rousing Edward VII to attend a Command Performance of *John Bull's Other Island*, given at the theatre in March 1905. The growth of interest in an enterprise originally aimed exclusively at the leisured matinée public is well reflected in the gradual addition of evening performances which ultimately eclipsed the matinées. Moreover it was largely the success of the Shaw plays which enabled the management to undertake such notable, but less popular, productions as the Greek plays and plays by Continental and unproven English authors.

After the Vedrenne-Barker management quitted the Court in 1907 there was little difficulty in finding a stage for the production of Shaw's plays, and in 1911 *Fanny's First Play* achieved a record run of 624 performances, due perhaps as much to external factors as to the merits of the play itself. Yet Shaw's appeal in England was still largely restricted to the discriminating, and his work had received widespread recognition both on the Continent and in America before the production by Tree of *Pygmalion* in 1914 marked his acceptance by the gods of the English theatre—on both sides of the curtain.

The fame accruing to Shaw from the Court Theatre productions naturally fostered the writing of more 'blue-book drama', very little of which will bear re-examination, for Shaw's imitators, in following his example of putting social issues squarely on the stage, overlooked the profound understanding of the stage which Shaw brought to this task. *Votes for Women* by Elizabeth Robins, the actress and novelist, was done with some success at the Court, and so long as women's suffrage remained at issue its Trafalgar Square scene, with the arguments for and against vigorously stated, could hold an audience. But the foundations on which this platform was erected are seen, with the realization of full adult suffrage, to be a commonplace collection of the clichés of Society drama, while many other examples of 'blue-book drama' lack even a Trafalgar Square scene to commend them.

Social Drama

A more substantial body of social drama did grow up in the years before 1914, but though clearly inspired by Shaw's lead, its practitioners used methods largely opposed to Shaw's. For them a serious purpose could only be achieved in a serious mood, and laughter must be banished to the wings. There must be no turning Shavian somersaults to catch the audience off its guard; settings should be contemporary and style sternly realistic. There could be no place in strict social drama for the flights of fancy or virtuoso writing in which Shaw indulged. For this reason the imprint of Ibsen is more plainly marked on English social drama than that of Shaw himself.

In this social school John Galsworthy soon became the recognized head, for his first play, *The Silver Box*, was done at the Court, and several later plays achieved considerable critical though little popular success. Both his approach and his methods were entirely opposed to the dominant school of Society drama. Rejecting the fashionable drawing-room for the office, the steelworks, or the prison-cell, Galsworthy sought to let the stage reflect the life of the nation as widely as its news-papers. But his methods were the reverse of journalistic, and the restraint and simplicity of his treatment contrast forcibly with the calculated manipulation of melodrama, into whose preserves he ventured for his themes.

Galsworthy's reaction from the methods of Victorian drama, salutary in its day, has lost much of its appeal with the disappearance of the style it opposed. His store of compassion is abundantly shown in *Strife* and *Justice*, the two major plays he wrote before 1914. Here there is a steady refusal to allot blame for the suffering of a whole community (in *Strife*) and a single family (in *Justice*). The briefest comparison with Boucicault's *The Long Strike* and Taylor's *Ticket-of-Leave Man* respectively will suggest the measure of Galsworthy's reforms. For him there are no villains, only human beings and human imperfections. Yet, separated from their context, Galsworthy's plays reveal increasingly the conflict of passion and compassion, and it is their lack of passion which later generations remark. This conflict was one which Galsworthy himself appears to have recognized, for without compromising his beliefs, he had recourse in such post-war plays as *The Skin Game*, *Loyalties*, and *Escape* to well-tried forms, directed towards a more positive effect in the theatre. Thus by a curious and unkind paradox, his plays maintain their precarious hold on the stage to-day by what little he borrowed from others, rather than by his own courage and convictions.

It was not only as an author but also as actor and producer that the Court seasons established the reputation of Harley Granville Barker. By playing a number of Shaw parts for the Stage Society he had shown early promise. By repeating these parts and also creating several major rôles he turned that promise into performance, and then—characteristically—abandoned acting. He was also responsible for the production of the majority of the plays not by Shaw which were done at the Court, and his deeply considered, scrupulously balanced treatment of the author's text established the prestige of the producer in the English theatre on the ground already prepared by Robertson, Gilbert, and Pinero for the playwrights and Hare, Irving, and Tree for the actor-managers. Barker's sternly intellectual approach to his task set the tone for an anti-Romantic revolt in the theatre. His insistence on lucidity of argument and refinement of effect marked a conscious opposition to the large emotions and broad effects of Romantic drama. To him no detail was insignificant, and it was by the impeccable playing of the small parts as well as the unfailing co-ordination of the whole that his productions excited attention. In this respect he had an initial advantage over the actor-managers, since the new intellectual drama sketched its background far more thoroughly than the few bold strokes of Romantic drama.

Barker's plays have, by virtue of his associations, been assigned to the school of English social drama. A re-examination may suggest that it was technique rather than theme which made the strongest appeal to him. In particular, he seems constantly drawn on to point the contrast between the outward appearance and inner essence of the scene he is describing. This interest had already emerged in *The Marrying of Ann Leete*, an early piece done by the Stage Society and largely devoted to the endless variations danced by an effete section of Georgian society. But behind this façade the creative impulse is stirring in the soul of John Abud, the gardener, and it is that impulse which the heroine answers when claiming him for her husband, instead of the brilliant match arranged for her.

Mask and face are more sharply defined in the two plays which followed. The production of *Waste* was prevented by the censor; yet the same creative impulse can be seen at work in Henry Trebell, a brilliant politician, destined for Cabinet office. Nevertheless, the impulse drives him into the arms of another man's wife, and when she dies trying to prevent the birth of his child, the scandal wrecks his career and stings him to suicide. Clearly the contrast which fired Barker here is between the precise calculations of the politician and the uncontrolled urges of the man. In *The Voysey Inheritance*, successfully produced at the Court, there is a cognate contrast between the imposing façade of a solicitor's office and the secret speculation with trust funds which lies behind it. The demolition of this façade by the solicitor's son and successor when breaking the news to his horrified family is one of Barker's most rewarding scenes. For so delicate a purpose, however, he evidently felt the need of precision tools, and to this end evolved his own pattern of elaborately detailed stage business, balanced by moments of insight, expressed in almost visionary terms. Even so, the end of *The Voysey Inheritance* finds him straining towards a point scarcely attainable by theatrical means, as he tries to demonstrate the self-sacrifice behind the younger

137

Voysey's decision to shoulder his inheritance and repay his father's debts at the risk of prosecution.

If the end of this play is ineffective, there is a total lack of cohesion in a later piece, *The Madras House*. Appearance and essence are still the theme: this time in the world of linen-drapers. There is the same impulse to show behind the well-stocked windows of Messrs. Huxtable and Roberts the furtive and frustrated existence of those assistants who are compelled to 'live in'; and to contrast the luxury and elegance of the Bond Street Madras House with the barren self-indulgence of its clientèle, or the avowed sensuality of its founder, Constantine Madras, who has turned Mohammedan in the process. But neither purpose is reconciled with the demands of stage presentation and the baffled spectator is left straining eyes and ears in an attempt to follow the elusive thread of argument.

Faced with his failure to communicate his purpose in this play, Barker began to turn his back on the theatre as he knew it. That he subsequently devoted himself largely to translations from the German and Spanish suggests a mind essentially interpretative rather than creative, just as his graduation from actor to producer led all too soon to his virtually abandoning the theatre for the study. The record of his thirty years of meditation, valuable as it is, confirms the impression already made by his plays: that of a spirit too sensitive to abide the raw though invigorating atmosphere of the theatre.

The Repertory Movement

The impact of the Court seasons was by no means limited to London. A few months after Vedrenne and Barker quitted the Court in 1907, a repertory theatre was opened in Manchester under the direction of Miss A. E. F. Horniman, who had already been largely instrumental in establishing the Abbey Theatre in Dublin. In fact it was provincial soil that proved most fertile for the seeds sown at the Court. Whereas subsequent repertory seasons in London proved short-lived, the founding of the Manchester Gaiety was followed by the establishment of repertory theatres at Glasgow in 1909, at Liverpool in 1911, and at Birmingham in 1913. These theatres were devoted to the presentation of plays of intellectual as well as theatrical worth.

They also represented a return from the ubiquitous touring system to the stock system of the mid-Victorian theatre: a resident company presented plays in rotation, though not in the nightly rotation of the stock company.

Their particular achievement, however, was the encouragement of local playwrights—an object well enough realized at Manchester and Liverpool to produce a 'Lancashire school' of drama. Among the playwrights thus brought forward, Harold Brighouse, St. John Ervine, and Allan Monkhouse were all to win recognition beyond the boundaries of Lancashire, but the 'Lancashire school' is chiefly remembered for the work of Stanley Houghton, perhaps because his career was almost coeval with the life of the Manchester Gaiety, his first play being produced there in 1908 and his death at the age of thirty-two occurring in 1913. Moreover, the rapid maturing of his talent, well reflected in the succession of his plays produced at the Gaiety, is a splendid tribute to an apprenticeship served with a single company under enlightened direction. Thus, from the modest but marked promise of his one-act piece, *The Dear Departed*, he moved on to the partial success of two longer plays, *Independent Means* and *The Younger Generation*, then benefited by their mistakes to produce the masterly *Hindle Wakes*, the play which gave both author and theatre national, even international, eminence. That *Hindle Wakes* originally attracted notice by its power to shock is manifest. The story of Fanny Hawthorne who spends a weekend with her employer's son and then refuses his reluctant offer of marriage because he is not good enough for her, was a reversal of all the values which a century of melodrama had fostered. But the play's staying power depends on its solid workmanship, and still more on the delightful vein of irony which informs its arguments. In this play Houghton emulated Shaw in making his audience laugh and think at the same time. Indeed, the laughter which *Hindle Wakes* can still command is the quality which distinguishes it from many admirable but decidedly austere offerings of the 'Lancashire school', and from English social drama as a whole.

The repertory movement and the social drama which it fostered may perhaps be termed the *avant-garde* of the pre-war theatre in England—the enterprise to which the youngest,

139

boldest spirits gave both heart and hand. At the same time, this preoccupation with the repertory movement may well have distracted pioneers in the English theatre from the revolution in methods of stage presentation taking place under their noses. The efforts of Gordon Craig, for example, to achieve visual effects of the utmost grandeur with the simplest materials imaginatively lit, met with little response until he quitted his native country for the continental workshops of Reinhardt and Appia. Similarly the impact of the Diaghilev Ballet at Covent Garden in 1911 left the English public gasping, for their Russian designers, being trained outside the theatre, used line and colour in ways undreamed of by the conventional schools of the English theatre.

The Production of Shakespeare

No Shakespeare was presented during the Vedrenne-Barker seasons, but in fact the partnership had come into being when Vedrenne was manager of the Court. Barker was invited to produce *Two Gentlemen of Verona* there, and made some matinées of *Candida* his condition of acceptance. Thus Barker's subsequent and well-known productions of *The Winter's Tale*, *Twelfth Night*, and *A Midsummer Night's Dream* at the Savoy between 1912 and 1914 can be linked with the Court seasons, and in those productions he sought to apply to Shakespeare the principle which had informed his work at the Court: the faithful interpretation of the author's purpose. That involved the preservation without rearrangement of Shakespeare's text, which had suffered so severely at the actor-managers' hands, and there was an equally decisive rejection of the heavily realistic scenery of the actor-managers' theatre. Thus Barker had recourse to much simpler methods of staging Shakespeare than were then fashionable. The scholarly conjectural reconstructions of the Elizabethan playhouse gave him the basis for an apron-stage built out over the orchestra-pit, greatly assisting the swift sequence of full-stage scenes and front-scenes before a drop-curtain, and thus reducing waits and intervals to a minimum. More controversial was his insistence on a rate of speech much quicker than that practised by actors whose highly individual delivery often obscured Shakespeare's rhythms and even meaning. Perhaps most controversial of all was his employment (no doubt inspired by Diaghilev's example) of artists from outside the theatre, like Norman Wilkinson and Albert Rothenstein, whose unorthodox settings and costumes mystified many playgoers brought up on Grieve and Telbin.

Much of the credit for Barker's stimulating re-interpretation of Shakespeare should go to predecessors from whose experience he had profited. The age of the actor-managers had its palaces at the Lyceum and Her Majesty's, but it also had its outposts in hall and school, where actors less publicized than Irving or Tree conveyed much of the same magic by performing Shakespeare to audiences often seeing their first play. Frank Benson went direct from a season with Irving to found his own company in 1883, and for nearly fifty years he had one or more companies giving plain unvarnished Shakespeare all over the country. His insistence on athletic prowess in his actors led him to rate a straight bat almost as highly as a fine voice, but his own and his actors' athleticism was put to excellent use in their stage-fights and falls. Above all, Benson and his company were the mainstay of the annual Stratford-on-Avon Festivals for thirty years, from 1886 to 1916, the first regular series there. From 1886 Benson had a companion-in-arms in the Shakespearean crusade: in that year Ben Greet formed a touring company principally for performances in schools and in the open air. Greet's arduous and little publicized labours for Shakespearean production were splendidly rewarded during the war years when he and his company were invited to raise the Shakespearean banner at the Old Vic, and kept it flying there while the actor-managers were striking their flags on all sides.

No doubt the difficulties under which Benson and Greet worked, especially their lack of funds, limited the standards they achieved, but it was their insistence on the delivery of Shakespeare's text and not its decoration that pointed the way to Barker's famed and influential productions at the Savoy. Above all, Benson's and Greet's devotion to their appointed tasks, without hope of material reward, inspired in their companies many men and women who graced the pre-war stage and in the post-war years upheld the standards of the English theatre amid the trials of a troubled epoch. These were the practitioners of the Shakespearean drama; among its theorists one who certainly inspired Barker's reforms was William Poel, most of whose work was done not in the professional theatre but with largely amateur casts for special performances, and particularly with the Elizabethan Stage Society of which he was for many years Director. Poel's work was by no means confined to Shakespeare, and his productions of *Dr. Faustus* and of *Everyman* (which he virtually re-discovered) were among his most successful. But it was in the field of Shakespearean production and appreciation that his influence was most strongly felt. By preaching and practising a return to the principles of Elizabethan staging for a fuller understanding of Shakespeare's work, Poel succeeded in enriching the scope of stage and study alike. Neither his own lapses as a producer (particularly in cutting the text) nor the limitations of Elizabethan staging for the general public should be allowed to obscure the stimulus which Poel's work gave to Shakespearean production and criticism. Of its effect on Barker the evidence is as clear in the *Prefaces to Shakespeare* as it was in the productions at the Savoy.

Melodrama and Musical Comedy

Germinal as the Court seasons proved both in writing and production, it would be false to suggest that the last chapter of the Victorian theatre was dominated by the work achieved and the principles evolved there. Social drama did not oust melodrama any more than the repertory movement dislodged the actor-managers. If the Adelphi forsook melodrama after Terriss's violent end,[1] there was still Drury Lane to keep the audience gasping at the horse-race and the train-smash in *The Whip*. Indeed the Lyceum made reparation for the Adelphi's defection, when after Irving's withdrawal it eventually passed into the hands of the celebrated Melville brothers, whose enthusiasms combined elaborate family pantomime with melodrama of the most sensational kind. *A Girl's Cross-Roads; The Girl Who Lost Her Character; The Bad Girl of the Family; Driven From Home; The Great World of London; A World of Sin; That*

---

[1] On 16 December 1897 he was stabbed at the stage-door of the Adelphi by Richard Archer Prince, an actor who believed himself slighted by Terriss, and who was subsequently found insane.

Wretch of a Woman; A Disgrace to Her Sex; The Worst Woman in London—all titles of melodramas produced by the Melvilles —provide the synopsis of a Melville melodrama in themselves. Though Henry Arthur Jones abandoned the vein of *The Silver King* and *The Dancing Girl* for Society comedy, he had a spiritual successor in Hall Caine, whose *Eternal City* was produced by Tree, *The Manxman* by Wilson Barrett and Lewis Waller, and *The Christian* by Matheson Lang—all with resounding success. The knell of melodrama was rung not by the repertory movement but by the moving picture, which found as it gained confidence that it could perform all the tricks expected of spectacular melodrama, and proceeded in the post-war years to put most of the theatres which had housed melodrama out of business.

Perhaps the taste of the pre-1914 audience is best reflected in the tremendous appeal of musical comedy, for the emergence of this highly genteel form of entertainment from its very different origins in the Victorian burlesque and music hall was a tribute to the refinement of its devotees. The first step in that process had been taken when John Hollingshead opened the Gaiety in 1868. In the next twenty years Hollingshead made the Gaiety the home of English burlesque, where, in his own bland phrase, 'the sacred lamp was kept burning'. The character of burlesque at the Gaiety during these years was determined far more by the company whom Hollingshead recruited than by the authors whose work he commissioned. In Fred Leslie and Nellie Farren he could depend on artists of extraordinary versatility around whom the majority of Gaiety burlesques were constructed. But the Gaiety also recruited many players who, like Marie Wilton before them, turned their burlesque training to advantage elsewhere. Three of them, Toole, Edward Terry, and Seymour Hicks, gave their names to the theatres they subsequently managed.

Hollingshead's sacred lamp burnt brightly for the male playgoer, at whom the lavish display of tights by the Gaiety chorus was firmly directed, but it is doubtful whether the ladies who made up so large a section of the Savoy audience ventured further east along the Strand to the Gaiety. When George Edwardes became manager of the Gaiety, therefore, he made it his mission to woo the audience whom Gilbert had coaxed into the Savoy. This he achieved by refining the burlesque element and developing the romantic side of the Gaiety's entertainment by elaborating Gilbert's tribute in *Utopia Limited* to 'the bright and beautiful English girl'. The birth of English musical comedy was thus attended by a dazzling assembly of fairy godmothers: *The Shop Girl, My Girl, The Circus Girl, A Runaway Girl* were all musical comedies produced by Edwardes at the Gaiety.

His triumph in establishing the musical comedy as a polite and highly fashionable form of entertainment was greatly helped by the emergence of a generation of English theatre composers gifted with both humour and melody. The success of Leslie Stuart, Sidney Jones, Paul Rubens and Lionel Monckton gave the composer an advantage over the librettist which had not been Sullivan's at the Savoy, and to the work of these English composers Franz Lehár added his own contribution and provided in *The Merry Widow* (heavily adapted for the English stage) the most successful musical comedy of all. The popularity of this new style of musical play encouraged other theatres to turn to this form of entertainment: Daly's, the new Prince of Wales's, and the Shaftesbury were three which, in the twenty years preceding 1914, combined to uphold the prestige of the English musical stage. The musical comedies which they housed were tailor-made to late-Victorian and Edwardian taste: leisurely, lavish and ingenuous—so that the cause of their original success has often limited their appeal for later audiences. The music of Edward German, however, established a more substantial claim to recognition, and his command of both lyrical and elegiac melody raised his musical plays to the level of *opéra comique* rather than *opéra bouffe*. For this reason the popularity of *Tom Jones* and *Merrie England* remains undiminished, while the majority of Gaiety and Daly's pieces have become musical memories.

The triumph of musical comedy left unsatisfied the stronger appetites for which burlesque had previously catered, and to this public the music halls now made an added appeal. The last years of the century saw a remarkable expansion of these, not only in London but throughout the country, so that Music Hall could now rank as a national institution. The giants of the Edwardian music hall, a Marie Lloyd, a Dan Leno, or an Albert Chevalier, could count on a far wider following even than such idols of the mid-Victorian audience as George Leybourne or Alfred Vance. The ranks of the music-hall public were filled largely by bridging the gap between the heavy swell and the working man who had been its first patrons. The shopkeeper and his wife thus began to patronize the music hall at the time that their customers were discarding their prejudice against the theatre. This change in the composition of the music-hall audience called for corresponding changes in the bill of fare, amongst which the popularity in the Edwardian era of the sketch and short play was particularly striking. But this increasing appeal to the family audience caused the music hall to neglect the sharper, more sophisticated flavour which Victorian burlesque had in part supplied. To this taste may be attributed the reappearance in the theatre of Planché's 'dramatick review'—at first in such simple forms as the Pelissier Follies, but soon to evolve, especially during the first World War period, as the modern 'revue'.

The Development of Society Drama

The large audience which patronized musical comedy in search of relaxation did not lose its more sober taste for Society drama. The successors of Jones and Pinero in popular favour were not Shaw or Galsworthy but men like Alfred Sutro, who could concoct highly romantic and dramatic situations against brilliantly fashionable backgrounds. Sutro's work is markedly that of a Society dramatist: even his titles seem to reflect an after-dinner glow of well-being with *The Perfect Lover, Mollentrave on Women,* or *The Fascinating Mr. Vanderveldt.* Their author plainly owed a large debt to Jones's example. They share a partiality for the unrequited love of a strong man for a beautiful woman, which Sutro introduces in *The Builder of Bridges,* and an imagination limelit rather than sunlit, as Archer noted of Jones, which informs such a climax as that in *John Glayde's Honour* when the great American financier is faced with the simultaneous collapse of his marriage and his financial empire:

JOHN *makes a mighty effort: he rises; the numbed muscles obey him; his hands unclasp; he tries in a voice he cannot entirely control, a voice that does not seem his, to resume his dictation.*

JOHN. Also . . . shares of . . . all . . . subsidiary . . . (*He stops: he cannot go on. His head sinks on his chest, his eyes close, he stands motionless. There is silence. The curtain slowly falls.*)

There is also in several of Sutro's plays that awkward note of criticism of the self-indulgence practised by smart Society which is evident in some of Jones's early plays. *The Walls of Jericho*, one of Sutro's greatest successes, thus juxtaposes the cunning and callous world of the Marquis of Steventon and the direct good nature of Australian pioneers, one of whom has married the Marquis's elder daughter. Sutro also shared Jones's gifts, especially his gift for reproducing the accents of the aristocracy, and the ladies' bridge-party in *The Walls of Jericho* outdoes Jones in the authenticity of its idiom. Both writers were at their best when least ambitious, and the more modest, though still highly select, settings of *The Perplexed Husband* and *The Two Virtues* show Sutro at his most pleasing. One tells the familiar story of a wife with Feminist leanings who learns wisdom from a tolerant husband. The other suggests mildly enough that Charity is a Virtue in women as well as Chastity. Both contrive to entertain without becoming ponderous, though they may seem thin fare to spectators who have dined less handsomely than the Edwardian audience.

There is also a high proportion of titles among the characters drawn by St. John Hankin, whose work is usually grouped with that of the social dramatists, since he was introduced to the general public at the Court. In fact, only his first play, *The Two Mr. Wetherbys*, claims to be a 'middle-class comedy', and proves its worth with a nice sense of irony in depicting one brother, 'bad' but happy in his freedom, and the other 'good' but profoundly miserable in his matrimonial chains. Neither of his two plays produced at the Court shows Hankin at his best: *The Charity That Began at Home* is little more successful in satirizing the impractical philanthropy of Lady Denniston and her daughter than Jones's handling of a similar theme in *The Crusaders* or Pinero's in *The Hobby-Horse*. The satirical treatment of

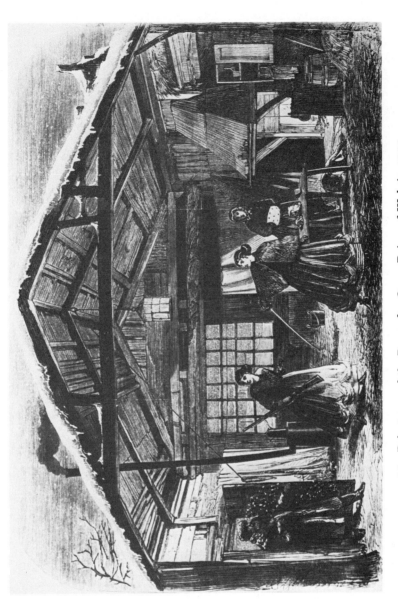

15. *Robertson and the Bancrofts: Ours, Prince of Wales's, 1866*

16. *George Alexander at the St. James's: John Glayde's Honour, 1907*

provincial pretensions in *The Return of the Prodigal* is equally superficial, though this play is redeemed by an engaging portrait of the black sheep of the family.

The Cassilis Engagement, however, is a great advance on its predecessors, and unfolds with extraordinary skill the story of a young actress, engaged to Geoffrey, the darling son of Mrs. Cassilis, who lures the girl into betraying her own and her mother's vulgarity. Hankin here states all that Robertson found it prudent to omit from *Caste*. Similarly in *The Last of the De Mullins* Hankin tackles the subject of the unmarried mother dear to so many Society dramatists, but insists that for Janet De Mullin motherhood and a career are more important than the respect of her effete family or the security of a belated offer of marriage. Hankin's death at the age of thirty-nine ended abruptly a career which lay closer to orthodoxy than perhaps critics, then and since, have allowed: only the growing confidence of treatment distinguishes his work from that of his fellow Society dramatists.

The most accurate picture of this final phase of Society drama is presented by the early plays of Somerset Maugham, for Maugham's acute intelligence enabled him to gauge popular taste, and his exact craftsmanship qualified him to meet it. When an early essay in social drama called *A Man of Honour* achieved little more than a Stage Society production he deftly turned to the writing of Society comedies with rewarding parts for the principal players. Thus *Jack Straw* plots the triumph over the leaders of Society at Taverner Court of an engaging impostor such as Charles Hawtrey regularly played, and in *Lady Frederick* a woman with no more of a past than her addiction to the rouge-pot turns away a young admirer by putting on her complexion in his presence. In the pre-1914 war years Maugham experimented in the styles of his various colleagues, taking a hint from Sutro in *Smith*, by allowing the honest hard-working parlour-maid to win the love of a pioneer who returns from Rhodesia to find his old circle possessed by the pursuit of pleasure; or trying his hand at Society melodrama in the Jones manner with *The Tenth Man*.

When success brought confidence, however, Maugham was in a position not merely to meet public taste but to guide it. In

The Land of Promise he was able to leave the English drawing-room for the Canadian log-cabin, and his story of a lady's companion who finds fulfilment and ultimately love as the wife of a settler is told with restraint and feeling. Like Haddon Chambers and H. H. Davies before him, Maugham was able to refine the technique of Society drama into the greater naturalism and subtler emotion of modern English drama, and in so doing to place himself among the most influential of the post-war playwrights. The pre-war audience, for instance, would have found little to approve in *The Sacred Flame* or *The Constant Wife*, and even when attempting Society comedy in his later plays Maugham was able, as in *Our Betters* and *The Circle*, to pursue his theme with a logic totally unacceptable to Edwardian playgoers. His plays would be rewarding in any context, but they are particularly valuable for the light they throw on the passing of one generation in the theatre and the coming of another.

Changes

The war years from 1914 to 1918 brought great prosperity to the London theatre, but at the same time brought great changes by enormously increasing the demand for light entertainment at the expense of more substantial matter. Musical comedy, farce, and revue prospered; Shakespeare and even Society drama were eclipsed. This prosperity also attracted to theatrical speculation men hitherto unconnected with the theatre, who largely replaced the leading actor-managers, now out of touch with a public that seemed to have changed overnight. While it lasted, this prosperity served to conceal the revolution in theatrical management. The end of the war, and the withdrawal of the wartime audiences, disclosed how completely the scene had changed. The popular audience, always the backbone of the actor-managers' theatre, was now largely captured by the enormous expansion of the cinema. The Society which had given glamour and prestige to the last chapter of the Victorian theatre was reduced and reorganized. Most of the actor-managers who had shaped the pre-war theatre had disappeared. Only in the provinces could a Martin Harvey keep the old traditions continuously alive.

The result was a major reduction of theatrical activity, now organized on strictly competitive and commercial lines, and catering to a smaller, more sophisticated audience than before 1914. The post-war theatre produced playwrights of intelligence, actors of accomplishment, and, especially in its outposts, leaders with courage and imagination, but the splendour and the stability of the actor-managers' era had vanished.

The Victorian theatre was always a popular theatre. For much of its history it was exclusively a popular theatre, and in consequence neglected the significance of what it presented in order to develop the means of presentation, striving to embellish what the audience saw and ignoring what they heard. In its last twenty years the Victorian theatre developed from a popular into a national institution; and though its breadth of appeal often led to an acceptance of common standards, it also made possible the general acceptance of work at first recognized only by a section. Since 1918 the English theatre has never regained its popular character. Certain enterprises, particularly the production of Shakespeare, have drawn an audience from every quarter, but elsewhere the competition of the cinema has proved too strong and the theatre has been left with a limited public. A minority can often refine and reform, but unless it can ultimately pass on its standards to the public as a whole, its influence will be transitory. The new patron of the theatre is the State, which by a familiar English compromise, prefers rather to assist certain chosen enterprises than to take direct responsibility for a National Theatre. Every increase in the exercise of that patronage, however, will also increase the danger of separating the theatre from the public by making the theatre independent of the public.

The Victorian theatre was entirely dependent on its public, and Victorian drama is now only intelligible through an understanding of that public. Because of its sudden growth and material changes any reconstruction of the Victorian theatre calls for a sustained effort of historical imagination. Yet it was this expansion that ultimately led to the modern English theatre and modern English drama. Caught up in the urgency of its fortunes, the theatre to-day, as always, is concerned principally with the present. It may dream of the future, but has no time for the past. Nevertheless, the past is part of the same design as the present, and the future will be fashioned from both. The theatre may ignore the past but cannot escape it.

English drama has had its hours of greatness, punctuating periods of limited or little literary interest. Some of these hours have been long, as the fifty years which separate Marlowe from Milton, some brief, as the decade into which the finest work of Sheridan and Goldsmith is crowded. These chapters in the history of the English theatre have been as clearly revealed as scholarship and the scanty materials which survive will permit, but the periods dividing them remain largely unillumined. Yet the theatre during these periods was active, often expanding and developing, even if its drama remained uninspired. By the dictate of the alphabet Shakespeare, Sheridan and Shaw stand side by side on the library shelf, and by the dictate of the public their plays command the English repertory. Of other playwrights who shaped the course of English drama the playgoer sees and learns little. These forgotten men and the times in which they lived and worked are part of the pattern of the English theatre. To ignore them is to neglect the whole pattern as well as its parts.

AFTERWORD 1978

It would be an unhappy comment on both author and subject if after twenty-two years there was nothing to alter or add. The enlarged bibliography which is appended testifies to the scholarship directed towards the Victorian theatre in that time. The following notes attempt to rectify some of the omissions or correct some of the stresses which the wisdom of others and a little self-education have disclosed.

These two sources are of course closely linked, but a source available though not drawn on in 1956, the two Reports of Select Committees of the House of Commons (1832 and 1866), is consistently used, as being rich and still comparatively rare.

Perhaps it is allowable to repeat that, while the book's title has very properly been extended, its purpose remains that of a Survey.

The Crown and the Theatre

Not surprisingly in view of the limited English commanded by at least the early Hanoverians, there was little Royal theatregoing in the eighteenth century. George III risked assassination to hear a play, and later Mrs. Siddons was called to Windsor to calm his troubled mind by her art, but the interest of his sons was personal and confined to the dressing-room. George IV told the actor William Dowton: 'I do not go to those theatres because they are so large; I am not comfortable', and the Select Committee of 1832 heard several witnesses attribute the decline of the drama to the Crown's lack of interest.

From her childhood Victoria was an ardent theatregoer, but her taste leant strongly towards opera and ballet, as did her subjects', and this preference was greatly strengthened by marriage to the musically minded Prince Albert. The record of Royal theatregoing in the 1840s shows an overwhelming predominance of opera and French drama, as annually presented at the St. James's. In 1847 (the year of Jenny Lind's triumphant

151

London debut) the Queen saw thirty-two performances of opera, fourteen of French plays, and two English, one being by amateurs.

Both the theatrical profession and the public began consequently to demonstrate symptoms of xenophobia, and the series of command performances at Windsor Castle, beginning in December 1848 and continuing more or less regularly until the Prince Consort's death in 1861, went far to assuage this. It should, however, be stressed that the Windsor theatricals fell far short of establishing a Court Theatre. They were essentially performances arranged for the Royal family as part of their Christmas festivities. While a number of careers were greatly advanced in consequence (notably those of Charles and Ellen Kean, Alfred Wigan, and Frederick Robson), the experiment in 1858 of transferring the performances to London to mark the marriage of the Princess Royal provoked intense theatrical jealousy and vindicated the Windsor compromise, to which a rapid return was made.

Nevertheless the Windsor performances, which were loyally English but almost equally divided between Shakespeare and contemporary plays (many of them brief comedies and farces), opened the Queen's eyes to theatrical fare outside the opera-house, and where the Queen looked, her subjects increasingly turned. Since by the 1850s Drury Lane had virtually and Covent Garden absolutely ceased to be a playhouse, Royal playgoing took the Queen and her family predictably to the Haymarket and the Princess's, several of Kean's Shakespeare productions being mounted at Windsor before opening in his own theatre. Less predictable was the Queen's patronage of theatres she had earlier only occasionally visited (the Lyceum, the Olympic), or avoided (the Adelphi). This widening of her theatrical horizon led to an enlargement of her theatrical taste. To her youthful and often half-hearted support for Sheridan Knowles or Bulwer-Lytton was added a great and growing delight in melodrama and farce. *The Corsican Brothers* gained much from the publicity attending her four visits in two months, and another Boucicault piece, *The Colleen Bawn*, proved to be the last she saw in a theatre, since she interpreted her widow's status so strictly as to debar her from entering one. Less publicised were her visits to the Olympic, drawn by the management of Alfred Wigan, whose appearances with Kean, both as hero (Orlando, Bassanio) and villain (Château-Renaud) had captivated her.

At the Olympic she saw and surprisingly approved of *Still Waters Run Deep* (apparently finding no offence in the midnight assignation of a wife and a known profligate), and became a devotee of Frederick Robson, both in his legitimate repertoire, such as *Daddy Hardacre* and *Boots at the Swan*, and more particularly in his unique extravaganza performances, which often contained more pathos than laughter.

It can be argued that by spreading her theatrical patronage so widely in the 1850s, Victoria contributed materially to that transformation of theatrical taste which is usually assigned to the Bancrofts' management at the Prince of Wales's ten years later. Not only were Kean, Wigan, and Robson the forerunners of Irving, Bancroft, and Toole, but dramatists like Boucicault and Taylor anticipated the work of W. G. Wills and Robertson amongst others. More generally, the tone and conduct of the Princess's and Olympic set standards which the Prince of Wales's, the Lyceum, and the Savoy had to strive hard to surpass in the following decades.

Although her self-denial after 1861 deprived the Queen of a chance to hear Robertson's 'cup-and-saucer comedies' or see Irving in his first triumphs, her example was taken up by her children, particularly her heir (whose interest in the theatre, unlike his great-uncles', stretched further than the stage-door), so that Royal attendance at important theatrical occasions became an accurate yardstick of the increasingly fashionable character of London audiences. The career of Lillie Langtry interestingly reverses that of 'Perdita' Robinson or Dorothy Jordan, in that Royal favour led her to, rather than distracted her from, the stage.

The command performances, mainly at Windsor and Balmoral, in which from the late 1880s the Queen was able to renew her love for the theatre without breaking her resolve never to enter the public playhouse again, are a further manifestation of the new status of the actor, which of course found concrete form in the knighthoods she conferred on Irving and

Bancroft. Not surprisingly her taste reverted largely to that of her youth; she saw substantially more opera than drama, and although she delighted in *The Gondoliers*, she did not flinch from *Carmen* or *Cavalleria Rusticana*, as she had once condemned *Rigoletto* and shunned *La Traviata*. Of the plays she saw, proven favourites like *The Bells*, *Becket*, or *A Pair of Spectacles* pleased her most. There was no suggestion of sampling *The Second Mrs. Tanqueray*, still less *Ghosts*.

Her son was to make amends for this; by 1890 he was attending the theatre 67 times in one year, and although his personal taste seems to have been self-indulgent, he would loyally sit through *John Bull's Other Island* at the Court (breaking a chair in the process, allegedly by laughing), while his son saw one act of this play at No. 10 Downing Street as part of his Coronation celebrations.

The Provincial Theatre

Just as in the Victorian theatre limelight was developed to give emphasis to the leading performer, so in Victorian theatre history light falls mostly on the London stage and London actor. Nevertheless the nineteenth century was as much an era of change in the provincial playhouse as in the capital. The circuits which had been assiduously and on the whole profitably built up in the last quarter of the preceding century, were seriously threatened by shifts in the population brought about by the Industrial Revolution and by technical advances (also the product of that movement) which made impossible demands on the often improvised stages of the older travelling companies.

By the 1790s a clearly established dual system of theatrical organization had emerged: a handful of theatres in cities of historic importance (Bath, Norwich, York, and Bristol among them) held Royal patents authorizing Theatres Royal to play extended, though by no means continuous, seasons. In addition an Act of 1788, empowering magistrates to license up to sixty consecutive performances, provided a secure basis for strolling companies making short visits to smaller centres (timed to coincide with such crowd-collecting functions as assizes, race-meetings, and fairs). This system worked acceptably at both levels: the Theatres Royal were regarded as training-ground for tomorrow's London favourites, while the circuits flourished on more modest fare and less illustrious companies. The Commons enquiry of 1832 heard testimony after testimony to the 'golden days' before the turn of the century.

The Satanic mills of Industrial Britain, with their sweated labour, called for a redeployment of theatrical resources. Manchester, Birmingham, Sheffield, and Glasgow found themselves on the theatrical map, and offered cheap entertainment as a concomitant to cheap gin which numbed the fatigue and misery of the factory workers. This audience was not only sweated and brutalized, it was largely illiterate. The compact and mainly classical repertoire of the Georgian theatre fell on deaf ears and stunted imaginations. Spectacle and sensation were even more necessary to the provincial playgoer than to the metropolitan, who could count on what remained of the great acting traditions. Such Theatres Royal as could afford to, equipped themselves with gas-lighting, 'sink and rise' trap equipment, transformation scenes, and every mechanical aid. The strolling companies found themselves unable to compete, and the old circuits withered and died away. Even theatres in the industrial towns could only survive by stooping to the audience's level: the manager of the Royal Amphitheatre, Liverpool, told the 1832 Committee: 'We never play "regular" drama', and E. W. Elton, a leading provincial actor, admitted he was glad to receive £3 a week, only a few years after Edmund Kean earned £10,000 per annum.

Increasingly, provincial managers sought to fill their houses by inviting London performers—a recourse much assisted by the introduction of first mail coach and then rail travel, but ruinous to the pride and standards of the resident company. These stars travelled alone, or with a single supporting actor, and rehearsals were perforce minimal. Kean, playing Shylock at York, baffled an inexperienced Tubal:

He didn't come to rehearsal, and although Lee, his secretary, rehearsed carefully enough, I did not know where to find Kean at night, for he crossed here, there, and everywhere, and prowled about like a caged tiger. I never took my eyes off him. I dodged him up and down,

155

crossed when he crossed, took up my cues, and got on pretty fairly, till he thoroughly flabbergasted me by hissing: 'Get out of my focus! Blast you! Get out of my focus!'[1]

But Kean and the York audience did not fare too badly, since the inexperienced Tubal was the young Samuel Phelps. On the other hand, Macready, a martinet at rehearsal, suffered torments from the indisciplined and archaic methods of the provincial companies with which he played, as at Salisbury in 1835:

after some search found the theatre, and went through the rehearsal. My Lady Macbeth was a relic of a style gone by, the veritable 'ti-tum-to' 'jerk and duck and twist' in a most engaging manner. Tried to act Macbeth, but, 'confusion to my Lady!' it was too farcical, and would have been good as Dollalolla, but quite a travesty in the part she played. Nearly betrayed on one occasion my anger at one of the performers, but was very thankful I subdued it before an opportunity for explosion was given; most happily I did not expose myself. The end of the play found me very much exhausted.[2]

The increase in standards of ensemble playing in London during the 1850s and 1860s gradually penetrated to the provinces. Rail travel made possible the touring of complete companies, with scenery and costumes, 'direct from the West End', a mortal blow to the stock company but in general a boon to the provincial playgoer. The start of the touring company is usually associated with Robertson's comedies—appropriately, since their delicate interplay of sentiment and laughter lay beyond the powers of a travelling star with local support, or the 'ti-tum-to' of the old actors with their 'lines of business'. It is interesting that 1867, the year of *Caste*, marked the opening in Bristol of the New Theatre Royal (later the Prince's) which gradually drove the old house, dating from 1766 and boasting its patent for ninety years, into obscurity. The New Theatre Royal started out with a resident company but before long was exclusively a touring house.

[1] John and Edward Coleman: *Memoirs of Samuel Phelps* (London, 1886), p. 67.
[2] William Toynbee (Editor): *The Diaries of William Charles Macready* (London 1912), Vol. I, p. 219.

The last quarter of the century and the first decade of the present were the heyday of the touring company, with London successes not merely toured after their initial run but duplicated during that run. Tours of musical plays were especially prolific: at one point the D'Oyly Carte had four companies on the road as well as that occupying the Savoy. It was against this often (though not inevitably) 'carbon-copy' technique that the repertory movement was called into being, appropriately in those industrial cities (Manchester, Glasgow, Liverpool, Birmingham) where the need for eye-filling, pain-killing spectacle had demolished the foundations of the Georgian theatre in the provinces.

Comedy and Farce

The doubts entertained by the Victorian theatre itself as to its capacity for comedy may be detected in the apologetic manner with which this *genre* was often announced: thus 'comedietta', '*petite comedie*', and 'farcical comedy' are found more frequently than the forthright 'comedy'. As has been seen, H. J. Byron struck a note of defiance when describing his play, *Cyril's Success*, as 'original, and a comedy—and, even in these vicious dramatic days—in five acts! There!' The content of Victorian comedy often tells a similar tale; the vast majority are mixed with sentiment (*Money*) or melodrama (*Still Waters Run Deep*), and many with both. A modern editor is forced to conclude: 'A nineteenth-century play can be termed a comedy, I believe, when the pathetic and potentially tragic, or melodramatic elements do not overwhelm the comic and are kept at least in equal balance with them.'[1] If the musical stage nurtured the only continuous strain of true Victorian comedy in the shape of burlesque and extravaganza, it was because melody and spectacle provided the elements of sentiment and sensation respectively in fuller measure than the legitimate drama could encompass.

Sentiment and melodrama are not wholly absent from Victorian farce; the indignities heaped on the central character suggest a grotesque variation of the perils of the melodramatic

---

[1] M. R. Booth: *English Plays of the Nineteenth Century III: Comedies* (London, 1973), p. 31.

hero, and the final reconciliation and curtain 'tag' echo the cliff-hanging climax of the sensation drama. But since the farce was until the 1870s mostly an afterpiece, providing contrast to the preceding entertainments, it could not risk too close a comparison with them. In this respect it was a direct descendant of the Georgian farce, but important differences emerged as the century progressed. The pervasive if imprecise tone of the eighteenth-century afterpiece was aristocratic: heroes were well born, heroines well dowered, though neither they nor the playwright could survive without a quota of comic servants. The increasingly artisan character of the Victorian audience fostered a stage peopled with manual workers. In the best-remembered of Victorian farces Box is a printer, Cox a hatter, and Mrs. Bouncer a lodging-house keeper. This distinction extends beyond the *dramatis personae*: in Georgian farce the plot is freely lubricated with wine or ale; the Victorian farce runs on food, and is doggedly domestic, both in the sense of being housebound (there are few 'exteriors', since the wide open spaces were the arena of melodrama) and of defending the domestic virtues against all odds.

The huge consumption of food in such farces has been analysed in some detail.[1] Of course eating is a staple diet of farce throughout the ages, but the elaborate meals served in the Victorian variety mark a change in staging techniques as well as audience composition. In Buckstone's *An Alarming Sacrifice* and J. S. Coyne's *How To Settle Accounts With Your Laundress*, the hard-pressed hero has to serve such delicacies as fowl, lobster, kidneys, champagne, celery, bread, ale, pepper, butter, vinegar, and mustard at his own table. This *verismo* is a reflection of the increased attention to detail in staging more often associated with box-sets, practicable doors, and upholstered furniture. In *Drawing Room, Second Floor, and Attics* by John Maddison Morton the hero is seen climbing up one chimney onto the roof, down another chimney into a lady's boudoir, has a fire lit beneath him, falls through two windows, and breaks everything in sight. Clearly such adventures could never have

[1] See especially M. R. Booth's article: 'Early Victorian Farce: Dionysus Domesticated' in *Nineteenth Century British Theatre* edited by Kenneth Richards and Peter Thomson (London, 1971) and his Introduction to *English Plays of the Nineteenth Century IV: Farces* (London, 1973).

been staged against a background of flats-in-grooves and painted furnishings, as provided by the Georgian theatre. In stressing the innovations of 'cup-and-saucer comedy' at the Prince of Wales's under Robertson and the Bancrofts, it is easy to lose sight of 'knife-and-fork farce' at the Adelphi or Lyceum.

The gradual emergence of farce as a full-length form in the later years of the century is generally and rightly attributed to the naturalization of the French school represented by Labiche, Hénnequin, Delacour, Feydeau, and others. It is also pointed out that their work was not only naturalized but neutralized, its sexual innuendo being diluted to suit a teetotal taste. Significantly this dilution was entrusted to hands practised in mixing other, innocuous brews. W. S. Gilbert, sternest of tutors, twice adapted both *Le Réveillon* (as *Committed for Trial* and *On Bail*) and *Un Chapeau de Paille d'Italie* (as *The Wedding March* and *Haste to the Wedding*); James Albery, one of Robertson's few disciples, was responsible for *Pink Dominos*; and F. C. Burnand, Editor of *Punch*, for *Betsy* (a vastly different child from its French playmate, *Bébé*).

It may be questioned whether such well-connected godparents were needed, since the Victorian paterfamilias could be relied on to bring up his progeny in a suitably respectable manner. Pinero's particular achievement in his Court farces was to launch his characters on a series of fast-moving, improbable but not impossible situations without once treading on the censorious playgoer's toes. Even more striking is the Victorian public's partiality for the strong dramas of the French masterbuilder, Sardou (*A Scrap of Paper*, *Diplomacy*, *Tosca*), while rejecting his highly sophisticated farce, *Divorçons*, which defeated all attempts to transplant it in English soil. Instead audiences welcomed *Charley's Aunt*—'from Brazil, where the nuts come from'.

Comic Acting

While the evolution of tragic acting from Kemble and Mrs. Siddons to Kean, followed by Macready, Fechter, Irving and Forbes-Robertson, has been repeatedly charted, historians have proved reluctant to map the course of comic acting during the same period. This is entirely understandable, since tragic acting can be illustrated from ground familiar to the reader (the great tragic rôles of Shakespeare, with an occasional foray into the by-ways of the repertoire), but comedy is to a large extent contemporary and ephemeral. There are few 'great' comic parts in English drama (even Shakespeare and Sheridan scarcely offer rôles equivalent to Alceste or Tartuffe), and the Victorian tragic actors were notably reluctant to play Shakespearean comedy, and generally unsuccessful when they did so (e.g. Irving as Malvolio and Tree as Falstaff in *Henry IV*, though not in *The Merry Wives*). Benedick was perhaps the only Shakespearean comic rôle consistently popular with nineteenth-century actor-managers, a subject worthy of speculation.

Such attention as has been paid to comic acting in this period indicates a development from 'tradition' (represented by Munden, Liston, Buckstone, and upheld with refinements by Farren), modified by the younger Mathews, who undoubtedly rejected 'traditional' methods but whose achievements were limited by his physical powers and the legal restrictions obtaining during his formative years, to the 'reserved force' and truth to life of the Bancroft school. This outline certainly does injustice to the significant changes brought about in the 1850s, when the climate of theatrical opinion made possible the work of (for example) the Wigans and Robson at the Olympic or Wright and Bedford at the Adelphi. Nor should the success of the Keans in Shakespeare and 'gentlemanly melodrama' at the Princess's obscure the place of comedy in their repertoire, originally given by performers like Harley and the Keeleys, whose roots lay in the past but whose methods pointed to the future. The increasing delicacy of English theatrical method in the 1850s (to which both writer and actor contributed) produced a fertile soil for the 'cup and saucer comedies' and tea-table technique much admired then and since.

A less obvious contributor to this process was Samuel Phelps, whose reign at Sadler's Wells during the years following the Theatre Regulation Act is rightly remembered for demonstrating in the bracing North London climate a Shakespearean spirit that the West End signally failed to emulate. Phelps also made a valuable contribution to comic acting. His physique prevented his becoming a great tragic actor; he was short and sturdy enough to be 'serviceable' (a term of which he would certainly be proud). But his range embraced comedy (Falstaff, Bottom, Sir Peter Teazle) in a measure wholly denied to Kean, still more Macready or Irving. In sheer versatility Phelps could link arms with Garrick in the previous century and Olivier in the next. He alone of the nineteenth-century actor-managers could play with distinction Macbeth and Malvolio on succeeding nights. It is salutary to compare this record with that not only of the recognized Shakespearean performers, but also of recognized comic stars. When Madame Vestris revived *The Merry Wives of Windsor*, Charles James Mathews played Slender; when the Bancrofts staged their only Shakespeare, Bancroft played Morocco and engaged Ellen Terry for Portia. Mrs. Bancroft did not appear.

Late Victorian Melodrama

The Society drama of the 1890s combined the strong situations of nineteenth-century melodrama with the refined technique of Robertson and the (usually French in origin) plays which succeeded his in the Bancrofts' repertory. In noting the importance to Irving and Tree of melodramas, old and new, it is easy to lose sight of many other practitioners of the genre, both fashionable (Terriss, Wilson Barrett, Martin-Harvey) and unfashionable (the unsung heroes of the Britannia, Hoxton, or the Whitechapel Pavilion). Most of the fashionable performers included Shakespeare in their repertoire, often with considerable success: Martin-Harvey as Richard III, Lewis Waller as Henry V. The theatrical fare of the actor-managers' heyday spanned imperishable masterpieces and perishable fustian.

In demonstrating the more abiding literary qualities of selected Society dramas (*The Second Mrs. Tanqueray*, *Mrs. Dane's Defence*, all three of Wilde's), there is a temptation to ignore plays and playwrights who contributed much to the refinement and appeal of the late Victorian stage, without setting their names to any lasting theatrical testament. Nevertheless, certain distinctions can be made, even in the work of these forgotten craftsmen, between the melodramatic school before the 1860s and afterwards. For example, religious themes, acceptable in the first half of the century only if shrouded in Gothic gloom, were regularly central to later melodramas: the nonconformist conscience did not stifle *The Sign of the Cross* (written and acted by Wilson Barrett) or *The Christian* (Hall Caine). Indeed church and chapel leaders increasingly pointed to these religious melodramas as evidence of the theatre's growing responsibility. It is notable that Wilson Barrett could build a career on *The Sign of the Cross*, whilst an ambitious 'problem play' with a clergyman hero, *Michael and his Lost Angel*, provoked opposition and failed— presumably because it claimed a profundity that was neither justified nor wanted.

Again, while Society drama increasingly exploited aristocratic backgrounds, even before the 1890s (as in *Diplomacy* or *The Profligate*) the traditional strongholds of melodrama kept pace with this ennobling trend. The Drury Lane melodramas of Augustus Harris, Cecil Raleigh, and Henry Hamilton between 1880 and 1914 are scarcely less crowded with title and rank than the playbills of the St. James's or the Haymarket. They also threw open the doors of Mayfair drawing-rooms but by no means confined themselves to such localities. Battles by sea and land took their protagonists all over the world, and if they chose not to cross the ocean, they still offered a panorama which unrolled race-courses, railway-stations, boat-races, and even aerobatics before their wide-eyed public.

In the last phase of the Victorian theatre it is often helpful to distinguish between romantic drama, such as *The Only Way* or *The Prisoner of Zenda*, in which the author and actor between them struck a note to which the audience responded wholeheartedly, and melodrama, in which part at least of the audience came to scoff, while their simpler brethren remained to worship, as in the Melville melodramas at the Lyceum. The importance to the evolution of modern British drama of the 'problem play' and the social drama which grew out of it can easily obscure the ground-bass of stirring sentiment which sounded in the majority of theatres until the 1914–18 War shattered the illusion on and off the stage.

The Playwright's Right to Pay

The meagre returns of the playwright's craft in the first half of the nineteenth century have been regularly pointed out. It could hardly be argued that his Georgian predecessor was richly rewarded; the traditional claim to the profits of the third, sixth, ninth, and twentieth (if any) nights of the initial run was a modest and unpredictable bounty. Many factors— political, personal, above all climatic—might ruin the chances of even a popular playwright. Thomas Morton, whose experience spanned forty years, told the 1832 Committee: 'I have often watched the clouds, very often.' In fact the Georgian playwright frequently earned more from publication than performance of his play, since his was still a play-reading age. Even so, the leading dramatists were mostly men of letters (Goldsmith, Cumberland, Kelly), or men of the theatre (Garrick, Colman, Sheridan), as well as authors of plays.

Nevertheless, the last decade of the old century and first of the new, with their increase in the size of the patent theatres, larger audiences, longer runs, and steady encroachment of minor houses, marked in many ways a new deal for playwrights, and this era saw the emergence of the professional, writing exclusively for the theatre, sometimes to rewarding effect. George Colman the younger claimed to have earned £1000 each from *John Bull* and *The Africans*, and Frederick Reynolds, after a career of nearly sixty years, owned to earning £19,000, no dazzling fortune, but in his words: 'a sum unequalled in the history of dramatic writing'.

Perhaps it was the earnings of such as Colman and Reynolds that increasingly nudged managers towards a lump-sum payment for their writers. Established practitioners like Sheridan Knowles or John Poole could command £100 per act from the patent theatres (the method of calculation, suggestive of pounds of sausages, is characteristic of the age), but afterpieces were worth only £100 or £150 at the most. These figures seem even shabbier when account is taken of a drop to £10 for publication rights. Small wonder that from the 1830s playwrights struggled to keep their work out of print and retain some bargaining power, although the sinister practice of 'feeing the copyist' was mentioned to the 1832 Committee by

163

more than one witness, and Douglas Jerrold went so far as to name the ring-leader:

> ...Mr. Kenneth, at the corner of Bow Street, will supply any gentleman with any manuscript on the lowest of terms.
>
> Q1798. How does he procure them, is it by short-hand writer in the theatre?
>
> A1799. He steals them somehow; he has no right to them.[1]

The grossest exploitation of the playwright obtained in the minor theatres, where writers were often employed as 'resident dramatists' for the derisory sum of £10 a week, and their work claimed as the property of the house. The cruellest sufferer from this system was probably Jerrold himself, whose *Black-Ey'd Susan* earned him £60 from the manager of the Surrey, and was then played all over the English-speaking world for the rest of the century. Not surprisingly the sweated dramatist became demoralized: Jerrold told the Committee 'the public has ceased to look on plays as part of the literature of the country', and W. T. Moncrieff described one of his biggest successes, *Tom and Jerry*, as 'mixed up with all sorts of trash', and thought another, *Giovanni in London*, 'ought not to have been licensed'.

Almost the sole immediate outcome of the Committee's hearings was the Dramatic Copyright Act of 1833, and the foundation of the Dramatic Author's Society in the same year. Neither, in fact, proved effective, as long as the theatre remained depressed and the author, alone or in association, lacked respect. But with the gradual restoration of prosperity to the former and prestige to the latter, the situation changed. Tom Taylor received only £150 for *Our American Cousin*, but his contemporary, Boucicault, exploited his appeal both as actor and sensation-dramatist to drive a hard bargain with his Irish pieces, claiming half of the net profits throughout their run (assessed by his fellow-witness before the 1866 Select Committee as bringing him upwards of £300 a week).

The principle of 'sharing terms' or a royalty was the foundation-stone upon which the prosperity of the late Victorian playwright was built. T. W. Robertson, who had been com-

[1] *House of Commons: British Sessional Papers 1831-2*, Vol. VII, p. 157.

pelled to borrow £10 to 'buy back' *David Garrick* from the publisher, Lacy, was treated with great consideration by the Bancrofts, who paid him a royalty from the start which rose to £5 a night. By the end of his unhappily brief life he was earning £4000 a year. While the playwright's position had improved at home, it remained unprotected abroad—notably in North America, as the history of 'pirated' productions of Gilbert and Sullivan illustrates. The Berne Convention of 1886 and the American copyright law of 1891 completed the work begun by Boucicault and the Bancrofts, and made possible such handsome returns as Pinero's £30,000 from the initial success of *The Second Mrs. Tanqueray*. The fortunes left by W. S. Gilbert (£111,971), J. M. Barrie (£167,694), and above all G. B. Shaw (£367,233) are, of course, only a portion of their ultimate earnings, thanks to the establishment of dramatic copyright.

A Century of Dramatic Critics

If the nineteenth century was the age of popular theatre in England, it was also the age of the popular press. Increasing technical resources in the hands of publishers and increasing literacy in their potential customers led to much variety of printing, and one manifestation of this was the growth of dramatic criticism. By a curious paradox, as the dramatist lost his literary status, so the critic gained prestige and power. From its Georgian rôle as an unsigned and irregular form of gossip-column, theatrical journalism evolved into a highly personal and considered exercise in aesthetics. Starting with the publication of Leigh Hunt's *Critical Essays on the Performers of the London Theatres* in 1807, dramatic critics not only carried out their nightly task authoritatively and expansively but produced collected judgements in popular and profitable editions. At the end of the century G. B. Shaw was playing David to the Goliath of Irving as impudently as Hunt had slung his stones at John Philip Kemble. Nor was this exercise restricted to the giants of the stage; between 1800 and 1830 over 160 theatrical periodicals were published, many of them appearing daily and a fair proportion in the provinces.

It is tempting to ask: does the theatre make its critics or the

critics their theatre? Certain occasions were decreed momentous by great judges; for example, Hazlitt's attendance in a thin
house at Drury Lane on 26 January 1814, when the mature
Kean first appeared there. The first quarter of the nineteenth
century found actors worthy of their critics: Kemble, Mrs.
Siddons, Kean, and Macready to fire Leigh Hunt and Hazlitt
to praise or punishment; Elliston and Munden to warm the
corners of Lamb's heart and Elia's Essays. In the last decade
Archer was on guard to defend Ibsen against the Pecksniffs, and
Shaw to recognize in Forbes-Robertson's playing of Shakespeare what he missed in Irving's.

Between these two peaks lay a wide and in some sense
featureless plain. Critics were active; players gave of their
best, often under the worst conditions. Yet G. H. Lewes had
to look back to Macready and even summon up childhood
memories of Edmund Kean, or hail Salvini and Ristori from
their foreign shores, if his note were to sound reverential.
When fixing his gaze on his own day and race, he was driven
to sharpening a hatchet for Charles Kean, dismissing his Macbeth as 'one whose crime is that of a common murderer, with
perhaps a tendency towards Methodism'. Henry Morley
rated good intentions above absolute standards when he praised
the high-toned (if low-budget) productions of Phelps at Sadler's
Wells before the expensive and scholarly but laboured efforts
of Kean at the Princess's. We may insist that Lewes would
have recognized the unknown Edmund as unequivocally as
Hazlitt; we may suspect that Leigh Hunt would have detected
the second-rate in Phelps as clearly as he condemned the
pedantic in Kemble. We may insist and suspect, but we do not
know.

The increasingly frenzied attacks which Clement Scott
launched on Ibsen in the 1890s have obscured the prestige which
his recognition conferred on actor-managers of the 1870s and
1880s, not only Bancroft (for whom he wrote) and Irving (by
whom he was paid) but the growing circle of authoritative
actors (Wyndham, the Kendals, Hare, and Tree amongst them).
Scott's dual responsibility as critic of the *Daily Telegraph* and
editor of *The Theatre* gave him immense power, which he was
not superhuman enough to exercise without abuse. Neverthe-

less, the continuity of his work (twenty-nine years on the *Telegraph*, twenty on *The Theatre*) gave theatrical journalism a stability it had never previously achieved. Hazlitt's regular career as a dramatic critic covered only five years, Leigh Hunt's four.

In the 1890s this stability was challenged by a number of men, some young (Shaw, Walkley, Beerbohm), some not so young (Archer). They swept away the weeds and undergrowth of the dramatic columns, planting new seeds and carving new careers in the process. One may doubt what would have been the fate of the Court seasons in the next decade if they had been judged by Scott, or even only by Archer, to whom Shaw and Granville-Barker were always too clever by half. Fortunately Walkley, Beerbohm, and MacCarthy were on hand and themselves clever enough to recognize more than mere cleverness when they saw it.

Victorian plays in revival

The place of Victorian drama in the modern repertoire remains controversial. At the end of the period Shaw and Wilde stand unchallenged and unchallengeable. Their plays and the Savoy Operas are the only examples of Victorian stagecraft which even a regular playgoer is likely to see, unless he searches diligently. In recent years a vogue for Victorian music hall has spilled over into an interest in Victorian melodrama, but both are marked by self-indulgence on the part of performers and audience. Entertaining as a production of *East Lynne* or *Lady Audley's Secret* in the manner of 'The Good Old Days' may be, it reveals little of the aims of the originators of such pieces, or of the command they exercised over their audiences.

This condescension is especially dangerous now that the National Theatre is in operation and the Arts Council confers a substantial measure of financial independence on many other theatres, in London and the provinces. Their directors are emancipated from public approval in a way the Victorian actor-manager never knew, and the necessity to study that public and its predecessors is thus largely obviated. Such excursions into the nineteenth-century repertoire as the London stage has recently undertaken seem curiously centrifugal. Thus the

Royal Shakespeare Company has scored substantial successes with two revivals: *London Assurance*, in which Boucicault's imitation of Goldsmith proved a great deal more entertaining in performance than on the page; and *Wild Oats*, a play which looks back to the theatrical traditions of the age which preceded its own. Similarly *The Shaughraun*, with which the Abbey Theatre succeeded stirringly enough to bring it to the World Theatre season in 1968, charmed by its Irish qualities, disarming the criticism Anglo-Saxons level at their own sensation-dramas.

The modern theatre in fact welcomes Victorian fun but resists Victorian plays with further pretensions, cold-shouldering *Engaged* at the National Theatre (announced as 'by the Gilbert of Gilbert-and-Sullivan') because it was not also by the Sullivan of Gilbert-and-Sullivan. A. W. Pinero's hold on the modern stage is no less incomplete: *The Magistrate*, *The Schoolmistress*, and *Dandy Dick* recur and are welcomed; recently *The Amazons* and *The Cabinet Minister* have been revived. *Trelawny of the 'Wells'* (skilfully if rather oddly staged by the National Theatre as a tribute to T. W. Robertson on the centenary of *Society*) gives pleasure, both as a play and a musical. But performances of *The Second Mrs. Tanqueray* are rare, and an undercast production of *The Gay Lord Quex* failed to make a special case for this piece, either as bedroom farce or 'problem play'.

Perhaps the most puzzling feature of the contemporary theatre's interest in the Victorian repertoire is its regular involvement with *The Bells*. The aura which Irving's triumph as Mathias still throws over this play consistently tempts actors and managements to present it, and no less consistently the performance is dismissed as sub-Irving, and therefore sub-standard. Whatever the truth of this verdict (which no living playgoer can arbitrate), it begs another issue: *The Bells* became the mainstay of the Lyceum repertoire not only because of Irving's performance, but also because the text gave certain insights into the Burgomaster's mind not previously attempted in the theatre but subsequently commonplaces of psychological analysis in both fact and fiction. Where *The Bells* seemed a revelation to Irving's audiences, it seems trite to today's public. Unlike *London Assurance* or *Caste*, this is a play which reads better than it acts.

Retrospect and Prospect

If interest in the performance of Victorian plays is still limited and partial, interest in the study of the Victorian theatre grows apace, as the substantially larger bibliography of this edition and the appearance of *Nineteenth Century Theatre Research*, a journal specially devoted to the subject, amply demonstrate. The neglect of Victorian drama which marked the first half of the twentieth century sprang partly from pride in that period's own dramatic achievements and partly from consciousness that fiction, poetry, philosophy, and historiography far outstripped the writing of plays in Victoria's reign. Assessment of Victorian drama's competitors having reached a satisfying (if not surfeiting) point, attention naturally turned back to the theatre.

Since the Victorians themselves so underrated their playwrights as to print their work as ephemera, a priority was the republication of these playwrights in legible form. Anthologies of Victorian drama have appeared in regular, though not rapid, sequence, and the demand now is for collections either of individual authors or of individual *genres*. A theatre so essentially visual in its appeal can often be better illustrated than written about, and pictorial coverage not only of the Victorian stage but of the Victorian public and its routine continues to be a prerequisite.

In one respect the scarcity of Victorian plays in performance and the increase of scholarship focussed on the Victorian theatre can and must complement each other. Commentary on other periods of English drama, above all Elizabethan drama, can assume a more or less close acquaintance with the subject under discussion, often on both page and stage. Since neither is widely true of the Victorian drama, its historians must convey both the first impressions of the playgoer and the second impressions of the fireside critic. The very fact that the theatre played a larger part in the lives of a larger proportion of Victoria's subjects than those of any other British monarch before or since calls for a sustained matching of scholarship with imagination from that theatre's recorders. Often they have first to create the playhouse, the public, and the performance, and then assess it. The task is exacting, but exciting.

PLAY-LIST, 1792–1914

This is a select list of plays and playwrights. Further information for the period 1792–1914 is to be found in the various Handlists appended to Allardyce Nicoll's *History of English Drama,*
The dates given here, unless otherwise stated, are of the play's first· London performance, including suburban or private performances but not copyright performances. The date of publication is given only when it substantially precedes production. Collaborations, wherever possible, have been listed under both authors.

THOMAS HOLCROFT, 1745–1809: *The Road to Ruin,* 1792. *The Deserted Daughter,* 1795. *He's Much to Blame,* 1798. *Deaf and Dumb,* 1801. *A Tale of Mystery,* 1802. *Hear Both Sides,* 1803.

RICHARD BRINSLEY SHERIDAN, 1751–1816: *Pizarro,* 1799.

ELIZABETH INCHBALD, 1753–1821: *Everyone Has His Fault,* 1793. *Wives as They Were and Maids as They Are,* 1797. *Lovers' Vows,* 1798.

WILLIAM BARRYMORE, 1758–1830: *The Dog of Montargis,* 1814. *Wallace, the Hero of Scotland,* 1818. *Gilderoy, the Bonny Boy,* 1822.

JOANNA BAILLIE, 1762–1851: *De Monfort,* 1800. *The Family Legend,* 1815; *published* 1810. *Ethwald; published* 1802. *Constantine Palaeologus; published* 1804. *Orra; published* 1812.

GEORGE COLMAN the younger, 1762–1836: *New Hay at the Old Market,* 1795. *The Iron Chest,* 1796. *The Heir-at-Law,* 1797. *Blue Beard,* 1798. *Feudal Times,* 1799. *The Poor Gentleman,* 1801. *Love Laughs at Locksmiths,* 1803. *John Bull,* 1803. *Who Wants a Guinea?* 1805. *The Africans,* 1808.

ISAAC POCOCK, 1762–1835: *The Miller and His Men,* 1813. *The Magpie or the Maid?* 1815. *Robinson Crusoe,* 1817. *The Robber's Bride,* 1829.

THOMAS MORTON (?)1764–1838: *The Way to Get Married,* 1796. *A Cure for the Heart-Ache,* 1797. *Secrets Worth Knowing,* 1798. *Speed the Plough,* 1800. *The School of Reform,* 1805. *The Slave,* 1816.

JOHN TOBIN, 1770–1804: *The Honey Moon*, 1805. *The Curfew*, 1807.

WILLIAM WORDSWORTH, 1770–1850: *The Borderers; published* 1842.

SAMUEL TAYLOR COLERIDGE, 1772–1834: *Remorse*, 1813. *Wallenstein (two parts); published* 1800.

MATTHEW LEWIS, 1775–1818: *The Castle Spectre*, 1797. *Adelmorn the Outlaw*, 1801. *Adelgitha*, 1807. *One O'Clock*, 1811. *Timour the Tartar*, 1811.

BENJAMIN THOMPSON (?)1776–1816: *The Stranger*, 1798. *Don Carlos; published* 1798. *Emilia Galotti; published* 1800. *The Robbers; published* 1800. *Stella; published* 1800.

JAMES KENNEY, 1780–1849: *Raising the Wind*, 1803. *Matrimony*, 1804. *The Blind Boy*, 1807. *Love, Law and Physic*, 1812.

GEORGE GORDON, LORD BYRON, 1788–1824: *Marino Faliero*, 1821. *Werner*, 1830; *published* 1823. *Manfred*, 1834; *published* 1817. *Sardanapalus*, 1834; *published* 1821. *The Two Foscari*, 1837; *published* 1821. *Cain; published* 1821.

JAMES SHERIDAN KNOWLES, 1788–1862: *Virginius*, 1820. *Caius Gracchus*, 1823. *William Tell*, 1825. *The Hunchback*, 1832. *The Wife*, 1833. *The Love Chase*, 1837. *Love*, 1839.

PERCY BYSSHE SHELLEY, 1792–1822: *The Cenci*, 1886; *published* 1819. *Prometheus Unbound; published* 1820.

EDWARD FITZBALL, 1792–1873: *The Pilot*, 1825. *The Flying Dutchman*, 1827. *The Inchcape Bell*, 1828. *The Red Rover*, 1829. *Jonathan Bradford*, 1833. *Paul Clifford*, 1835. *Thalaba, the Destroyer*, 1836. *Maritana*, 1845. *Uncle Tom's Cabin*, 1852.

THOMAS MONCRIEFF, 1794–1857: *Giovanni in London*, 1817. *The Lear of Private Life*, 1820. *Tom and Jerry*, 1821. *The Cataract of the Ganges*, 1823. *Eugene Aram*, 1832.

THOMAS NOON TALFOURD, 1795–1854: *Ion*, 1836.

JAMES ROBINSON PLANCHÉ, 1796–1880: *The Vampyre*, 1820. *Success*, 1825. *Oberon*, 1826. *Olympic Revels*, 1831. *Olympic Devils*, 1831. *The Paphian Bower*, 1832. *High, Low, Jack, and the Game*, 1833. *The Deep Deep Sea*, 1833. *Telemachus*, 1834. *Riquet with the Tuft*, 1836. *Puss in Boots*, 1837. *The Drama's Levée*, 1838. *Blue*

Beard, 1839. *The Sleeping Beauty in the Wood*, 1840. *Beauty and the Beast*, 1841. *The White Cat*, 1842. *The Fair One with the Golden Locks*, 1843. *The Drama at Home*, 1844. *The Golden Fleece*, 1845. *The Bee and the Orange Tree*, 1846. *The Birds*, 1846. *The Invisible Prince*, 1846. *The Golden Branch*, 1847. *Theseus and Ariadne*, 1848. *The King of the Peacocks*, 1848. *The Seven Champions of Christendom*, 1849. *The Island of Jewels*, 1849. *Cymon and Iphigenia*, 1850. *King Charming*, 1850. *The Queen of the Frogs*, 1850. *The Prince of the Happy Land*, 1851. *The Good Woman in the Wood*, 1852. *The Camp at the Olympic*, 1853. *Mr. Buckstone's Ascent of Mount Parnassus*, 1853. *Mr. Buckstone's Voyage Round the Globe*, 1854. *The Yellow Dwarf*, 1854. *The New Haymarket Spring Meeting*, 1855. *Orpheus in the Haymarket*, 1865.

JOHN BALDWIN BUCKSTONE, 1802–79: *Luke the Labourer*, 1826. *Jack Sheppard*, 1839. *The Green Bushes*, 1845. *The Flowers of the Forest*, 1847. *An Alarming Sacrifice*, 1849.

EDWARD BULWER-LYTTON, BARON LYTTON, 1803–73: *The Duchess de la Vallière*, 1837. *The Lady of Lyons*, 1838. *Richelieu*, 1839. *The Sea-Captain*, 1839. *Money*, 1840. *Not So Bad As We Seem*, 1851.

DOUGLAS WILLIAM JERROLD, 1803–57: *Fifteen Years of a Drunkard's Life*, 1828. *Black-Ey'd Susan*, 1829. *The Mutiny at the Nore*, 1830. *The Factory Girl*, 1832. *The Rent Day*, 1832. *Bubbles of the Day*, 1842. *The Prisoner of War*, 1842. *Time Works Wonders*, 1845.

THOMAS BEDDOES, 1803–49: *Death's Jest-Book; published* 1850.

WILLIAM BAYLE BERNARD, 1807–75: *Casco Bay*, 1827. *The Conquering Game*, 1832. *The Nervous Man*, 1833. *The Farmer's Story*, 1836. *Marie Ducange*, 1841. *A Storm in a Teacup*, 1854.

ALFRED, LORD TENNYSON, 1809–92: *Queen Mary*, 1876. *The Falcon*, 1879. *The Cup*, 1881. *The Promise of May*, 1882. *Becket*, 1893; *published* 1879. *The Foresters*, 1893. *Harold; published* 1877.

JOHN MADDISON MORTON, 1811–91: *Lend Me Five Shillings*, 1846. *Box and Cox*, 1847. *Woodcock's Little Game*, 1864. *Drawing Room, Second Floor and Attics*, 1864.

ROBERT BROWNING, 1812–89: *Strafford*, 1837. *A Blot in the 'Scutcheon*, 1843. *Colombe's Birthday*, 1853; *published* 1844. *Pippa Passes; published* 1841. *King Victor and King Charles; published* 1842.

CHARLES READE, 1814–84: *The Ladies' Battle*, 1851. *Masks and Faces*, 1852. *Gold*, 1853. *Two Loves and a Life*, 1854. *The Courier of Lyons*, 1854. *The King's Rival*, 1854. *Foul Play*, 1858. *It's Never Too Late To Mend*, 1865. *The Wandering Heir*, 1873. *Drink*, 1879.

TOM TAYLOR, 1817–80: *To Parents and Guardians*, 1846. *Masks and Faces*, 1852. *Plot and Passion*, 1853. *The King's Rival*, 1854. *Two Loves and a Life*, 1854. *Still Waters Run Deep*, 1855. *The Contested Election*, 1859. *The Fool's Revenge*, 1859. *Our American Cousin*, 1861. *The Ticket-of-Leave Man*, 1865. *Settling Day*, 1865. *New Men and Old Acres*, 1869. *'Twixt Axe and Crown*, 1870. *Joan of Arc*, 1871. *Lady Clancarty*, 1874. *Anne Boleyn*, 1876.

DION BOUCICAULT, (?)1820–90: *London Assurance*, 1841. *Used Up*, 1844. *Don Cæsar de Bazan*, 1844. *The Corsican Brothers*, 1852. *Faust and Marguerite*, 1854. *Louis XI*, 1855. *Foul Play*, 1858. *Jessie Brown*, 1858. *The Colleen Bawn*, 1860. *The Octoroon*, 1861. *The Poor of New York*, 1864 (as *The Streets of London*). *Arrah-na-Pogue*, 1865. *Rip Van Winkle*, 1865. *The Long Strike*, 1866. *After Dark*, 1868. *Formosa*, 1869. *The Shaughraun*, 1875. *The O'Dowd*, 1880.

WILLIAM BROUGH, 1826–70: *Perdita, the Royal Milkmaid*, 1856. *The Area Belle*, 1863. *The Field of the Cloth of Gold*, 1868.

WILLIAM BLANCHARD JERROLD, 1826–84: *Cool as a Cucumber*, 1851.

LEOPOLD LEWIS, 1828–90: *The Bells*, 1871.

WILLIAM GORMAN WILLS, 1828–91: *Charles I*, 1872. *Eugene Aram*, 1873. *Olivia*, 1878. *Vanderdecken*, 1878. *Iolanthe*, 1878. *William and Susan*, 1880. *Faust*, 1885. *A Chapter from Don Quixote*, 1895.

THOMAS WILLIAM ROBERTSON, 1829–71: *The Battle of Life*, 1847 (Norwich). *The Ladies' Battle*, 1851. *Faust and Marguerite*, 1854. *The Half-Caste*, 1856. *The Cantab*, 1861. *David Garrick*, 1864. *Society*, 1865. *Ours*, 1866. *Caste*, 1867. *Play*, 1868. *Progress*, 1869. *School*, 1869. *Home*, 1869. *M.P.*, 1870. *Birth*, 1870 (Bristol). *The Nightingale*, 1870. *War*, 1871.

HENRY JAMES BYRON, 1834–84: *The Maid and the Magpie*, 1858. *The Rosebud of Stinging-Nettle Farm*, 1863. *La! Sonnambula!* 1865. *Lucia di Lammermoor*, 1865. *Cyril's Success*, 1868. *Uncle Dick's Darling*, 1869. *Married in Haste*, 1875. *Our Boys*, 1875.

SIR WILLIAM SCHWENCK GILBERT, 1836–1911: *Dulcamara,* 1866. *The Merry Zingara,* 1868. *The Palace of Truth,* 1870. *The Princess,* 1870. *Thespis,* 1871. *Pygmalion and Galatea,* 1871. *The Wicked World,* 1873. *The Wedding March,* 1873. *Charity,* 1874. *Sweethearts,* 1874. *Committed for Trial,* 1874. *Trial by Jury,* 1875. *Dan'l Druce, Blacksmith,* 1876. *Engaged,* 1877. *The Sorcerer,* 1877. *On Bail,* 1877. *H.M.S. Pinafore,* 1878. *The Pirates of Penzance,* 1880. *Patience,* 1881. *Iolanthe,* 1882. *Princess Ida,* 1884. *The Mikado,* 1885. *Ruddigore,* 1887. *The Yeomen of the Guard,* 1888. *The Gondoliers,* 1889. *Haste to the Wedding,* 1892. *Utopia (Limited),* 1893. *The Grand Duke,* 1896. *Fallen Fairies,* 1909.

ALGERNON CHARLES SWINBURNE, 1837–1909: *Locrine,* 1899; *published* 1887. *Chastelard; published* 1865. *Atalanta in Calydon; published* 1865. *Bothwell; published* 1874. *Mary Stuart; published* 1881.

JAMES ALBERY, 1838–89: *Two Roses,* 1870. *Pickwick,* 1871. *Pink Dominos,* 1877. *The Crisis,* 1878. *Duty,* 1879.

SIR CHARLES L. YOUNG, 1840–87: *Shadows,* 1871. *Gilded Youth,* 1872 (Brighton). *Petticoat Perfidy,* 1885. *Jim the Penman,* 1887.

CLEMENT SCOTT, 1841–1904 and B. C. STEPHENSON, 1839–1906: *Peril,* 1876. *Diplomacy,* 1878.

SYDNEY GRUNDY, 1848–1914: *Mammon,* 1877. *The Snowball,* 1879. *The Glass of Fashion,* 1883. *The Silver Shield,* 1885. *A Wife's Sacrifice,* 1886. *The Bells of Haslemere,* 1887. *A Fool's Paradise,* 1889. *A Pair of Spectacles,* 1890. *Haddon Hall,* 1892. *Sowing the Wind,* 1893. *A Bunch of Violets,* 1894. *The New Woman,* 1894. *The Degenerates,* 1899. *Business is Business,* 1905.

HENRY ARTHUR JONES, 1851–1931: *The Silver King,* 1882. *Saints and Sinners,* 1884. *Wealth,* 1889. *The Middleman,* 1889. *Judah,* 1890. *The Crusaders,* 1891. *The Dancing Girl,* 1891. *The Bauble Shop,* 1893. *The Tempter,* 1893. *The Case of Rebellious Susan,* 1894. *The Masqueraders,* 1894. *The Triumph of the Philistines,* 1895. *Michael and His Lost Angel,* 1896. *The Rogue's Comedy,* 1896. *The Liars,* 1897. *The Physician,* 1897. *The Manœuvres of Jane,* 1898. *Mrs. Dane's Defence,* 1900. *Whitewashing Julia,* 1903. *The Heroic Stubbs,* 1906. *The Hypocrites,* 1906. *Dolly Reforming Herself,* 1908. *The Ogre,* 1911. *Mary Goes First,* 1913.

SIR HALL CAINE, 1853–1931: *The Manxman,* 1895. *The Christian,* 1899. *The Eternal City,* 1902.

175

PAUL POTTER, 1854–1921: *Trilby*, 1895.

OSCAR WILDE, 1854–1900: *Lady Windermere's Fan*, 1892. *A Woman of No Importance*, 1893. *An Ideal Husband*, 1895. *The Importance of Being Earnest*, 1895. *Salome*, 1896; *published* 1893.

SIR ARTHUR WING PINERO, 1855–1934: *The Money-Spinner*, 1881. *The Squire*, 1881. *Lords and Commons*, 1883. *The Iron Master*, 1884. *The Magistrate*, 1885. *In Chancery*, 1885. *Mayfair*, 1885. *The School-Mistress*, 1886. *The Hobby-Horse*, 1886. *Dandy Dick*, 1887. *Sweet Lavender*, 1888. *The Profligate*, 1889. *The Weaker Sex*, 1889. *The Cabinet Minister*, 1890. *Lady Bountiful*, 1891. *The Times*, 1891. *The Amazons*, 1893. *The Second Mrs. Tanqueray*, 1893. *The Benefit of the Doubt*, 1895. *The Notorious Mrs. Ebbsmith*, 1895. *The Princess and the Butterfly*, 1897. *Trelawny of the 'Wells'*, 1898. *The Gay Lord Quex*, 1899. *Iris*, 1901. *Letty*, 1903. *His House in Order*, 1906. *The Thunderbolt*, 1908. *Mid-Channel*, 1909. *Preserving Mr. Panmure*, 1911. *The 'Mind the Paint' Girl*, 1912.

MICHAEL MORTON, 1855–1931: *Colonel Newcome*, 1906.

GEORGE BERNARD SHAW, 1856–1950: *Widowers' Houses*, 1892. *Arms and the Man*, 1894. *You Never Can Tell*, 1899; *published* 1898. *The Devil's Disciple*, 1899. *Candida*, 1900; *published* 1898. *Captain Brassbound's Conversion*, 1900. *The Man of Destiny*, 1901; *published* 1898. *Mrs. Warren's Profession*, 1902; *published* 1898. *John Bull's Other Island*, 1904. *Man and Superman*, 1905; *published* 1903. *Major Barbara*, 1905. *The Philanderer*, 1905; *published* 1898. *The Doctor's Dilemma*, 1906. *Cæsar and Cleopatra*, 1907; *published* 1901. *Getting Married*, 1908. *Misalliance*, 1910. *Fanny's First Play*, 1911. *Androcles and the Lion*, 1913. *Pygmalion*, 1913.

R. C. CARTON, 1856–1928: *Sunlight and Shadow*, 1890. *Liberty Hall*, 1892. *Lord and Lady Algy*, 1898. *Wheels within Wheels*, 1899. *Lady Huntsworth's Experiment*, 1900. *Mr. Hopkinson*, 1905. *Public Opinion*, 1905. *The Bear Leaders*, 1912.

BRANDON THOMAS, 1857–1914: *Charley's Aunt*, 1892.

SIR JAMES MATTHEW BARRIE, 1860–1937: *Walker, London*, 1892. *The Professor's Love Story*, 1894. *The Little Minister*, 1897. *The Wedding Guest*, 1900. *The Admirable Crichton*, 1902. *Quality Street*, 1902. *Peter Pan*, 1904. *Alice-Sit-By-The-Fire*, 1905. *What Every Woman Knows*, 1908. *The Twelve-Pound Look*, 1910. *Rosalind*, 1912. *The Will*, 1913.

CHARLES HADDON CHAMBERS, 1860–1921: *Captain Swift,* 1888. *The Idler,* 1891. *John-A-Dreams,* 1894. *The Tyranny of Tears,* 1899. *The Awakening,* 1901. *Passers By,* 1911.

ALFRED SUTRO, 1863–1933: A *Marriage Has Been Arranged,* 1902. *The Walls of Jericho,* 1904. *Mollentrave on Women,* 1905. *The Perfect Lover,* 1905. *The Fascinating Mr. Vanderveldt,* 1906. *John Glayde's Honour,* 1907. *The Barrier,* 1907. *The Builder of Bridges,* 1908. *The Perplexed Husband,* 1911. *The Two Virtues,* 1914.

LAURENCE HOUSMAN, 1865–1959: *Prunella,* 1904.

ELIZABETH ROBINS, 1865–1952: *Votes for Women,* 1907.

JOHN GALSWORTHY, 1867–1933: *The Silver Box,* 1906. *Strife,* 1909. *Justice,* 1910. *The Eldest Son,* 1912. *The Pigeon,* 1912. *The Fugitive,* 1913. *The Mob,* 1914.

STEPHEN PHILLIPS, 1868–1915: *Herod,* 1900. *Paolo and Francesca,* 1902. *Ulysses,* 1902. *Nero,* 1906. *Faust,* 1908.

ST. JOHN HANKIN, 1869–1909: *The Two Mr. Wetherbys,* 1903. *The Return of the Prodigal,* 1905. *The Charity That Began At Home,* 1906. *The Cassilis Engagement,* 1907. *The Last of the De Mullins,* 1908.

WILLIAM SOMERSET MAUGHAM, 1874–1965: *A Man of Honour,* 1903. *Lady Frederick,* 1907. *Jack Straw,* 1908. *Mrs. Dot,* 1908. *Penelope,* 1909. *Smith,* 1909. *Grace,* 1910. *The Tenth Man,* 1910. *Loaves and Fishes,* 1911. *Landed Gentry,* 1913. *The Land of Promise,* 1914.

HUBERT HENRY DAVIES, 1876–1917: *Cousin Kate,* 1903. *Mrs. Gorringe's Necklace,* 1903. *Captain Drew on Leave,* 1905. *The Mollusc,* 1907. *Lady Epping's Lawsuit,* 1908. *Outcast,* 1914.

HARLEY GRANVILLE BARKER, 1877–1946: *The Marrying of Ann Leete,* 1901. *Prunella,* 1904. *The Voysey Inheritance,* 1905. *Waste,* 1907. *The Madras House,* 1910.

RUDOLF BESIER, 1878–1942: *The Virgin Goddess,* 1906. *Don,* 1909. *Lady Patricia,* 1911.

STANLEY HOUGHTON, 1881–1913: *The Dear Departed,* 1908. *Independent Means,* 1909. *The Younger Generation,* 1910. *Hindle Wakes,* 1912.

A BIBLIOGRAPHY
OF THE ENGLISH THEATRE
1792–1914

Books are arranged under the following headings:

Biography and Autobiography
General Studies
Bibliographies and Works of Reference
A Selection of Periodicals
Anthologies of Plays

*The place of publication is London,
unless otherwise stated.*

Biography and Autobiography

Subject	Title	Author	Date
JAMES ALBERY	*Introduction to Dramatic Works*	Wyndham Albery (Editor)	1939
SIR GEORGE ALEXANDER	*Sir George Alexander and the St. James's Theatre*	A. E. W. Mason	1935
GEORGE W. ALLTREE	*Footlight Memories*		1932
JAMES R. ANDERSON	*An Actor's Life*	W. E. Adams (Editor)	1902
MARY ANDERSON	*Mary Anderson*	J. M. Farrar	1884
	The Stage Life of Mary Anderson	William Winter	1884 New York
	A Few Memories		1896
	A Few More Memories		1936
FRANK ARCHER	*An Actor's Notebooks*		1912
WILLIAM ARCHER	*William Archer: His Life, Work and Friendships*	Charles Archer	1931
	The Dramatic Criticism of William Archer	Hans Schmid	1964

179

Subject	Title	Author	Date
MRS. ELIZABETH ARIA	*My Sentimental Self*		1922
GEORGE ARLISS	*On the Stage*		1928
	George Arliss: by Himself		1940
SIR GEORGE ARTHUR	*From Phelps to Gielgud*		1936
OSCAR ASCHE	*Oscar Asche: His Life, by Himself*		1929
LENA ASHWELL	*Modern Troubadours*		1922
	Myself a Player		1936
JOANNA BAILLIE	*Life and Works of Joanna Baillie*	M. S. Corhart New Haven, Connecticut	1923
GEORGE PLEYDELL BANCROFT	*Stage and Bar*		1939
SIR SQUIRE and LADY BANCROFT	*Mr. and Mrs. Bancroft: On and Off the Stage*		1886
	Recollections of Sixty Years		1909
	Empty Chairs	Sir Squire Bancroft	1925
JOHN BANNISTER	*Memoirs of John Bannister, Comedian*	John Adolphus	1838
HARLEY GRANVILLE BARKER	*Harley Granville Barker*	C. B. Purdom	1955
J. H. BARNES	*Forty Years on the Stage*		1914
SIR JAMES BARRIE	*J. M. Barrie and the Theatre*	H. M. Walbrook	1922
	Barrie	F. J. H. Darton	1928
	Barrie	T. Moult	1928
	Barrie: The Story of a Genius	J. A. Hammerton	1929
	J. M. Barrie	W. A. Darlington	1938
	James Matthew Barrie	J. A. Roy New York	1938
	The Story of J.M.B.	Denis Mackail	1941
	Letters of J. M. Barrie	Viola Meynell (Editor)	1942
	J. M. Barrie	Roger Lancelyn Green	1960

Subject	Title	Author	Date
SIR JAMES BARRIE (*continued*)	*J. M. Barrie: the Man behind the Image*	Janet Dunbar	1970
	Sir James Barrie	Harry M. Geduld New York	1971
RUTLAND BARRINGTON	*Rutland Barrington* *More Rutland Barrington*		1908 1911
ISABEL BATEMAN	*From Theatre to Convent: Memories of Mother Isabel Mary, C.S.M.V.*	Various	1936
ARTHUR À BECKETT	*Green Room Recollections*		1896
PAUL BEDFORD	*Recollections and Wanderings*		1864
FRED BELTON	*Random Recollections of an Old Actor*		1880
GIOVANNI BELZONI	*Pharaoh's Fool*	Maurice Willson Disher	1957
LADY (CONSTANCE) BENSON	*Mainly Players*		1926
SIR FRANK BENSON	*My Memoirs*		1930
	Benson and the Bensonians	J. C. Trewin	1960
JOHN BERNARD	*Retrospections of the Stage*	W. B. Bernard (Editor) New York	1830
W. H. WEST BETTY	*An Authentical Biographical sketch of W. H. West Betty*	G. D. Harley	1804
	Memoirs		1848
	The Prodigy	Giles Playfair	1967
GEORGE W. BISHOP	*My Betters*		1957
E. L. BLANCHARD	*Life and Reminiscences*	Clement Scott and Cecil Howard (Editors)	1891
SYDNEY BLOW	*The Ghost Walks on Fridays*		1935
	Through Stage Doors		1958
JESSIE BOND	*Life and Reminiscences*	Ethel MacGeorge	1930

Subject	Title	Author	Date
J. B. BOOTH	*Pink Parade*		1933
	Sporting Times		1938
	The Days We Knew		1943
DION BOUCICAULT	*The Career of Dion Boucicault*	Townsend Walsh	1915 New York
	Dion Boucicault	Robert Hogan	1969 New York
G. V. BROOKE	*The Life of Gustavus Vaughan Brooke*	W. J. Lawrence	1892 Belfast
CHARLES BROOKFIELD	*Random Reminiscences*		1902
THE BROUGH FAMILY	*Prompt Copy: the Brough Story*	Jean Webster Brough	1952
JOHN BROUGHAM	*John Brougham: An Autobiography*	William Winter (Editor) New York	1881
EDWARD BULWER-LYTTON, 1ST BARON LYTTON	*Bulwer and Macready*	Charles H. Shattuck (Editor) Urbana, Illinois	1958
ALFRED BUNN	*The Stage, Both Before and Behind the Curtain*		1840
SIR FRANCIS BURNAND	*Records and Reminiscences*		1904
PERCY BURTON	*Adventures among Immortals*		1938
GEORGE GORDON, LORD BYRON	*Byron and the Theatre*	Boleslaw Taborski	1973 Salzburg
	The Style of Lord Byron's Plays	Pauline M. Lim	1973 Salzburg
	The Major Characters of Lord Byron's Dramas	Allen Percy Whitmore	1974 Salzburg
MRS. CHARLES CALVERT	*Sixty-eight Years on the Stage*	Harold Simpson (Editor)	1911
MRS. PATRICK CAMPBELL	*My Life and Some Letters*		1922
	Bernard Shaw and Mrs. Patrick Campbell: Their Correspondence	Alan Dent (Editor)	1952
	Mrs. Patrick Campbell	Alan Dent	1961

Subject	Title	Author	Date
ALICE COMYNS CARR	Reminiscences	Eve Adams (Editor)	1925
R. D'OYLY CARTE	Gilbert, Sullivan and D'Oyly Carte	François Cellier and C. Bridgeman	1914
JOSEPH A. CAVE	A Jubilee of Dramatic Life and Incident	Robert Soutar (Editor)	1905
ALBERT CHEVALIER	Albert Chevalier, A Record, by Himself	Bryan Daly (Editor)	1895
	Before I Forget		1901
O. B. CLARENCE	No Complaints		1943
WILLIE CLARKSON	The Strange Life of Willie Clarkson	H. J. Greenwall	1936
HAYDEN COFFIN	Hayden Coffin's Book		1930
JOHN COLEMAN	Players and Playwrights I have Known		1888
	Fifty Years of an Actor's Life		1904
CONSTANCE COLLIER	Harlequinade		1929
HORACE F. COLLINS	My Best Riches		1941
GEORGE COLMAN (the younger)	Random Records		1830
	Memoirs of the Colman Family	R. B. Peake	1841
	George Colman, the Younger	J. F. Bagster-Collins New York	1946
HENRY COMPTON	Memoirs	Charles and Edward Compton (Editors)	1879
THE CONQUEST FAMILY	Conquest : The Story of a Theatre Family	F. Fleetwood and B. Conquest	1953
ITALIA CONTI	The Conti Story	Joan Selby-Lowndes	1954
GEORGE FREDERICK COOKE	The Life of George Frederick Cooke	William Dunlap	1813
FREDERICK FOX COOPER	Nothing Extenuate : The Life of Frederick Fox Cooper	F. Renad Cooper	1964

Subject	Title	Author	Date
'CORIN'	The Truth About the Stage		1885
ROBERT COURTNEIDGE	I Was an Actor Once		1930
JOSEPH COWELL	Thirty Years among the Players of England and America		1845
EDITH CRAIG	'Edy': Recollections of Edith Craig	Eleanor Adlard (Editor)	1949
EDWARD GORDON CRAIG	Gordon Craig and the Theatre	Enid Rose	1931
	Edward Gordon Craig	Janet Leeper	1949
	Index to the Story of My Days		1957
	Edward Gordon Craig	Denis Bablet trans. Daphne Woodward	1966
	Gordon Craig: The Story of his Life	Edward Craig	1968
J. RUSSELL CRAUFORD	Ramblings of an Old Mummer		1909
WILLIAM CRESWICK	An Autobiography		1885
CHARLOTTE CUSHMAN	Bright Particular Star: the Life and Times of Charlotte Cushman	Joseph Leach	1972 New Haven, Connecticut
W. C. DAY	Behind the Footlights		1885
THOMAS J. DIBDIN	Reminiscences		1827
CHARLES DIBDIN (the younger)	Professional and Literary Memoirs	George Speaight (Editor)	1956
WALTER DONALDSON	Recollections of an Actor		1865
ALBERT DOUGLASS	Memories of Mummers and the Old Standard Theatre		1924
	Footlight Reflections		1934
SIR GERALD DU MAURIER	Gerald: A Portrait	Daphne Du Maurier	1934

Subject	Title	Author	Date
THE EAST FAMILY	'Neath the Mask: The Story of the East Family	John M. East	1967
W. G. ELIOT	In My Anecdotage		1925
'MISS ELLERSLIE'	The Diary of an Actress	H. C. Shuttleworth (Editor)	1885
R. W. ELLISTON	The Life and Enterprises of Robert William Elliston	George Raymond	1844
	Robert William Elliston, Manager	Christopher Murray	1975
THOMAS W. ERLE	Letters from a Theatrical Scene-Painter		1880
E. C. EVERARD	Memoirs of an Unfortunate Son of Thespis		1818
ELIZABETH FAGAN ('ELIZABETH KIRBY')	From the Wings		1922
SIDNEY FAREBROTHER	Through an Old Stage Door		1937
HELENA FAUCIT	Helena Faucit	Sir Theodore Martin	1900
CHARLES FECHTER	Charles A. Fechter	Kate Field	1882
EDWARD FITZBALL	Thirty-five Years of a Dramatic Author's Life		1859
CHARLES FROHMAN	Charles Frohman: Manager and Man	Isaac F. Marcosson and Daniel Frohman	1916
JOHN GALSWORTHY	John Galsworthy	Sheila Kaye-Smith	1916
	John Galsworthy as a Dramatic Artist	R. H. Coats	1926
	John Galsworthy: A Survey	Leon Schatit	1929
	John Galsworthy	Herman Ould	1934
	Life and Letters of John Galsworthy	H. V. Marrot	1935
	John Galsworthy	Catherine Dupré	1975
ROBERT GANTHONY	Random Recollections		1898

Subject	Title	Author	Date
SIR W. S. GILBERT	The Savoy Opera	Percy Fitzgerald	1894
	W. S. Gilbert	Edith A. Browne	1907
	Gilbert, Sullivan and D'Oyly Carte	François Cellier and C. Bridgeman	1914
	The Gilbert and Sullivan Opera	H. M. Walbrook	1922
	W. S. Gilbert, His Life and Works	Sidney Dark and Rowland Grey	1923
	The Story of the Savoy Opera	S. J. A. Fitzgerald	1924
	The Story of Gilbert and Sullivan	Isaac Goldberg	1929
	Gilbertian Characters	G. Lambton	1931
	Gilbert and Sullivan	Hesketh Pearson	1935
	The World of Gilbert and Sullivan	W. A. Darlington	1950
	Gilbert and Sullivan	Arthur Jacobs	1951
	The Gilbert and Sullivan Book	Leslie Baily	1952
	Gilbert and Sullivan Opera	Audrey Williamson	1953
	Gilbert: His Life and Strife	Hesketh Pearson	1957
	The Gilbert and Sullivan Book (revised edition)	Leslie Baily	1957
	A Picture History of Gilbert and Sullivan	Raymond Mander and Joe Mitchenson (Editors)	1962
	The First Night Gilbert and Sullivan	Reginald Allen New York	1963
	Gilbert before Sullivan	Jane W. Stedman (Editor) Chicago	1967
	W. S. Gilbert: A Century of Scholarship and Commentary	John Bush Jones (Editor) New York	1970
	Gilbert and Sullivan: Papers Presented at the Kansas Conference	James Helyar (Editor) Lawrence, Kansas	1971
	The Gilbert and Sullivan Companion	Leslie Ayre	1972
	The Osprey Guide to Gilbert and Sullivan	Michael Hardwick Reading	1972

Subject	Title	Author	Date
SIR W. S. GILBERT (continued)	Gilbert and Sullivan and their World	Leslie Baily	1973
	W. S. Gilbert	Max Keith Sutton	1975 Boston
	Gilbert and Sullivan. Lost Cords and Discords	Caryl Brahms	1975
HARLEY GRANVILLE-BARKER	Bernard Shaw's Letters to Granville-Barker	C. B. Purdom (Editor)	1957
	A Drama of Political Man	Margery M. Morgan	1961
J. M. GLOVER	Jimmy Glover: His Book		1911
	Jimmy Glover and His Friends		1913
	Hims: Ancient and Modern		1926
J. F. GRAHAM	An Old Stock-Actor's Memories		1930
GEORGE GRAVES	Gaieties and Gravities		1931
SIR PHILIP BEN GREET	Ben Greet and the Old Vic	Winifred F. E. C. Isaac	1964
J. T. GREIN	J. T. Grein: The Story of a Pioneer	Michael Orme	1936
	J. T. Grein: Ambassador of the Theatre, 1862–1935	N. H. G. Schoonderwoerd	1963 Assen
JOSEPH GRIMALDI	Memoirs of Joseph Grimaldi	Charles Dickens (Editor)	1838
	Life of Joseph Grimaldi	H. D. Miles	1939
	Grimaldi	Richard Findlater	1955
	Memoirs, edited by Charles Dickens	Revised by Richard Findlater	1968
GEORGE GROSSMITH (the elder)	A Society Clown: Reminiscences		1888
	Piano and I		1910
WEEDON GROSSMITH	From Studio to Stage		1912
COSMO HAMILTON	Unwritten History		1924

Subject	Title	Author	Date
F. C. VERNON HARCOURT	From Stage to Cross		1902
SIR JOHN HARE	John Hare, Comedian	T. Edgar Pemberton	1895
JOSEPH HARKER	Studio and Stage		1924
FRANK HARRIS	Frank Harris	Hugh Kingsmill Lunn New York	1932
	My Life and Loves		1964
SIR JOHN MARTIN HARVEY	Martin Harvey: Some Pages of His Life	George Edgar	1912
	The Book of Martin Harvey		1930
	The Autobiography of Sir John Martin Harvey		1933
	The Last Romantic	M. Willson Disher	1948
SIR CHARLES HAWTREY	The Truth at Last	W. Somerset Maugham (Editor)	1924
H. G. HIBBERT	Fifty Years of a Londoner's Life		1916
	A Playgoer's Memories		1920
SIR SEYMOUR HICKS	Twenty-four Years of an Actor's Life		1910
	Between Ourselves		1930
	Night Lights		1938
	Me and My Missus		1939
	Vintage Years		1943
THOMAS HOLCROFT	Memoirs	Continued by William Hazlitt	1816
JOHN HOLLINGSHEAD	Footlights		1883
	My Lifetime		1895
	Gaiety Chronicles		1898
	Good Old Gaiety		1903
THE HONRI FAMILY	Peter Honri Presents	Peter Honri Farnborough	1973
MISS A. E. F. HORNIMAN	Miss Horniman and the Gaiety Theatre, Manchester	Rex Pogson	1952

Subject	Title	Author	Date
MISS A. E. F. HORNIMAN *(continued)*	*Miss Annie F. Horniman and the Abbey Theatre, Dublin*	James W. Flannery	1971 Dublin
J. BANNISTER HOWARD	*Fifty Years a Showman*		1938
KEBLE HOWARD	*My Motley Life*		1927
J. B. HOWE	*A Cosmopolitan Actor*		1886
P. HUTCHINSON	*Masquerade*		1936
ELIZABETH INCHBALD	*Memoirs of Mrs. Inchbald*	James Boaden	1833
	Elizabeth Inchbald and Her Circle	S. R. Littlewood	1921
SIR HENRY IRVING	*Irving as Hamlet*	Sir Edward Russell	1875
	The Fashionable Tragedian	William Archer and R. W. Lowe	1877
	Henry Irving, Actor and Manager	William Archer	1883
	Henry Irving, Actor and Manager	'Irvingite' (Frank A. Marshall)	1883
	Henry Irving : A Short Account of his Public Life		1883
	Henry Irving's Impressions of America	Joseph Hatton	1884
	Henry Irving in England and America	Frederick Daly	1884
	Henry Irving	Austin Brereton	1884
	Henry Irving : A Record of Twenty Years at the Lyceum	Percy Fitzgerald	1895
	Sir Henry Irving	Percy Russell	1895
	From 'The Bells' to 'King Arthur'	Clement Scott	1896
	Sir Henry Irving	Walter Calvert	1897
	Henry Irving : A Record and Review	Charles Hiatt	1899
	Some Notes for a Life of Henry Irving	Joseph Hatton	1902

Subject	Title	Author	Date
SIR HENRY IRVING (continued)	The Lyceum and Henry Irving	Austin Brereton	1903
	Sir Henry Irving	Haldane MacFall	1905
	Henry Irving	Austin Brereton	1905
	Henry Irving	Christopher St. John	1905
	Henry Irving	Mortimer Menpes	1906
	Personal Reminiscences of Henry Irving	Bram Stoker	1906
	Impressions of Henry Irving	W. H. Pollock	1908
	Life of Henry Irving	Austin Brereton	1908
	Henry Irving	E. Gordon Craig	1930
	The Shadow of Henry Irving	Henry Arthur Jones	1931
	We Saw Him Act	H. A. Saintsbury (Editor)	1939
	Henry Irving	Laurence Irving	1951
	Henry Irving and the Victorian Theatre	Madeleine Bingham	1978
H. B. IRVING	H. B. Irving	Mabel E. Wotton	1912
	'H.B.' and Laurence Irving	Austin Brereton	1922
LAURENCE IRVING	'H.B.' and Laurence Irving	Austin Brereton	1922
THE IRVING FAMILY	The Successors	Laurence Irving	1967
JEROME K. JEROME	On the Stage and Off		1885
	My Life and Times		1926
DOUGLAS JERROLD	Douglas Jerrold: Dramatist and Wit	Walter Jerrold	1914
	Douglas Jerrold	Richard M. Kelly New York	1972
HENRY ARTHUR JONES	Henry Arthur Jones	P. Shorey	1925
	Life and Letters of Henry Arthur Jones	Doris Arthur Jones	1930
	Henry Arthur Jones and Modern Drama	R. A. Cordell New York	1932

Subject	Title	Author	Date
DOROTHY JORDAN	Life of Mrs. Jordan	James Boaden	1831
	The Public and Private Life of Mrs. Jordan		c. 1833
	Mrs. Jordan	P. W. Serjeant	1913
	The Story of Dorothy Jordan	Clare Jerrold	1914
	Mrs. Jordan and Her Family	A. Aspinall (Editor)	1951
	Mrs. Jordan: Portrait of an Actress	Brian Fothergill	1965
JAMES JUPP	The Gaiety Stage Door		1923
WHITFORD KANE	Are We All Met?		1931
CHARLES KEAN	Life and Theatrical Times of Charles Kean	J. W. Cole	1859
	Emigrant in Motley: Unpublished Letters of Charles and Ellen Kean	J. M. D. Hardwick (Editor)	1954
EDMUND KEAN	Life of Edmund Kean	Barry Cornwall	1835
	Life of Edmund Kean	F. W. Hawkins	1869
	Life and Adventures of Edmund Kean	J. Fitzgerald Molloy	1881
	Edmund Kean	N. H. Hillebrand	1933 New York
	Kean	Giles W. Playfair	1939
	The Sun's Bright Child	Julius Berstl	1946
	Mad Genius	M. Willson Disher	1950
	Edmund Kean: Fire from Heaven	Raymond Fitzsimmons	1976
JOHN KEATS	The English Theatre and John Keats	Harry R. Beaudry	1973 Salzburg
ROBERT and MARY ANNE KEELEY	The Keeleys on the Stage and at Home	Walter Goodman	1895
FANNY KELLY	Lamb's 'Barbara S.' The Life of Frances Maria Kelly	L. E. Holman	1935
	Fanny Kelly of Drury Lane	Basil Francis	1950
CHARLES KEMBLE	Charles Kemble: Man of the Theatre	Jane Williamson	1970 Lincoln, Nebraska

Subject	Title	Author	Date
FANNY KEMBLE	*Journal of Frances Anne Kemble*		1835
	Records of a Girlhood		1835
	Records of Later Life		1878
	Fanny Kemble, Actress	Dorothy de Bear Bobbé	1932
	Fanny Kemble	L. S. Driver Chapel Hill, N.C.	1933
	Fanny Kemble	M. N. Armstrong	1938
	Affectionately Yours, Fanny	Henry Gibbs	1947
	Fanny Kemble	Robert Rushmore New York	1970
	Fanny, the American Kemble. Her Journals and Unpublished Letters	Fanny Kemble Wirth (Editor) Tallahassee, Florida	1972
	Fanny Kemble and the Lovely Land	Constance Wright New York	1972
	Fanny Kemble	Dorothy Marshall	1977
JOHN PHILIP KEMBLE	*Life of John Philip Kemble*		1809
	An Authentic Narrative of Mr. Kemble's Retirement from the Stage		1817
	Memoirs of John Philip Kemble	John Ambrose Williams	1817
	Memoirs of the Life of John Philip Kemble	James Boaden	1825
	John Philip Kemble : The Actor in His Theatre	Herschel Baker Cambridge, Mass.	1942
THE KEMBLE FAMILY	*The Kembles : An Account of the Kemble Family*	Percy Fitzgerald	1871
DAME MADGE KENDAL	*Dramatic Opinions*		1890
	Dame Madge Kendal, by Herself	Rudolph de Cordova (Editor)	1933
W. H. and DAME MADGE KENDAL	*The Kendals : A Biography*	T. Edgar Pemberton	1900
BART KENNEDY	*Footlights*		1928

Subject	Title	Author	Date
FRED KERR	Recollections of a Defective Memory		1930
NELSON KEYES	'Bunch': A Biography of Nelson Keyes	John Paddy Carstairs	1941
GERTRUDE KINGSTON	Curtsey While You're Thinking		1937
EDWARD KNOBLOCK	Round the Room		1933
JAMES SHERIDAN KNOWLES	The Life of James Sheridan Knowles	Richard Brinsley Knowles	1872
	Sheridan Knowles and the Theatre of His Time	Leslie H. Meeks Bloomington, Indiana	1933
MATHESON LANG	Mr. Wu Looks Back		1940
LILLIE LANGTRY	Days I Knew		1921
	The Gilded Lily: The Life and Loves of the Fabulous Lily Langtry	Ernest Dudley	1958
	Lillie Langtry	Noel B. Gerson	1972
	The Prince and the Lily	James Brough	1975
MARK LEMON	Reminiscences of Mark Lemon	Joseph Hatton	1872
	Mark Lemon, First Editor of 'Punch'	Adrian A. Arthur Norman, Oklahoma	1965
DAN LENO	Dan Leno: Hys Booke		1899
	Dan Leno	J. Hickory Wood	1905
FRED LESLIE	Recollections of Fred Leslie	W. T. Vincent	1894
W. H. LEVERTON	Through the Box-Office Window: Memories of Fifty Years at the Haymarket	W. H. Leverton and J. B. Booth	1932
CHARLES LEE LEWES	Memoirs of Charles Lee Lewes		1805
MATTHEW ('MONK') LEWIS	The Life of Matthew Gregory Lewis	H. Colburn	1831
	A Life of Matthew Gregory Lewis	Louis F. Peck Cambridge, Mass.	1961

Subject	Title	Author	Date
LEON M. LION	*The Surprise of My Life*		1938
MARIE LLOYD	*Our Marie*	Naomi Jacob	1936
	Marie Lloyd and Music Hall	Daniel Farson	1972
ROBERT LORAINE	*Robert Loraine: Soldier, Actor, Airman*	Winifred Loraine	1938
THE LUPINO FAMILY	*From the Stocks to the Stars*	Stanley Lupino	1934
SIR HENRY A. LYTTON	*The Secrets of a Savoyard*		1922
	A Wandering Minstrel		1933
LILLAH McCARTHY	*Myself and My Friends*		1933
WILLIAM CHARLES MACREADY	*Biography of William C. Macready, Tragedian*	R. H. Littleton	1850
	Macready's Reminiscences	Sir Frederick Pollock (Editor)	1875
	Macready As I Knew Him	Lady Pollock	1884
	William Charles Macready	William Archer	1890
	A Life of William Charles Macready	W. T. Price New York	1894
	Macready	Sir Theodore Martin	1906
	Diaries of William Charles Macready	William Toynbee (Editor)	1912
	Macready	J. C. Trewin	1955
	Bulwer and Macready	Charles H. Shattuck (Editor) Urbana, Illinois	1958
	William Charles Macready: The Eminent Tragedian	Alan S. Downer Cambridge, Mass.	1966
	The Journals of William Charles Macready 1832–1851	J. C. Trewin (Editor)	1968
H. F. MALTBY	*Ring Up the Curtain*		1950
CHARLES MATHEWS (the elder)	*Memoirs of Charles Mathews, Comedian*	Ann Mathews	1838–9
	Forgotten Facts in the Memoirs of Charles Mathews	S. J. Arnold	1839

Subject	Title	Author	Date
	Memoirs of Charles Mathews (abridged edition)	Edmund Yates (Editor)	1860
MRS. CHARLES MATHEWS	*Anecdotes of Actors* *Tea-table Talk*		1844 1857
CHARLES JAMES MATHEWS	*Life of Charles James Mathews*	Charles Dickens, junior (Editor)	1879
C. R. MATURIN	*Charles Robert Maturin: His Life and Works*	N. Idman	1923
CYRIL MAUDE	*The Haymarket Theatre*	Cyril and Ralph Maude	1903
	Behind the Scenes with Cyril Maude		1927
	Worlds Away	Pamela Maude	1964
MARK MELFORD	*Life in a Booth and Something More*		1913
HARRIOT MELLON	*Memoirs of Harriot, Duchess of St. Albans*	Mrs. Cornwell Baron-Wilson	1839
	Memoirs of Miss Mellon, afterwards Duchess of St. Albans		1886
	The Jolly Duchess	C. E. Pearce	1915
ADAH ISAACS MENKEN	*The Naked Lady*	Bernard Falk	1934
	Reckless Lady	Nathaniel S. Fleischer	1941
	Queen of the Plaza: A Biography of Adah Isaacs Menken	Paul Lewis	1964 New York
HERMAN C. MERIVALE	*Bar, Stage and Platform*		1902
JESSIE MILLWARD	*Myself and Others*		1923
RUBY MILLER	*Champagne from my Slipper*		1963
EVA MOORE	*Exits and Entrances*		1923
MARY MOORE	*Charles Wyndham and Mary Moore*	Mary Moore	1925
CHARLES MORTON	*Sixty Years of Stage Service*	W. H. Morton and H. C. Newton	1905

Subject	Title	Author	Date
WILLIAM MORTON	*I Remember*		1934
JOSEPH SHEPHERD MUNDEN	*Memoirs of Joseph Shepherd Munden, Comedian*	T. Shepherd Munden	1844
W. H. MURRAY	*A Memoir of W. H. Murray*		1851
JULIA NEILSON	*This For Remembrance*		1940
ADELAIDE NEILSON	*Lilian Adelaide Neilson*	M. A. De Leine	1881
	Adelaide Neilson	Laura C. Holloway	1885
		New York	
H. CHANCE NEWTON ('CARADOS')	*Cues and Curtain Calls*		1928
JOHN O'KEEFE	*Recollections of the Life of John O'Keefe*		1826
'AN OLD PLAYGOER'	*Random Recollections of the Stage*	P. Hanley	*c.* 1883
'AN OLD STAGER'	*Stage Reminiscences*	Matthew Mackintosh	1866
ELIZA O' NEIL	*Memoirs of Miss O'Neil*	Charles Inigo Jones	1816
LOUIS N. PARKER	*Several of My Lives*		1928
'PETER PATERSON'	*Confessions of a Strolling Player*	J. G. Bertram	1852
	Glimpses of Real Life	J. G. Bertram	1864
SYDNEY PAXTON	*Stage See-Saws*		1917
HESKETH PEARSON	*Modern Men and Mummers*		1921
F. KINSEY PEILE	*Candied Peel : Tales Without Prejudice*		1931
CHARLES REECE PEMBERTON	*Charles Reece Pemberton*	W. J. Fox and John Fowler (Editors)	1843
W. S. PENLEY	*Penley on Himself*		1896 Bristol
SAMUEL PHELPS	*Life of Samuel Phelps*	Fitzgerald	1846
	Memoirs of Samuel Phelps	John and Edward Coleman	1886

Subject	Title	Author	Date
SAMUEL PHELPS (*continued*)	*Life and Lifework of Samuel Phelps*	W. May Phelps and J. Forbes Robertson	1886
	Samuel Phelps and Sadler's Wells Theatre	Shirley S. Allen Middletown, Connecticut	1971
F. C. PHILLIPS	*My Varied Life*		1914
WATTS PHILLIPS	*Watts Phillips: Artist and Playwright*	E. Watts Phillips	1891
SIR A. W. PINERO	*Arthur Wing Pinero*	H. Hamilton Fyfe	1902
	Sir Arthur Pinero's Plays and Players	H. Hamilton Fyfe	1930
	Sir Arthur Pinero	W. D. Dunkel Chicago	1941
	Arthur Wing Pinero	Walter Lazenby New York	1972
	The Collected Letters of Sir Arthur Pinero	J. P. Wearing (Editor) Minneapolis	1974
JAMES ROBINSON PLANCHÉ	*Recollections and Reflections*		1872
WILLIAM POEL	*William Poel and His Stage Productions*		1932
	William Poel and the Elizabethan Revival	Robert Speaight	1954
JOHN POOLE	*Sketches and Recollections*		1835
NANCY PRICE	*Shadows on the Hills*		1938
CHARLES READE	*Charles Reade*	John Coleman	1903
	Charles Reade	Malcolm Elwin	1931
	Charles Reade: A Study in Victorian Authorship	Wayne Burns New York	1961
ADA REEVE	*Take It For a Fact*		1954
JOHN REEVE	*Life of John Reeve*	Douglas Banister	1838
	The Late John Reeve	W. Leman Rede	1838
WYBERT REEVE	*From Life*		1892
FREDERICK REYNOLDS	*Life and Times of Frederick Reynolds*		1826
	A Playwright's Adventures		1831

Subject	Title	Author	Date
SAMUEL WILLIAM RILEY	*The Itinerant*		1808, 1816–17, 1827
ARTHUR ROBERTS	*Adventures of Arthur Roberts*		1896
	Fifty Years of Spoof		1927
SIR JOHNSTON FORBES ROBERTSON	*A Player Under Three Reigns*		1925
T. W. ROBERTSON	*Memoir* in *Principal Dramatic Works of T. W. Robertson*	T. W. Robertson (the younger)	1889
	Life and Writings of T. W. Robertson	T. Edgar Pemberton	1893
	T. W. Robertson: His Plays and Stagecraft	Maynard Savin Providence, Rhode Island	1950
W. GRAHAM ROBERTSON	*Time Was*		1931
ELIZABETH ROBINS	*Theatre and Friendship*		1932
	Both Sides of the Curtain		1940
FREDERICK ROBSON	*Robson: A Sketch*	G. A. Sala	1864
WILLIAM ROBSON	*The Old Playgoer*		1846
PHILIP RODWAY	*Philip Rodway and a Tale of Two Theatres*	Phyllis Rodway and L. H. Slingsby Birmingham	1934
RICHARD RYAN	*Dramatic Table Talk*		1825
GEORGE AUGUSTUS SALA	*Life and Adventures*		1894
CLEMENT SCOTT	*Thirty Years at the Play*		1892
	Old Days in Bohemian London: Recollections of Clement Scott	Margaret Clement Scott	1919
GEORGE BERNARD SHAW	*George Bernard Shaw: His Plays*	H. L. Mencken	1905
	Bernard Shaw	Holbrook Jackson	1907
	George Bernard Shaw	G. K. Chesterton	1910

Subject	Title	Author	Date
GEORGE BERNARD SHAW (*continued*)	*Bernard Shaw: His Life and Works*	Archibald Henderson	1911
	The Quintessence of Bernard Shaw	H. C. Duffin	1920
	Bernard Shaw	Edward Shanks	1924
	Shaw	J. S. Collis	1925
	Ellen Terry and Bernard Shaw (The Shaw-Terry Letters)	Christopher St. John (Editor)	1930
	Bernard Shaw	Frank Harris	1931
	Bernard Shaw: His Life and Personality	Hesketh Pearson	1948
	Sixteen Self-Sketches		1949
	The Real Bernard Shaw	Maurice Colbourne	1949
	Shaw	C. E. M. Joad	1949
	The Universe of G.B.S.	W. Irvine	1949 New York
	Bernard Shaw	Eric Bentley	1950
	A Good Man Fallen Among Fabians	Alick West	1950
	Shaw	Sir Desmond McCarthy	1951
	Bernard Shaw	A. C. Ward	1951
	Bernard Shaw	R. F. Rattray	1951
	Thirty Years with G.B.S.	Blanche Patch	1951
	G.B.S.: A Postscript	Hesketh Pearson	1951
	Bernard Shaw and Mrs. Patrick Campbell: Their Correspondence	Alan Dent (Editor)	1952
	Bernard Shaw	St. John Ervine	1956
	Bernard Shaw: Man of the Century	Archibald Henderson	1956
	Bernard Shaw: Advice to a Young Critic	E. J. West (Editor)	1956
	Jesting Apostle: The Private life of Bernard Shaw	Stephen Winsten	1956
	Bernard Shaw 1856–1950 (revised edition)	Eric Bentley	1957 New York
	Bernard Shaw's Letters to Granville-Barker	C. B. Purdom (Editor)	1957

Subject	Title	Author	Date
GEORGE BERNARD SHAW (continued)	Bernard Shaw and the Nineteenth Century Tradition	Julian B. Kaye Norman, Oklahoma	1958
	Shaw on Theatre	E. J. West (Editor) New York	1958
	Shaw the Villager and Human Being	Allan Chappelow	1961
	How to Become a Musical Critic	Dan H. Laurence (Editor)	1961
	Bernard Shaw: His Life and Personality (revised edition)	Hesketh Pearson	1961
	Shaw: the Style and the Man	Richard M. Ohmann Middletown, Connecticut	1962
	Bernard Shaw: A Pictorial Biography	Margaret Shenfield	1962
	The Loves of George Bernard Shaw	C. G. L. Ducann	1963
	G.B.S. and the Lunatic	Lawrence Langner New York	1963
	Shaw and the Nineteenth Century Theatre	Martin Meisel	1963
	A Guide to the Plays of Bernard Shaw	C. B. Purdom	1963
	Private Shaw and Public Shaw	Stanley Weintraub	1963
	Bernard Shaw: Man and Writer	Audrey Williamson	1963
	George Bernard Shaw	H. E. Woodbridge Carbondale, Illinois	1963
	Shaw of Dublin: The Formative Years	B. C. Rosset University Park, Pennsylvania	1964
	G. B. Shaw: A Collection of Critical Essays	R. J. Kauffman Englewood Cliffs, New Jersey	1965
	Bernard Shaw: Collected Letters Vol. I 1874–1897	Dan H. Laurence (Editor)	1965
	Shaw and the Charlatan Genius	John O'Donovan	1965

Subject	Title	Author	Date
GEORGE BERNARD SHAW (continued)	The Unrepentant Pilgrim	J. Percy Smith	1965
	Shaw in his Time	Ivor Brown	1967
	The Shaws of Synge Street	John O'Donovan Dixon, California	1966
	Bernard Shaw and the Theatre in the Nineties	Harold Fromm Lawrence, Kansas	1967
	Bernard Shaw and the Arts of Destroying Ideals	C. Carpenter Madison, Wis.	1969
	Shaw, the Dramatist	Louis Crompton Lincoln, Neb.	1969
	Shaw	A. M. Gibbs Edinburgh	1969
	Shaw : A Reassessment	Colin Wilson	1969
	Shaw, An Autobiography Vol. I 1856–1898	Stanley Weintraub (Editor)	1969
	Vol. II 1898–1950 : The Playwright Years		1970
	Bernard Shaw, Director	Bernard Dukore	1971
	Bernard Shaw : Playwright and Preacher	L. Hugo	1971
	Bernard Shaw : Collected Letters Vol. II 1898–1910	Dan H. Laurence (Editor)	1972
	The Shavian Playground	Margery M. Morgan	1972
	Victorian Stage Puppeteer. Bernard Shaw's Crusade	Alan P. Barr	1973
	Bernard Shaw and the Art of the Drama	Charles A. Berst Urbana, Illinois	1973
	The Bernard Shaw Companion	Michael and Mollie Hardwick	1973
	The Cart and the Trumpet : the Plays of George Bernard Shaw	Maurice Valency	1973
	Bernard Shaw : Pygmalion to Many Players	Vincent Wall Ann Arbor, Michigan	1973
	The Marriage of Contraries : Bernard Shaw's Middle Plays	J. L. Wisenthal Cambridge, Mass.	1974

Subject	Title	Author	Date
GEORGE BERNARD SHAW (*continued*)	*George Bernard Shaw's Historical Plays*	R. N. Roy	1977
	Fabian Feminist: Bernard Shaw and Women	R. Weintraub	1977
GEORGE SHELTON	*It's Smee*		1928
RICHARD BRINSLEY SHERIDAN	*Memoirs of Richard Brinsley Sheridan*	William Hone	1816
	Memoirs of the Public and Private Life of R. B. Sheridan	John Watkins	1818
	Memoirs of the Rt. Hon. Richard Brinsley Sheridan	Thomas Moore	1825
	Memoir of Mr. Sheridan	William Smythe	1840
	Sheridan	Walter Sichel	1909
	Sheridan: A Ghost Story	E. M. Butler	1931
	Sheridan	W. A. Darlington	1933
	Harlequin Sheridan	R. Crompton Rhodes	1933
	Sheridan of Drury Lane	Alice Glasgow New York	1940
	Sheridan	Lewis Gibbs	1947
	The Letters of Richard Brinsley Sheridan	Cecil Price (Editor)	1966
SARAH SIDDONS	*Memoirs of Mrs. Siddons*	James Boaden	1827
	Life of Mrs. Siddons	Thomas Campbell	1834
	Mrs. Siddons	Nina A. Kennard	1887
	The Incomparable Siddons	Mrs. Clement Parsons	1909
	The Private Life of Mrs. Siddons	Naomi Royde-Smith	1931
	Mrs. Siddons, Tragic Actress	Yvonne French	1936
	Mrs. Siddons	Roger Manvell	1970
	A Troubled Grandeur: The Story of England's Great Actress, Mrs. Siddons	Marian Jonson Boston, Mass.	1972

Subject	Title	Author	Date
GEORGE R. SIMS	*My Life*		1917
ALBERT SMITH	*The Baron of Piccadilly. The Travels and Entertainments of Albert Smith 1816–1860*	Raymond Fitzsimmons	1967
EMILY SOLDENE	*My Theatrical and Musical Recollections*		1897
E. A. SOTHERN	*Edward Askew Sothern: A Memoir*	T. Edgar Pemberton	1889
EDWARD STIRLING	*Old Drury Lane*		1881
FANNY STIRLING	*The Stage Life of Mrs. Stirling*	Percy Allen	1922
BRAM STOKER	*The Man Who Wrote Dracula: A Biography of Bram Stoker*	Daniel Farson	1975
SIR ARTHUR SULLIVAN	*The Savoy Opera*	Percy Fitzgerald	1894
	Gilbert, Sullivan and D'Oyly Carte	François Cellier and C. Bridgeman	1914
	The Gilbert and Sullivan Opera	H. M. Walbrook	1922
	The Story of the Savoy Opera	S. J. A. Fitzgerald	1924
	Gilbert and Sullivan	A. H. Godwin	1926
	Sir Arthur Sullivan	Herbert Sullivan and Newman Flower	1928
	The Story of Gilbert and Sullivan	Isaac Goldberg	1929
	Gilbert and Sullivan	Hesketh Pearson	1935
	The World of Gilbert and Sullivan	W. A. Darlington	1950
	Gilbert and Sullivan	Arthur Jacobs	1951
	The Gilbert and Sullivan Book	Leslie Baily	1952
	Gilbert and Sullivan Opera	Audrey Williamson	1953
	The Gilbert and Sullivan Book (revised edition)	Leslie Baily	1957

Subject	Title	Author	Date
SIR ARTHUR SULLIVAN (continued)	A Picture History of Gilbert and Sullivan	Raymond Mander and Joe Mitchenson (Editors)	1962
	The First Night Gilbert and Sullivan	Reginald Allen New York	1963
	Gilbert and Sullivan: Papers Presented at the Kansas Conference	James Helyar (Editor) Lawrence, Kansas	1971
	Sir Arthur Sullivan	Percy M. Young	1971
	The Gilbert and Sullivan Companion	Leslie Ayre	1972
	The Osprey Guide to Gilbert and Sullivan	Michael Hardwick Reading	1972
	Gilbert and Sullivan and their World	Leslie Baily	1973
	Gilbert and Sullivan. Lost Cords and Discords	Caryl Brahms	1975
BARRY SULLIVAN	Barry Sullivan	W. J. Lawrence	1893
	Barry Sullivan and His Contemporaries	Robert Sillard	1901
ALFRED SUTRO	Celebrities and Simple Souls		1933
HERBERT SWEARS	When All's Said and Done		1937
TOM TAYLOR	Tom Taylor and the Victorian Drama	Winton Tolles New York	1940
MARIE TEMPEST	Marie Tempest: Her Biography	Hector Bolitho	1936
ELLALINE TERRISS	Ellaline Terris, by Herself		1928
	A Little Piece of String		1955
WILLIAM TERRISS	The Life of William Terriss, Actor	Arthur J. Smythe	1898
ELLEN TERRY	Miss Ellen Terry	Walter Calvert	1897
	Ellen Terry and Her Impersonations	Charles Hiatt	1898
	Ellen Terry: An Appreciation	Clement Scott New York	1900
	Ellen Terry and Her Sisters	T. Edgar Pemberton	1902

Subject	Title	Author	Date
ELLEN TERRY (*continued*)	*Ellen Terry*	Christopher St. John	1907
	The Story of My Life		1908
	The Heart of Ellen Terry		1928
	Ellen Terry and Bernard Shaw (The Shaw-Terry Letters)	Christopher St. John (Editor)	1930
	Ellen Terry and Her Secret Self	E. Gordon Craig	1931
	Ellen Terry's Memoirs	Edith Craig and Christopher St. John (Editors)	1933
	Ellen Terry	Roger Manvell	1968
	Bright Star: A Portrait of Ellen Terry	Constance Fechter New York	1970
	Lover or Nothing: The Life and Times of Ellen Terry	Tom Prideaux	1976
THE TERRY FAMILY	*A Pride of Terrys*	Marguerite Steen	1962
ERNEST THESIGER	*Practically True*		1927
JOHN TOBIN	*Memoirs of John Tobin*	Miss Benger	1820
J. L. TOOLE	*Reminiscences of J. L. Toole*	Joseph Hatton (Editor)	1889
SIR HERBERT TREE	*Herbert Beerbohm Tree*	Mrs. George Cran	1907
	Herbert Beerbohm Tree	Max Beerbohm and others	1920
	Beerbohm Tree: His Life and Laughter	Hesketh Pearson	1956
VIOLA TREE	*Castles in the Air*		1926
MRS. ALEC TWEEDIE	*Behind the Footlights*		1904
IRENE VANBRUGH	*To Tell My Story*		1948
VIOLET VANBRUGH	*Dare to be Wise*		1925
GEORGE VANDENHOFF	*Dramatic Reminiscences*	H. S. Carleton (Editor)	1860
	An Actor's Notebook		1865
MADAME VESTRIS	*Madame Vestris and Her Times*	C. E. Pearce	1923

Subject	Title	Author	Date
MADAME VESTRIS (continued)	The Witch of Wych Street	L. Waitzkin Cambridge, Mass.	1933
	Madame Vestris: A Theatrical Biography	Clifford John Williams	1973
	Madame Vestris and the London Stage	William Appleton New York	1974
JAMES W. WALLACK	A Sketch of the Life of James William Wallack	T. H. Morell New York	1865
GENEVIEVE WARD	Genevieve Ward	Z. B. Gustafson	1881
	Both Sides of the Curtain	Genevieve Ward and R. Whiteing	1918
ALFRED WAREING	Alfred Wareing	Winifred F. E. C. Isaac	1951
THE WEBSTER FAMILY	The Same, Only Different: Four Generations of a Great Theatre Family	Margaret Webster	1969
RALPH WEWITZER	Dramatic Reminiscences		c. 1812
SAMUEL WILD	'Old Wild's': A Nursery of Strolling Players	'Trim' (William Broadley Megson)	1888
OSCAR WILDE	Oscar Wilde, a Study	André Gide	1905
	Oscar Wilde	L. C. Ingleby	1907
	Oscar Wilde, Art and Morality	Stuart Mason	1912
	Oscar Wilde	Arthur Ransome	1912
	Oscar Wilde, His Life and Confessions	Frank Harris	1916
	Oscar Wilde	Hesketh Pearson	1948
	Oscar Wilde	St. John Ervine	1951
	Oscar Wilde: A Pictorial Biography	Vyvyan Holland	1960
	The Letters of Oscar Wilde	Rupert Hart-Davies (Editor)	1962
	Oscar Wilde: The Aftermath	H. Montgomery Hyde	1963
	Oscar Wilde, His Life and Confessions (revised edition)	Frank Harris	1965
	Oscar Wilde	Philippe Jullian trans. Violet Wyndham	1969

Subject	Title	Author	Date
OSCAR WILDE (*continued*)	*The Unrecorded Life of Oscar Wilde*	Rupert Croft-Cooke	1972
	Oscar Wilde	Michael Fido	1973
	Oscar Wilde	H. Montgomery Hyde	1976
	Oscar Wilde	Louis Kronenberger Boston, Mass.	1976
	The Plays of Oscar Wilde	A. Bird	1977
	Oscar Wilde: Art and Egotism	R. Shewan	1977
BRANSBY WILLIAMS	*An Actor's Story*		1909
MONTAGUE WILLIAMS	*Leaves of a Life*		1890
W. G. WILLS	*W. G. Wills: Dramatist and Painter*	Freeman Wills	1898
SIR CHARLES WYNDHAM	*Sir Charles Wyndham*	T. Edgar Pemberton	1904
	Sir Charles Wyndham	Florence Shore	1908
	Charles Wyndham and Mary Moore	Mary Moore	1925
EDMUND YATES	*Recollections and Experiences*		1884
	Fifty Years of London Life		1885
CHARLES MAYNE YOUNG	*Charles Mayne Young, Tragedian*	J. C. Young	1871

General Studies

W. DAVENPORT ADAMS	*A Book of Burlesque* (1891)
JAMES AGATE	*A Short View of the English Stage* (1926)
	Those Were the Nights (1947)
REGINALD ALLEN	*W. S. Gilbert: An Anniversary Survey and Exhibition Checklist* (Charlottesville, Virginia, 1964)
C. ANDREWS	*The Drama Today* (1913)
WILLIAM ARCHER	*English Dramatists of Today* (1882)
	About the Theatre (1886)

WILLIAM ARCHER (*continued*)	'The Drama' in *The Reign of Victoria*, edited by Sir A. W. Ward (1887) *Study and Stage: A Yearbook of Criticism* (1899) *The Old Drama and the New* (1923)
C. F. ARMSTRONG	*A Century of Great Actors* (1912) *Shakespeare to Shaw* (1913)
DENNIS ARUNDELL	*The Story of Sadler's Wells* (1965)
V. C. CLINTON BADDELEY	*The Burlesque Tradition in the English Theatre after 1660* (1952) *All Right on the Night* (1954) *Some Pantomime Pedigrees* (1963)
H. BARTON BAKER	*Our Old Actors* (1878) *A History of the London Stage* (1904)
MICHAEL BAKER	*The Rise of the Victorian Actor* (1978)
MAURICE BARING	*Punch and Judy, and Other Essays* (1924)
H. GRANVILLE BARKER	'Exit Planché, Enter Gilbert' in *The Eighteen-Sixties: Essays by Fellows of the Royal Society of Literature*, edited by John Drinkwater (Cambridge, 1932) (Editor): *The Eighteen-Seventies: Essays by Fellows of the Royal Society of Literature* (Cambridge, 1929) 'The Coming of Ibsen' in *The Eighteen-Eighties: Essays by Fellows of the Royal Society of Literature*, edited by Walter de la Mare (Cambridge, 1930)
KATHLEEN BARKER	*The Theatre Royal, Bristol: The First Seventy Years* (Bristol, 1961) *The Theatre Royal, Bristol: Decline and Rebirth 1834–1943* (Bristol, 1966) *The Theatre Royal, Bristol, 1766–1966* (1974) *Bristol At Play* (Bradford-on-Avon, 1976)
LILIAN BAYLIS and CICELY HAMILTON	*The Old Vic* (1926)
MAX BEERBOHM	*Around Theatres* (1924) *More Theatres*, edited by Rupert Hart-Davis (1969) *Last Theatres*, edited by Rupert Hart-Davis (1970)
IAN BEVAN	*Royal Performance* (1954)
FREDERICK BINGHAM	*The History of the Richmond Theatre* (Richmond, Surrey, 1886)
M. E. BOARD	*The Story of the Bristol Stage* (1926)

JOHN BOOTH   *A Century of Theatre History, 1816–1916. The Old Vic* (1917)

MICHAEL R. BOOTH   *English Melodrama* (1965)

MICHAEL R. BOOTH and others   *The Revels History of Drama in English: Vol. VI 1750–1880* (1975)

ROBERT LOUIS BRANNAN   *Under the Management of Mr. Charles Dickens. His Production of 'The Frozen Deep'* (Ithaca, N.Y., 1966)

E. W. BRAYLEY   *Historical and Descriptive Accounts of the Theatres of London* (1826)

W. BRIDGES-ADAMS   'Theatre' in *Edwardian England 1901–1914*, edited by Simon Nowell-Smith (1964)

R. J. BROADBENT   *A History of Pantomime* (1901)
Annals of the Liverpool Stage (Liverpool, 1908)

C. BROWN and H. SIMPSON   *A Century of Famous Actresses, 1750–1850* (1913)

ELUNED BROWN (Editor)   *The London Theatre 1811–1866: Selections from the Diary of Henry Crabb Robinson* (1966)

T. L. G. BURLEY   *Playhouses and Players of East Anglia* (Norwich, 1928)

E. J. BURTON   *The British Theatre: Its Repertory and Practice 1100–1950* (1960)

GEORGE GORDON, LORD BYRON   *'Werner': A Tragedy. A Facsimile of the Acting Version by William Charles Macready.* Introduction by Marvin Spevack (Munich, 1970)

F. W. CHANDLER   *Aspects of Modern Drama* (1915)

D. F. CHESHIRE   *Music Hall in Britain* (Newton Abbott, 1970)

HAROLD CHILD   'Nineteenth Century Drama' in *The Cambridge History of English Literature*, edited by Sir A. W. Ward and A. R. Waller, Vol. XIII (Cambridge, 1916)

ALEC CLUNES   *The British Theatre* (1964)

L. W. CONOLLY   *The Censorship of English Drama 1737–1824* (San Marino, California, 1976)

DUTTON COOKE   *A Book of the Play* (1876)
Hours with the Players (1880)
Nights at the Play (1883)
On the Stage (1883)

WILLIAM COTTON — *The Story of the Drama in Exeter* (1887)

EDWARD GORDON CRAIG — *The Art of the Theatre* (1911)
Towards a New Theatre (1913)

G. CROFT — *Fifty Years of Shakespearean Playgoing* (1940)

J. W. CUNLIFFE — *Modern English Playwrights: A Short History of the English Drama from 1825* (New York, 1927)

ALFRED DARBYSHIRE — *The Art of the Victorian Stage* (1907)

W. A. DARLINGTON — *The Actor and His Audience* (1949)

SYDNEY DARK — *Stage Silhouettes* (1901)

F. J. H. DARTON — *Vincent Crummles, His Theatre and His Times* (1926)

BASIL DEAN — *The Repertory Theatre* (1911)

ERIC DELDERFIELD — *Cavalcade by Candlelight* (Exmouth, 1950)

ALAN DELGADO — *Victorian Entertainment* (Newton Abbott, 1971)

EDWARD J. DENT — *A Theatre for Everybody: The Story of the Old Vic and Sadler's Wells* (1945)

CHARLES DIBDIN (the younger) — *The History and Illustrations of the London Theatres* (1826)

JOHN DIPROSE — *Diprose's Book of the Stage and the Players* (c. 1877)

MAURICE WILLSON DISHER — *Clowns and Pantomimes* (1925)
Blood and Thunder: Mid-Victorian Melodrama and its Origins (1949)
Melodrama (1954)

BRIAN DOBBS — *Drury Lane: Three Centuries of the Theatre Royal* (1972)

FRANCES DONALDSON — *The Actor Managers* (1970)

WALTER DONALDSON — *Theatrical Portraits* (1870)

WILLIAM BODHAM DONNE — *Essays on the Drama* (1863)

JOSEPH W. DONOHUE Jnr. — *Dramatic Character in the English Romantic Age* (Princeton, New Jersey, 1970)
(Editor): *The Theatrical Manager in England and America. Player of a Perilous Game* (Princeton, New Jersey, 1971)
Theatre in the Age of Kean (Oxford, 1975)

JOHN DORAN — *In and About Drury Lane* (1881)

JOHN DORAN and R. W. LOWE — *Their Majesty's Servants: Annals of the English Stage from Thomas Betterton to Edmund Kean* (1888)

ALAN S. DOWNER (Editor) — *'King Richard III': Edmund Kean's Performance as recorded by James H. Hackett* (1958)

ASHLEY DUKES — *Modern Dramatists* (1912)

BARRY DUNCAN — *The St. James's Theatre: Its Strange and Complete History* (1964)

ARTHUR H. ENGELBACH — *Anecdotes of the Theatre* (1914)

B. IFOR EVANS — *A Short History of English Drama* (1948)

EDWARD FAGG — *The Old Old Vic: from Barrymore to Bayliss* (1936)

GERARD FAY — *The Abbey Theatre: Cradle of Genius* (1958)

P. M. A. FILON — *The English Stage*: translated by Frederick Whyte (1897)

RICHARD FINDLATER — *Six Great Actors* (1957)
The Player Kings (1971)
The Player Queens (1976)

PERCY FITZGERALD — *The Romance of the English Stage* (1874)
A Book of Theatrical Anecdotes (1874)
The World Behind the Scenes (1881)
A New History of the English Stage (1882)

RICHARD M. FLETCHER — *English Romantic Drama 1795–1843* (New York, 1966)

HORACE FOOTE — *A Companion to the Theatres and a Manual of the British Drama* (1829)

JOHN FORSTER and GEORGE HENRY LEWES — *Dramatic Essays*, edited by William Archer and R. W. Lowe (1896)

MIRIAM A. FRANC — *Ibsen in England* (1919)

J. GALT — *Lives of the Players* (1886)

PETER GAMMOND — *Your Own, Your Very Own!* (1973)

ROSAMUND GILDER — *Enter the Actress* (1931)

VICTOR GLASSTONE — *Victorian and Edwardian Theatres* (1975)

A. GODDARD — *Players of the Period* (1891)

J. T. GREIN — *Dramatic Criticism* (1899, 1900, 1902, 1904)

ROGER LANCELYN GREEN — *Fifty Years of Peter Pan* (1954)

DAVID GRIMSTEAD — *Melodrama Unveiled* (Chicago, 1968)

ARNOLD HARE — *The Georgian Theatre in Wessex* (1958)

WILLIAM HAZLITT — *A View of the English Stage* (1818)
Dramatic Essays, edited by William Archer and R. W. Lowe (1895)
Liber Amoris and *Dramatic Criticisms* (1948)

A. HENDERSON — *The Changing Drama* (1915)

J. HODGKINSON and REX POGSON — *The Early Manchester Theatre* (1960)

CHARLES BEECHER HOGAN (Editor) — *The London Stage : Part 5 1776–1800*, 3 vols. (Carbondale, Illinois, 1968)

ROBERT HOGAN and MICHAEL J. O'NEIL — *Joseph Holroyd's Abbey Theatre. A Selection from the Unpublished Journal, 'Impressions of a Dublin Playgoer'* (Carbondale, Illinois, 1967)

DIANA HOWARD — *London Theatres and Music Halls 1850–1900* (1970)

PERCEVAL P. HOWE — *The Repertory Theatre* (1910)

LYNTON HUDSON — *The English Stage, 1850–1950* (1951)

LEIGH HUNT — *Critical Essays on the Performers of the London Theatres* (1807)
Dramatic Essays, edited by William Archer and R. W. Lowe (1894)
Dramatic Criticism, 1808–31, edited by L. H. and C. W. Houtchens (1950)

ALAN HYMAN — *The Gaiety Years* (1975)

J. ISAACS (Editor) — *William Poel's Prompt Book of 'Fratricide Punished'* (1956)

HENRY JAMES — *The Scenic Art*, edited by Allan Wade (1949)

RICHARD JENKINS — *Memoirs of the Bristol Stage* (Bristol, 1826)

HENRY ARTHUR JONES — *The Renascence of the English Drama* (1894)

B. L. JOSEPH — *The Tragic Actor* (1959)

STEPHEN JOSEPH — *The Story of the Playhouse in England* (1963)

T. C. KEMP and J. C. TREWIN — *The Stratford Festival* (Birmingham, 1953)

C. L. KENNEY	*Poets and Profits at Drury Lane : a Theatre Narrative Suggested by F. B. Chatterton* (1875)
HENRY KNEPLER	*The Gilded Stage. The Years of the Great International Actresses* (New York, 1966)
JOSEPH KNIGHT	*Theatrical Notes* (1893)
	The History of the English Stage during the Reign of Victoria (Appendix to *The Stage in the Year 1900*) (1901)
DAVID KRAUSE (Editor)	*The Dolmen Boucicault, with an Introduction* (1964)
M. J. LANDA	*The Jew in Drama* (1926)
CHARLES LAMB	*Dramatic Essays*, edited by Brander Matthews (1891)
JACOB LARWOOD	*Theatrical Anecdotes* (1882)
JAMES LAVER	*Drama : Its Costume and Décor* (1951)
JANKO LAVRIN	*Aspects of Modernism from Wilde to Pinero* (1935)
RICHARD LEACROFT	*The Theatre Royal, Leicester 1836–1958* (Leicester, 1958)
	The Development of the English Playhouse (1975)
W. P. LENNOX	*Plays, Players and Playhouses* (1881)
E. LAURENCE LEVY	*Birmingham Theatrical Reminiscences* (Birmingham, 1920)
GEORGE HENRY LEWES	*On Actors and the Art of Acting* (1875)
GEORGE HENRY LEWES and JOHN FORSTER	*Dramatic Essays*, edited by William Archer and R. W. Lowe (1896)
THE MANCHESTER STAGE	*1880–1900* (1900)
RAYMOND MANDER and JOE MITCHENSON (Editors)	*Hamlet Through the Ages* (1952)
	Theatrical Companion to Shaw (1954)
	The Artist and the Theatre (1955)
	Theatrical Companion to Maugham (1955)
	A Picture History of the British Theatre (1957)
	The Theatres of London (1961)
	British Music Hall : A Story in Pictures (1965)
	The Lost Theatres of London (1968)
	Pantomime : A Story in Pictures (1973)
	British Music Hall: Revised Edition (1974)

KARL MANTZIUS   *A History of Theatrical Art in Ancient and Modern Times.* Vol. VI: Classicism and Romanticism; translated by Charles Archer (1921)

J. W. MARRIOTT   *The Theatre* (1931)

NORMAN MARSHALL   *The Producer and the Play* (1957)

THOMAS MARSHALL   *Lives of the Most Celebrated Actors and Actresses* (1848)

WESTLAND MARSTON   *Our Recent Actors* (1888)

GORDON MARTIN   *The Playbill, the Development of its Typographical Style* (Chicago, 1963)

SIR THEODORE MARTIN   *Essays on the Drama* (1st Series, 1874; 2nd Series, 1879)

CYRIL MAUDE   *The Haymarket* (1903)

DAVID MAYER III   *Harlequin in his Element* (Cambridge, Mass., 1969)

SIR DESMOND McCARTHY   *The Court Theatre, 1904–1907* (1907)

SAMUEL McKECHNIE   *Popular Entertainment Through the Ages* (1931)

WILFRED MELLERS   *Harmonious Meeting: A Study of the Relationship between English Music, Poetry and Theatre 1800–1900* (1965)

G. J. MELLOR   *The Northern Music Hall* (Newcastle-on-Tyne, 1970)

ALLAN MONKHOUSE   *Books and Plays* (1894)

C. E. MONTAGUE   *Dramatic Values* (1910)

A. E. MORGAN   *Tendencies of Modern English Drama* (1924)

HENRY MORLEY   *Journal of a London Playgoer, 1851–66* (1891)

MALCOLM MORLEY   *The Old Marylebone Theatre* (1960)
                  The Royal West London Theatre (1962)

MOWBRAY MORRIS   *Essays in Theatrical Criticism* (1882)

DANIEL NALBACH   *The King's Theatre 1704–1867. London's First Opera House* (1972)

ALFRED L. NELSON and GILBERT B. CROSS (Editors)   *Drury Lane Journal: Selections from James Winston's Diaries 1819–1827* (1974)

H. CHANCE NEWTON	*The Old Vic* (1920) *Crime and the Drama* (1927)
WATSON NICHOLSON	*The Struggle for a Free Stage in London* (1906)
ALLARDYCE NICOLL	*A History of English Drama 1660–1900. Vol. III. Late Eighteenth Century Drama:* Revised Edition (Cambridge, 1952) *Vol. IV. Early Nineteenth Century Drama:* Revised Edition (Cambridge, 1955) *Vol. V. Late Nineteenth Century Drama:* Revised Edition (Cambridge, 1959) *Vol. VI. Alphabetical Catalogue of Plays* (Cambridge, 1959) *The English Theatre* (1936) *British Drama:* Revised Edition (1947) *The Development of the Theatre :* Revised Edition (1948) *English Drama 1900–1930. The Beginnings of the Modern Period* (1973)
O. C. D. O'DELL	*Shakespeare from Betterton to Irving* (1921)
TERRY OTTEN	*The Deserted Stage : The Search for Dramatic Form in Nineteenth-Century England* (Athens, Ohio, 1972)
HESKETH PEARSON	*The Last Actor-Managers* (1950)
CAMILLO PELIZZI	*English Drama : the Last Great Phase* (1938)
T. EDGAR PEMBERTON	*The Birmingham Theatres* (Birmingham, 1890) *The Theatre Royal, Birmingham* (Birmingham, 1901) *The Criterion Theatre, 1876–1903* (1903)
BELVILLE S. PENLEY	*The Bath Stage* (1892)
W. MACQUEEN POPE	*Theatre Royal, Drury Lane* (1945) *Carriages at Eleven* (1947) *Haymarket, Theatre of Perfection* (1948) *Gaiety, Theatre of Enchantment* (1949) *Nights of Gladness* (1956) *Give Me Yesterday* (1958) *St. James's : Theatre of Distinction* (1958)
G. RENNIE POWELL	*The Bristol Stage* (Bristol, 1919)

CECIL PRICE — *The English Theatre in Wales* (Cardiff, 1948)

FRANK RAHILL — *The World of Melodrama* (University Park, Pennsylvania, 1967)

TERENCE REES — *'Thespis': A Gilbert Enigma* (1964)

T. MACDONALD RENDLE — *Jubilee of the Vaudeville Theatre* (1920)

ERNEST REYNOLDS — *Early Victorian Drama, 1830–70* (Cambridge, 1936)
Modern English Drama: A Survey of the Theatre from 1900 (1949)

CHARLES RICE — *The London Theatre in the Eighteen-Thirties*, edited by A. C. Sprague and Bertram Shuttleworth (1950)

KENNETH RICHARDS and PETER THOMSON (Editors) — *Nineteenth-Century British Theatre* (1971)

PETER ROBERTS — *The Old Vic Story: A Nation's Theatre 1818–1976* (1976)

CYRIL ROLLINS and R. JOHN WITTS (Editors) — *The D'Oyly Carte Opera Company in Gilbert and Sullivan Operas: A Record of Productions 1875–1961* (1962)

SYBIL ROSENFELD — *A Short History of Scenic Design in Great Britain* (Oxford, 1973)

GEORGE ROWELL — (Editor) *Victorian Dramatic Criticism* (1971)
Queen Victoria Goes To The Theatre (1978)

W. C. RUSSELL — *Representative Actors* (1888)

ST. JAMES'S THEATRE — *A Chronicle* (1900)

NEWELL WHEELER SAWYER — *The Comedy of Manners from Sheridan to Maugham* (Philadelphia, 1931)

ARTHUR H. SAXON — *Enter Foot and Horse: A History of Hippodrama in England and France* (New Haven, 1968)

SIR GEORGE SCHARF — *Recollections of the Scenic Effects of the Covent Garden Theatre* (1838)

CLEMENT SCOTT — *The Drama of Yesterday and Today* (1899)

R. F. SHARP — *A Short History of the English Stage to 1908* (1909)

CHARLES H. SHATTUCK (Editor)	*William Charles Macready's 'King John'* (Urbana, Illinois, 1963) *Mr. Macready Produces 'As You Like It'* (Urbana, Illinois, 1963) *The Shakespeare Prompt Books* (Urbana, Illinois, 1965) *John Philip Kemble Promptbooks: Vol. I: 'All's Well That Ends Well', 'As You Like It', 'The Comedy of Errors'* (Charlottesville, Pennsylvania, 1974)
GEORGE BERNARD SHAW	*Dramatic Opinions and Essays*, selected and introduced by James Huneker with an Introduction by Bernard Shaw (1907) *Our Theatres in the 'Nineties* (1932)
F. H. W. SHEPPARD (Editor)	*The Survey of London. Vol. 35: The Theatre Royal, Drury Lane, and the Royal Opera House, Covent Garden* (1970)
THOMAS SHEPPERD	*The Evolution of the Drama in Hull and District* (Hull, 1927)
ERROL SHERSON	*London's Lost Theatres of the Nineteenth Century* (1925)
ERNEST SHORT	*Theatrical Cavalcade* (1942) *Fifty Years of Vaudeville, 1894–1945* (1946) *Sixty Years of Theatre* (1951)
H. SIMPSON and C. BROWN	*A Century of Famous Actresses, 1750–1850* (1913)
JAMES L. SMITH	*Melodrama* (1973)
RICHARD SOUTHERN	*Changeable Scenery: Its Origin and Development in the British Theatre* (1952) *The Seven Ages of the Theatre* (1962) *The Victorian Theatre: A Pictorial Survey* (Newton Abbott, 1970)
GEORGE SPEAIGHT	*Juvenile Drama* (1946) *The History of the English Toy Theatre* (1969)
ROBERT SPEAIGHT	*Shakespeare on the Stage. An Illustrated History of Shakespearean Performance* (1973)
E. F. SPENCE	*Our Stage and its Critics* (n.d.)
A. C. SPRAGUE	*Shakespearean Players and Performances* (1954)
THE STAGE SOCIETY	*Ten Years of the Incorporated Stage Society, 1899–1909* (1909)

JOHN STOKES   *Resistible Theatres: Enterprise and Experiment in the Late Nineteenth-Century Theatre* (1972)

ARTHUR SYMONS   *Plays, Acting and Music* (1903)

DESMOND SHAWE-TAYLOR   *Covent Garden* (1948)

JOHN RUSSELL TAYLOR   *The Rise and Fall of the Well Made Play* (1967)

F. G. TOMLINS   *A Brief View of the English Drama* (1840)

J. C. TREWIN   *The Theatre Since 1900* (1951)
The Birmingham Repertory Theatre 1913–1963 (1963)
Shakespeare on the English Stage 1900–1964 (1964)
The Pomping Folk in the Nineteenth-Century Theatre (1968)
The Edwardian Theatre (Oxford, 1976)

SIR ST. VINCENT TROUBRIDGE   *The Benefit System in the British Theatre* (1967)

A. NICHOLAS VARDAC   *Stage to Screen: Theatrical Method from Garrick to Griffith* (Cambridge, Mass., 1949)

EDWARD WAGENKNECHT   *Seven Daughters of the Theatre* (Norman, Oklahoma, 1964)
Merely Players: a Great Actor Becomes the Second Author of his Parts by his Accents and his Physiognomy (Norman, Oklahoma, 1967)

A. B. WALKLEY   *Playhouse Impressions* (1892)
Dramatic Criticism (1903)
Drama and Life (1907)

LOU WARWICK   *Theatre Un-Royal. A History of the Theatre, Sometime Royal, Northampton* (Northampton, 1974)
Drama That Smells; or Early Drama in Northampton and Thereabouts (Northampton, 1975)

ERNEST BRADLEE WATSON   *Sheridan to Robertson: A Study of the Nineteenth Century London Stage* (Cambridge, Mass., 1926)

GUY TRACEY WATTS   *Theatrical Bristol* (Bristol, 1915)

J. P. WEARING   *The London Stage 1890–1899. 2 Vols.* (Metuchen, N.J., 1976)

FREDERIC WHYTE   *Actors of the Century* (1898)

HARCOURT WILLIAMS	*Old Vic Saga* (1949)
MICHAEL WILLIAMS	*Some Theatres, Past and Present* (1883)
ROBERT WILKINSON	*Theatrum Illustratum: Graphic and Historic Memorials of Ancient Playhouses, Modern Theatres and Places of Public Amusement* (1825)
A. E. WILSON	*Penny Plain, Twopence Coloured: A History of the Juvenile Drama* (1932) *Christmas Pantomime* (1934) *Pantomime Pageant* (1946) *The Edwardian Theatre* (1951) *The Lyceum* (1952) *East End Entertainment* (1954)
D. FORBES-WINSLOW	*Daly's: The Biography of a Theatre* (1944)
HENRY SAXE-WYNDHAM	*Annals of Covent Garden Theatre* (1905)

Bibliographies and Works of Reference

W. DAVENPORT ADAMS	*A Dictionary of the Drama* (1904). Vol. 1. A-G only; no others published
SILVIO D'AMICO (Editor)	*Enciclopedia della Spettacolo* (Rome, 1954–66)
WILLIAM ARCHER	*The Theatrical World for 1893, 1894, 1895, 1896, 1897* (1894–98)
J. F. ARNOTT and J. W. ROBINSON (Compilers)	*English Theatrical Literature 1559–1900. A Bibliography Incorporating Robert W. Lowe's 'A Bibliographical Account of English Theatrical Literature' Published in 1888* (1970)
BLANCH M. BAKER	*Dramatic Bibliography* (New York, 1933)
LIONEL CARSON (Editor)	*The Stage Guide* (1912)
LIONEL CARSON (Editor) and Others	*The Stage Year Book* (1908–28)
REGINALD CLARENCE (Editor)	*The Stage Cyclopedia* (1909)

L. W. CONOLLY and J. P. WEÁRING (Compilers)	*English Drama and Theatre 1800–1900: a guide to information sources* (Detroit, 1978)

THE DRAMATIC AND MUSICAL DIRECTORY OF THE UNITED KINGDOM (1883–4)

THE DRAMATIC SOUVENIR (1833)

WILLIAM R. DUBOIL	*English and American Stage Productions. An Annotated Checklist of Promptbooks 1800–1900 from the Nisbet-Snyder Collection, Northern Illinois University Libraries* (Boston, Mass., 1973)

THE ENTRACTE ANNUAL (1881–1906)

F. W. FAXON (Editor) and Others	*The Magazine Subject Index* (Part II: The Dramatic Index), Boston, Mass. (1908–continuing)
PHYLLIS HARTNOLL (Editor)	*The Oxford Companion to the Theatre* (1951) *The Oxford Companion to the Theatre* (Revised, illustrated edition, 1964; 3rd edition, 1967) *The Concise Oxford Companion to the Theatre* (1972)
VIOLET KENT (Editor) continued by	*The Player's Library: Catalogue of the Library of the British Drama League* (1930)
MARY GÁRNHAM (Editor)	*The Player's Library* (1950) *First Supplement* (1951) *Second Supplement* (1953) *Third Supplement* (1956)
EDWARD LEDGER (Editor) and Others	*The Era Almanack* (1868–1917)
ALFRED LOEWENBERG (Editor)	*A Bibliography of the Theatres of the British Isles (excluding London)* (1950)
R. W. LOWE	*A Bibliographical Account of English Theatrical Literature* (1888)
BRANDER MATTEWS and LAURENCE HUTTON	*Actors and Actresses of Great Britain and the United States from the Days of David Garrick to the Present Time* (New York, 1886)

BRITISH MUSEUM: CATALOGUE OF ADDITIONS AND MANUSCRIPTS
Plays Submitted to the Lord Chamberlain 1825–1851 (1964)

A. M. NAGLER *Sources of Theatrical History* (New York, 1952)

JOHN PARKER (Editor) *Who's Who in the Theatre* (1912; 16th Edition, 1977)
Originally

and Others *The Green Room Book:* edited by BAMPTON HUNT (1906) and by JOHN PARKER (1907–9)

C. E. PASCOE *The Dramatic List* (1879, 1880)
and Others *Dramatic Notes: A Year Book of the Stage* (1879–93)

ERSKINE REID and *The Dramatic Peerage* (1892)
HERBERT COMPTON

CLEMENT SCOTT (Editor) *The Theatre Annual* (1884–8)

CARL J. A. STRATMAN (Editor) *A Bibliography of British Dramatic Periodicals 1720–1960* (New York, 1962; revised edition, 1972)

STANLEY WELLS (General Editor) *English Drama (excluding Shakespeare). A Select Bibliographical Guide* (1975)

A Selection of Periodicals

The Drama, 1821–5

The Dramatic and Musical Review, 1842–7

The Era, 1838–1939

Oxberry's Dramatic Biography and Histronic Anecdotes, 1825–7

The Playgoer, 1901–4

Play Pictorial, 1903–39

The Stage, 1881—continuing

Tallis's Dramatic Magazine, 1850–1
continued as
Tallis's Drawing Room Table Book, 1851
and
Tallis's Shakespeare Gallery, 1852–3

The Theatre, 1877–8 (weekly)
1878–97 (monthly)

The Theatre, continued as *Playgoer and Society*, 1909–13

The Theatrical Examiner, 1823–8
The Theatrical Inquisitor, 1812–21
The Theatrical Journal, 1837–73
The Theatrical Observer, 1821–71
See also
Theatre Notebook (1946—continuing)
Theatre Research/Recherches Théâtrales (1959–75)
subsequently
Theatre Research International (1975—continuing)
Nineteenth-Century Theatre Research (Edmonton, Alberta, 1973—continuing)

Anthologies of Plays

L. R. N. ASHLEY	*Nineteenth-Century British Drama* (Glenview, Illinois, 1967)
J. O. BAILEY	*British Plays of the Nineteenth Century* (New York, 1966)
MICHAEL R. BOOTH	*English Plays of the Nineteenth Century.*
	I: *Dramas 1800–1850*
	II: *Dramas 1850–1900*
	III: *Comedies*
	IV: *Farces*
	V: *Pantomimes, Extravaganzas, and Burlesques* (1969–76)
	Hiss the Villain. Six English and American Melodramas (1964)
	The Magistrate, and Other Nineteenth-Century Plays (1974)
GERALD B. KAUVAR and GERALD C. SORENSON	*Nineteenth-Century English Verse Drama* (Rutherford, N.J., 1973)
MICHAEL KILGARIFF	*The Golden Age of Melodrama: Twelve Nineteenth-Century Melodramas* (1974)
J. W. MARRIOTT	*Great Modern British Plays* (1929)
MONTROSE J. MOSES	*Representative British Dramas, Victorian and Modern* (Boston, Mass., 1919)
GEORGE ROWELL	*Late Victorian Plays 1890–1914* (1968)
	Nineteenth-Century Plays (1953)

JAMES L. SMITH   *Victorian Melodramas* (1976)
GERALD WEALES   *Edwardian Plays* (New York, 1962)
STEPHEN   *The Hour of One : Six Gothic Melodramas* (1975)
  WISCHAUSEN

INDEX

Abbey Theatre, Dublin, 138, 168
Acis and Galatea, 16
acting: change of styles in, 22–9; and melodrama, 26, 60; of light comedy, 26–9; of burlesque, 67, 72; Robertson and, 81–2; Barker and, 140–1; of comedy, 159–61
actor-manager, the, xii, 104–7, 142; Barker as, 136, 140; in post-war times, 148–9
actors: and the Victorian play, 2, 81; the strolling player, 5–6; and stage design, 7–8; and scenery, 15; and Georgian repertory, 22; and changing styles, 22–9; and the audience, 31; and melodrama, 60; the actress as hero, 70; and burlesque, 72; Robertson and, 81–8; his prestige under Irving, 96–7, 105–6; Barker and, 140–1; in post-war years, 149
Adelphi Theatre, 7, 10, 12, 90, 105, 142, 152, 159
Admirable Crichton, The (Barrie), 128, 176
Africans, The (Colman the Younger), 163, 171
Alarming Sacrifice, An (Buckstone), 158, 173
Albert, Prince, 151, 152
Albery, James, 86–9, 159, 175
Alexander, Sir George, x, xiii, 82, 97, 105, 106, 117, 120: and English drama, 107, 112, 113
Alice-Sit-By-The-Fire (Barrie), 127, 176
Amazons, The (Pinero), 168, 176
America, 55, 95, 104, 134
amphitheatre, the, 9, 12
Androcles and the Lion (Shaw), 133, 176
Antony and Cleopatra, 107
Appia, Adolphe, 140
Archer, William, 52, 80, 121, 145, 166, 167: and Ibsen, 128

Aristophanes, 69, 71
Arms and the Man (Shaw), 131, 134, 176
Arrah-na-Pogue (Boucicault), 55, 57, 174
Asche, Oscar, 105
Assommoir, L' (Zola), 61
Astley's Amphitheatre, ix, 9, 12, 46
As You Like it, 9, 97
audience, the, 1–2: mob-rule by, 3–4, 6; and costume, 15; and spectacular drama, 18, 31, 38; and melodrama, 26, 60; and burletta, 66; and burlesque, 68, 72; the Bancrofts and, 82–4; and the touring company, 84; and the theatre's status, 92–3; and the Savoy Operas, 93, 95; Irving and, 96; its changing character, 103, 149; for Society drama, 108, 145, 147; Barrie and, 127; and intellectual drama, 128; and Shaw, 133; and musical comedy, 143–4; and Music Hall, 144–5
auditorium, ix, x, 82–3, 96; its changing character, 103
Augier, Guillaume Victor Émile, 58

Back to Methuselah (Shaw), 133
Bad Girl of the Family, The (F. Melville), 142
Baillie, Joanna, 31, 151
ballet, 4, 8; Diaghilev and, 140
Balmoral Castle, 153
Bancroft, Sir Squire, 98, 106, 154
Bancrofts, the, 4, 29, 85, 97; Robertson and, xiii, 73–4, 75, 76, 80, 82; and the Prince of Wales's, 82–3, 103, 153, 159; and the audience, 82–4, 92, 101; their acting 'school', 160; production of *The Merchant of Venice*, 161; payments to T. W. Robertson, 165; produce Clement Scott's work, 166

Barker, Harley Granville, 71, 72, 157, 167, 177; and his Shakespeare production, xii, 140–2; and Shaw, 134, 136; as actor-producer, 136–7; as dramatist, 137–8

Barrett, Wilson, 102, 118, 143, 161, 162

Barrie, Sir James, 63, 176; as Society dramatist, 127–8; his estate, 165

Barrymore, William, 46, 151

Bateman family, 95

Battle of Hexham, The (Colman the Younger), 43

Battle of Life, The (Robertson), 76, 174

Beauty and the Beast (Planché), 70, 173

Bébé (Hennequin and De Najac), 159

Becket (Tennyson), 37, 100, 154, 173

Beddoes, Thomas Lovell, 34, 173

Bedford, Paul, 160

Beerbohm, Sir Max, 167

Bells, The (Lewis), 98–9, 106, 154, 168, 174

Bells of Haslemere, The (Grundy), 90, 175

Benson, Sir Frank, 97, 141

Bernard, Charles, 59

Bernard, William Bayle, 18, 173

Besier, Rudolf, 100, 177

Betsy (Burnand), 159

Betty, William Henry West, 23

Birds, The (Planché), 69, 173

Birmingham Repertory Theatre, 138

Birth (Robertson), 77, 79, 84, 174

Black-Ey'd Susan (Jerrold), 48–50, 53, 164, 173

Blot in the 'Scutcheon, A (Browning), 36, 37, 173

Blue Beard (Planché), 43, 70, 172–3

blue-book drama, 129, 131, 134–5

Booth, Edwin, 42, 52

Booth, Junius Brutus, 4

Booth, Michael R., 157, 158

Boots at the Swan (Selby), 153

Borderers, The (Wordsworth), 33–4, 172

Bothwell (Swinburne), 32, 175

Boucicault, Dionysius Lardner, 17, 65, 80, 136, 153, 168, 174: his *London Assurance*, 28, 53, 63;

and melodrama, 54–7, 98; his earnings, 164

Bourchier, Arthur, 105

Box and Cox (Morton), 65–6, 158, 173

Brayton, Lily, 105

Brighouse, Harold, 139

Britannia Theatre, Hoxton, 161

Brooke, G. V., 25, 83

Brough, Robert and William, 66, 71, 174

Browning, Robert, 173: and the dramatic form, 36–7, 38

Buckingham, George Villiers, 2nd Duke of, 66, 67

Buckstone, John Baldwin, 26, 47, 68–9, 73, 158, 160, 173

Builder of Bridges, The (Sutro), 145, 177

Bulwer-Lytton, Edward, Baron Lytton, 38, 51–2, 58, 99, 100, 152, 173

Bunn, Alfred, xii

burlesque, 93; and burletta, 66; in the English theatre, 66–9, 143, 144, 145; Planché and, 67–9, 70–1; Planché's successors and, 71–4

burletta, 10, 18, 28, 46; and burlesque, 66

Burnand, Sir Francis, 66, 159

Byrne, James, 4

Byron, George Gordon, Lord, 17, 172: and the theatre, 32, 33, 34–6

Byron, H. J., 66, 72, 73, 94, 157, 174: as successor to Robertson, 87–9

Cabinet Minister, The (Pinero), 168, 176

Caesar and Cleopatra (Shaw), 130, 131, 176

Caigniez, Louis-Charles, 46

Cain (Lord Byron), 35, 172

Caine, Sir Hall, 143, 162, 175

Caius Gracchus (Knowles), 64, 172

Caleb Williams (Godwin), 42; *see also Iron Chest, The*

Campbell, Mrs. Patrick, 113, 120

Candida (Shaw), 131, 176

Capon, William, ix, 14, 15

Captain Brassbound's Conversion (Shaw), 131–2, 176

Captain Drew on Leave (Davies), 127, 177

Captain Swift (Chambers), 126, 177
Carmen (Bizet), 154
Carton, Richard Claude, 90, 126, 176
Case of Rebellious Susan, The (H. A. Jones), 121, 175
Cassilis Engagement, The (Hankin), 147, 177
Caste (Robertson), 75, 76, 77, 78, 79, 83, 128, 147, 156, 169, 174
Castle of Otranto, The (Walpole), 39
Castle Spectre, The (Lewis), 39, 43, 44, 45, 172
Cavalleria Rusticana (Mascagni), 154
Cenci, The (Shelley), 32, 33, 172
Chambers, Charles Haddon, 126, 148, 177
Chapeau de Paille d'Italie, Un (Labiche), 159
characterization: Robertson and, 77–8, 81, 82; Albery and, 86–7
Charity (Gilbert), 94, 175
Charity that Began at Home, The (Hankin), 146, 177
Charles I (Wills), 99, 174
Charley's Aunt (Thomas), 112, 159, 176
Chevalier, Albert, 145
Chien de Montargis, Le (Pixérécourt), 46
Christian, The (Caine), 143, 162, 175
Circle, The (Maugham), 148
Circus Girl, The, 144
Clandestine Marriage, The (Colman the elder), 41
classical themes, 67–8, 69, 71
Coburg Theatre, 12
Coelina: ou l'Enfant du Mystère (Pixérécourt), 46
Coleridge, Samuel Taylor, 24, 33, 34, 36, 172
Colleen Bawn, The (Boucicault), 55, 57, 152, 174
Collier, Constance, 107
Colman, George (the elder), 24, 42, 163
Colman, George (the younger), 10, 39, 163, 171: and comedy, 41–2, 63; and spectacle, 42–3
comedy: acting styles in, 25, 29, 159–60; Georgian drama and, 40; melodrama and, 42, 53; its eclipse, 63; and burlesque, 66, 74; 'cup-and-saucer', 79–80; Gilbert and, 94; Pinero and, 112; musical comedy, 143–5, 148; relation to farce, 156–9
Committed for Trial (Gilbert), 159, 175
Commons, House of, Report of Select Committee: on Dramatic Literature (1832), 151, 155, 163, 164; on Theatrical Licenses and Regulations (1866), 151, 164
composer, the, and musical comedy, 144
Conquering Game, The (Barnard), 18, 173
Conquest family, the, 70 n2
Constant Wife, The (Maugham), 148
Cooke, George Frederick, 105
Cooke, T. P., 26, 47–8, 55
Cool as a Cucumber (Jerrold), 65, 174
Copyright Acts, 107; Dramatic Copyright Act (1833), 164; Berne Convention (1886), 165; U.S. Copyright Law (1891), 165
Corsican Brothers, The (Boucicault), 17, 53–5, 83, 98, 152, 174
costume: antiquarianism in, 17, 51; in burlesque, 67
Courier of Lyons, The (Reade), 61, 98, 174
Court Favour (Planché), xiii
Court Masque, the, 14, 20
Court of Alexander, The (G. A. Stevens), 67
Court Theatre, 82, 112, 146: Shaw and the, 133–5; Granville Barker and the, 136–8, 140, 142, 154, 167
Covent Garden, x, 3, 11, 12, 15, 16, 22, 31, 33, 140, 152: its design, 6; becomes and opera house, 13; Vestris and, 19, 28, 29, 70; and gas-lighting, 21; and melodrama, 46
Coyne, J. S., 158
Craig, Gordon, 140
Craven, Hawes, xi, 96
Creswick, William, 13
Cricket on the Hearth, The (Dickens), 51

Criterion Theatre, 104
Critic, The (Sheridan), 67
Critical Essays on the Performers of the London Theatres (Leigh Hunt), 165
criticism, dramatic: and Ibsen, 129; Shaw and, 130; rôle of, 165–7
criticism, Romantic, 64
Crusaders, The (H. A. Jones), 121, 146, 175
Cumberland, Richard, 163
Cup, The (Tennyson), 38, 100, 173
Cuthbert, H., xi
Cymon and Iphigenia (Planché), 68, 173
Cyril's Success (H. J. Byron), 87, 88, 157, 174

Daddy Hardacre (Simpson), 153
Daily Telegraph, The, 166–7
Daly's Theatre, 144
Dame aux Camélias, La (Dumas), 58
Dance, Charles, 67
Dancing Girl, The (H. A. Jones), 119–20, 175
Dandy Dick (Pinero), 112, 168, 176
Dante (Sardou), 100
Davenant, Sir William, 7, 8
David Garrick (Robertson), 73, 75, 165, 174
Davies, Hubert Henry, 126–7, 148, 177
Dear Brutus (Barrie), 128
Dear Departed, The (Houghton), 139, 177
Death's Jest Book (Beddoes), 34, 173
Deep, Deep Sea, The (Planché), 67, 172
Delacour, Alfred-Charlemagne Lartigue, 61, 92, 159
Delavigne, Casimir, 53, 98
D'Ennery, Adolphe, 53, 91
Devil's Disciple, The (Shaw), 131, 176
Diaghilev Ballet, the, 140, 141
Dibdin, Charles, 48, 67
Dickens, Charles, 22, 50–1, 73
Diplomacy (Clement Scott and B. C. Stephenson), 85, 159, 162, 175
director, the, his beginning, 80–1
Disgrace to Her Sex, A (Melville), 143
Divorçons (Sardou and De Najac), 159
Doctor's Dilemma, The (Shaw), 133, 176

Dog of Montargis, The (Barrymore), 46, 171
Doll's House, A (Ibsen), 129, 131
Dolly Reforming Herself (H. A. Jones), 125, 127, 175
Don Caesar de Bazan (Dumanoir and D'Ennery), 53
Don Giovanni in London (Moncrieff), 164, 172
Don Juan (Flecker), 100
Don Quixote (Wills), 99, 174
Dora (Sardou), 85
Dorset Garden, 6
Dowton, William, 25, 151
D'Oyly Carte, Richard, 95
D'Oyly Carte Company, 157
drama: burletta and, 10; patent theatres and, 11; at the turn of the century, 31; the Romantics and, 32–8; melodrama and, 39–41; Dickens and, 50–1; Robertson and, 75–84, 85, 86, 87; Taylor and, 84–5; Albery and, 86–9; Grundy and, 0–2; the New Drama, 91–2; the Victorian theatre and, 149–50; revivals of Victorian plays, 167–9
   Bastille, 45–6
   intellectual, 128, 136–7
   Irish, 55–6, 57
   legitimate and illegitimate, 11
   native, 107–8
   nautical, 47–50
   poetic, 32–8, 100, 105
   Romantic, 54, 71
   social, 135–8, 142
   Society, xiii, 108ff, 145–8: Pinero and, 113–18; Jones and, 118–25; lesser dramatists, 126–7; Barrie and, 127–8; repertory and, 139; Maugham and, 149
Drama's Levée The (Planché), 11, 68–9, 172
Dramatic Authors' Society, 164
dramatic writing, 12: Browning and, 36–7; Romantic poets and, 38; James and, 101–2
Drawing Room, Second Floor and Attics (J. M. Morton), 158, 173
Dr. Faustus (Marlowe), 142
Drink (Reade), 61, 174
Driven from Home (Melville), 142

Drury Lane, 3, 4, 10, 11, 12, 15, 16, 22, 31, 66, 152: its design, ix, 6, 8; and melodrama, 13, 46, 48, 142; Byron and, 33, 34–5; and spectacle, 38, 43

Dryden, John, 63

Duchess de la Vallière (Bulwer-Lytton), 51, 173

Ducrow, Andrew, 9

Duke's Men, the, 8

Dulcamara (Gilbert), 93, 175

Dumanoir (Philippe-François Pinel), 53

Dumas, Alexandre, 17, 51

Dumas, Alexandre (the younger), 58, 98

Eagle Saloon, City Road, 12

East Lynne (Wood), 167

Edward VII, King, 153, 154

Edwardes, George, 143–5

Edwards, Sutherland, 91

Egan, Pierce, xiii, 47

Elizabethan Stage Society, 142

Elliston, Robert William, 10, 26, 48, 166

Elton, E. W., 155

Emperor and Galilean (Ibsen), 129–30

Enchanted Cottage, The (Pinero), 117

Enchanted Girdles, 4

Engaged (Gilbert), 94–5, 112, 168, 175

English Dramatists of To-day (Archer), 128

Erckmann-Chatrian, (pseudonym of Émile Erckmann and Louis Chatrian), 98

Ervine, St. John, 139

Escape (Galsworthy), 136

Essays of Elia (Lamb), 166

Eternal City, The (Caine), 143, 175

Eugene Aram (Wills), 99, 100, 174

Europe: English drama and, 38, 39–40, 43, 45–6, 134, 138, 140; and the Savoy Operas, 95

Everyman, 142

Examiner, The, 16, 18

Extravaganza, 93; Planché and, 69–71

Factory Girl, The (Jerrold), 50, 173

Fairy Blue and Fairy Red, 5

fairy tales, 69–71

Falcon, The (Tennyson), 38, 173

Fanny's First Play (Shaw), 133, 134, 176

farce, 65, 71, 87, 89, 148: Pinero and, 112; development of, 156–9

Farquhar, George, 53

Farren, Nellie, 143

Farren, William, senr., and William, jnr., 26, 160

Fascinating Mr. Vanderveldt, The (Sutro), 145, 177

Faust: (Wills), 99, 154; (Phillips), 100, 106, 177

Faust and Marguerite (Boucicault), 17, 20, 75, 174

Fechter, Charles, 19, 159

Fernandez, James, xi

Feudal Times (Colman the younger), 43, 171

Feydeau, Georges, 159

Fielding, Henry, 8, 66, 67, 72

Field of the Cloth of Gold, The (Brough), 71

films: melodrama and, 60, 143; and the theatre, 149

Fitzball, Edward, 23, 45, 47, 50, 56, 57, 59, 172

Flecker, James Elroy, 100

Flying Dutchman, The (Fitzball), 45, 172

Follies of a Day, The (Holcroft), 4

Foote, Samuel, 8, 27

Formosa (Boucicault), 57, 174

France: England's debt to the drama of, 29, 40, 43, 45–6, 51, 53, 55, 58, 90, 98, 110, 112; her fairy tales, 69, 70; the *pièce bien faite*, 58, 85, 109; Irving and, 98, 100; Society drama and, 109

Freischütz, Der, 45

Gaiety Theatre, x: and musical comedy, 143–4

Galsworthy, John, 61, 145, 177: and social drama, 135–6

Ganaches, Les (Sardou), 76

Garrick, David, 3, 6, 14, 15, 20, 24, 161

Garrick Theatre, 105: John Hare and the, 104, 113

Gay, John, 48, 93

Gay Lord Quex, The (Pinero), 115, 168, 176

Gendre, Le (Bernard), 59
George III, King, 151
George IV, King, 151
George V, King, 154
George Barnwell (Lillo), 40
German, Sir Edward, 144
Germany, English drama and, 34, 40, 43, 44
Getting Married (Shaw), 133, 176
Ghosts (Ibsen), 129, 154
Gilbert, Sir William Schwenk, 66, 69, 103, 106, 111, 136, 144, 175: as librettist, 72, 93–5; and Robertson, 81; adapts French farce, 159; estate of, 165; revival of *Engaged*, 168
Gilded Youth (Young), 90, 175
Gill, Basil, 107
Girl, My, 144
Girl's Cross-Roads, A (Melville), 142
Girl Who Lost Her Character, The (Melville), 142
Glasgow Repertory Theatre, 138
Glenny, Charles, xi
Godwin, William, 42
Goethe, Johann Wolfgang von, 38
Golden Fleece, The (Planché), 68, 173
Goldsmith, Oliver, 150, 163, 168
Gondoliers, The (Gilbert), 154, 175
Gothic cult: the Romantic poets and the, 33–6; and melodrama, 39, 43–6, 47, 50
Grangé (Pierre Eugène Baske), 54
Great World of London, The (Melville), 142
Grecian Theatre, 12
Greet, Sir Ben, 141
Grein, J. T., 129
Grieve, Thomas, 17, 141
Grimaldi, Joseph, 70
Grove, David, 23
Grundy, Sydney, 90–2, 110, 175

Haddon Hall (Grundy), 90, 175
Half-Caste, The (Robertson), 76, 174
Hamilton, Henry, 162
Hankin, St. John, 146–7, 177
Harding, Lyn, 107
Hare, Sir John, 29, 91, 92, 102, 107, 166: Robertson and, 78, 81, 82; and theatrical prestige, 101, 103,

105, 106, 136; and the Garrick, 104, 113
Harker, Joseph, xi, xiii, 96
Harlequinade, 70, 71
Harlequin and the Marble Rock, 5
Harley, John Pritt, 160
Harris, Sir Augustus, 162
Harris, Thomas, 33
Harvey, Sir John Martin, 97, 148, 161
Hassan (Flecker), 100
Haste to the Wedding (Gilbert), 159, 175
Hawtrey, Sir Charles, 109, 147
Haymarket Theatre, 8, 12, 21, 42, 66, 68, 69, 73, 83: the Bancrofts and the, 4, 82, 84, 101; and comic acting, 26; Tree and the, 105, 119; Queen Victoria visits, 152; Society drama at, 162
Hazlitt, William, 31, 166, 167
Heartbreak House (Shaw), 133
Hedda Gabler (Ibsen), 129
Hennequin, Alfred, 159
Henry V, x, 16
Henry VIII, 20
Her Majesty's Theatre, Tree and, xi, 105, 106–7, 141
Hicks, Sir Seymour, 143
His House in Order (Pinero), 115, 176
Hobby-Horse, The (Pinero), 113, 146, 176
Holcroft, Thomas, 4, 41, 43, 46, 171
Holland, Henry, ix, 6
Hollingshead, John, 143
Home (Robertson), 77, 174
Honey Moon, The (Tobin), 64, 172
Horniman, Annie Elizabeth Fredericka, 138
Houghton, Stanley, 139, 177
Housman, Laurence, 134, 177
How To Settle Accounts With Your Laundress (Coyne), 158
Hugo, Victor, 32, 38, 51, 58, 101
Hunchback, The (Knowles), 64, 172
Hunt, Leigh, 165–7

Ibsen, Henrik, 91, 101, 108, 166: the English theatre and, 128–9, 135; Shaw and, 129–30; 131, 133
Ideal Husband, An (Wilde), 110, 176

INDEX

Idler, The (Chambers), 126, 177

Importance of Being Earnest, The (Wilde), 94, 111–12, 176

Inchbald, Mrs., 44, 171

Independent Means (Houghton), 139, 177

Independent Theatre, 129, 134

Inkle and Yarico (Colman the younger), 42

Iolanthe: (Gilbert), 93, 175; (Wills), 99, 174

Ion (Talfourd), 31–2, 172

Iris (Pinero), 115, 176

Iron Chest, The (Colman the younger), 42, 99, 171

Iron Master, The (Pinero), 112, 176

Irving, Sir Henry, 21, 82, 104, 107, 131, 136: his character parts, 37, 42, 54, 65, 86–7, 97, 98, 100, 106; and the stage, 92; and the Lyceum, xi, 95–6, 104, 105, 106, 141; his leadership, 96–7; as actor, 97, 106, 107; his repertory, 98–101; his knighthood, 105–6, 153; attacked by Shaw, 165, 166; pays Clement Scott, 166; in *The Bells*, 166

Irving, Washington, 55

It's Never Too Late to Mend (Reade), 61, 174

Ivanhoe, adaptations of Scott's, 50

Jack Straw (Maugham), 147, 177

James, Charles S., xiii

James, Henry, 101

Jealous Wife, The (Colman the elder), 24, 41

Jerrold, Douglas William, 48–50, 53, 56, 65, 164, 173

Jerrold, William Blanchard, 65, 174

Jew and the Yorkshireman, The, 5

Jim the Penman (Young), 89–90, 175

John-a-Dreams (Chambers), 126, 177

John Bull (Colman the younger), 42, 163, 171

John Bull's Other Island (Shaw), 134, 154, 176

John Glayde's Honour (Sutro), xiii, 145, 177

Jonathan Bradford (Fitzball), 50, 59, 172

Jones, Henry Arthur, 90, 102, 108, 128, 175: as a dramatist, 118–25, 126, 127, 143, 145, 146, 147

Jones, Sidney, 144

Jordan, Dorothy, 153

Judah (H. A. Jones), 119, 175

Juif Polonais, Le (Erckmann-Chatrian), 98

Justice (Galsworthy), 61, 136, 177

Kean, Charles, 19, 21, 36, 83, 95, 99, 107, 153: and the Princess's, xi, 13, 16, 17–18, 20, 53, 75, 98; his acting style, 25, 55; parts played by, 42, 61; and Windsor Theatricals, 152; at the Princess's, 160; criticised, by G. H. Lewes, 166, and by Henry Morley, 166

Kean, Edmund, 4, 10, 159, 161: acting style, 24, 25; earnings in provinces, 155–6; reviewed, by Hazlitt, 166, and by G. H. Lewes, 166

Keeley, Robert and Mary Ann, 160

Kelly, Hugh, 163

Kemble, Charles, 17, 26

Kemble, John Philip, 3–4, 15, 159, 165, 166: and acting style, 24

Kendal (*née* Robertson), Madge, 75, 82, 91

Kendals, William and Madge, 101, 105, 112, 113, 166

Kenney, James, 64, 172

Killigrew, Thomas, 8

Kind der Liebe, Das (Kotzebue), 44

King Charming (Planché), 70, 173

King John, xi, 17, 106

King Lear, 16

King Rene's Daughter (Wills), 99

King's Men, the, 8

King's Rival, The (Taylor and Reade), 58, 62, 174

King's Theatre, Haymarket, 8

King Victor and King Charles (Browning), 37, 173

Knowles, James Sheridan, 31–2, 38, 64, 100, 152, 163, 172

Kotzebue, August von, 44

K.O.W. ('Keen on Waller') badge, 105

Labiche, Eugène, 91, 92, 159

Ladies' Battle, The (Robertson), 75, 174
Ladies of Samarkand, 4
Lady Audley's Secret (Braddon), 167
Lady Epping's Lawsuit (Davies), 127, 177
Lady Frederick (Maugham), 147, 177
Lady Huntsworth's Experiment (Carton), 126, 176
Lady of Lyons, The (Bulwer-Lytton), 51, 52, 59, 173
Lady Windermere's Fan (Wilde), 110, 111, 176
Lamb, Charles, 166
Lancashire drama, 139
Land of Promise, The (Maugham), 148, 177
Lang, John, 58
Lang, Matheson, xiii, 143
Langtry, Lillie, 153
La! Sonnambula! (H. J. Byron), 73, 174
Last Days of Pompeii, The (Bulwer-Lytton), 52
Last of the De Mullins, The (Hankin), 147, 177
'Lawrence, Slingsby' (G. H. Lewes), 29
Lawyer, The, 5
Lehár, Franz, 144
Leno, Dan, 145
Leslie, Fred, 143
Lewes, G. H., 29, 166
Lewis, Leopold, 98, 174
Lewis, Matthew Gregory ('Monk'), 39, 43–4, 172
Lewis, W. T., 65
Leybourne, George, 145
Liars, The (H. A. Jones), 125, 175
Licensing Acts, 5, 8, 10, 66, 93
Lie, The (H. A. Jones), 125
lighting, xii, 14: gas-, 21–2, 96; limelight, 21, 80, 96, 101; Irving and, 21, 96; electric-, 96, 101
Lillo, George, 40
limelight, xii, 21, 80, 96, 101
Lind, Jennie, 151
Liston, John, 25, 26, 67, 160
Little Eyolf (Ibsen), 130
Little Minister, The (Barrie), 127, 176
Little Theatre (Haymarket), 8, 9

Liverpool Repertory Theatre, 138, 139
Lloyd, Marie, 145
Lloyds, Frederick, 17
Löhr, Marie, 107
London Assurance (Boucicault), 19, 28, 53, 63, 168, 169, 174
Long Strike, The (Boucicault), 56, 174
Lord and Lady Algy (Carton), 126, 176
Lord Chamberlain, 10, 12, 58, 131
Louis XI (Boucicault), 53, 98, 174
Loutherbourg, Philip James de, 14, 15
Love Chase, The (Knowles), 64, 172
Lovers' Vows (Inchbald), 44, 171
Love's Labour's Lost, 19
Loyalties (Galsworthy), 136
Lucia di' Lammermoor (H. J. Byron), 73, 174
Luke the Labourer (Buckstone), 47, 173
Lyceum Theatre, 12, 19, 23, 102, 159: the Mathews and, 29; Vestris and 70; the Bancrofts and, 84; Irving and, 92, 95–9, 104, 105, 141, 153; the Melville brothers and, 142–3; Queen Victoria visits, 152
Lyons Mail, The (Reade), 98; *see also The Courier of Lyons*

Macbeth, 33
MacCarthy, Sir Desmond, 167
Macready, William Charles, 12, 13, 16, 19, 83, 161: his innovations in production, x, 16, 21; his acting, 24–5, 33, 36, 51, 53; on provincial companies, 156; criticism of, 159, 166
Madame Sans-Gêne (Sardou), 100
Madras House, The (Barker), 138, 177
Magic in Two Colours, 5
Magistrate, The (Pinero), 112, 168, 176
Magpie or the Maid?, The (Pocock), 46, 171
Maid and the Magpie, The (H. J Byron), 73, 174
Maître des Forges, Le (Ohnet), 112
Major Barbara (Shaw), 133, 176
Man and Superman (Shaw), 132–3, 134, 176

Manchester Gaiety Theatre, 138, 139

Manfred (Lord Byron), 35, 172

Man of Destiny, The (Shaw), 131, 176

Man of Honour, A (Maugham), 147, 177

Manxman, The (Caine), 143, 175

Marino Faliero (Lord Byron), 35, 172

Marriage of Figaro, The (Holcroft's version of), 4

Married in Haste (H. J. Byron), 87, 88–9, 174

Marrying of Ann Leete, The (Barker), 137, 177

Martyre (D'Ennery and Tarbe), 91

Mary Goes First (H. A. Jones), 125, 175

Mary Rose (Barrie), 128

Masks and Faces (Reade and Taylor), 61–3, 174

Masqueraders, The (H. A. Jones), 120, 175

Mathews, Charles, and comic acting, 26–7

Mathews, Charles James (and Mme Vestris), 12, 53, 65, 160, 161: and scenic reform, xiii, 18–19, 79; and Shakespeare production, 19–20; and comic acting, 27–9; and the Lyceum, 29

matinée performances, 103, 128, 134

Maude, Cyril, 105

Maugham, William Somerset, 177; and Society drama, 147–8

Mead, Tom, xi

mechanical devices, xii, 20–2, 43: the back-stage staff and, 23; the Corsican trap, 54

melodrama, 20, 23: and acting styles, 26; French, 29; the Gothic cult and, 39, 43–6; Colman and, 42–3; native, 46–52; nautical, 47–50; mid-Victorian, 53; Irish, 55; Boucicault's innovation, 57; films and, 60; eclipses comedy, 64; Robertson and, 76; Irving and, 98–9, 161; Jones and, 118–19; Galsworthy and, 135; at the Lyceum, 142–3; Tree and, 161; East End, 161; late Victorian, 161–2

Melville, Walter and Frederick, 142–3, 162

Menschenhass und Reue (Kotzebue), 44

Merrie England (German), 144

Merry Widow, The (Lehár), 144

Merry Wives of Windsor, The, 19

Merry Zingara, The (Gilbert), 93, 175

Michael and His Lost Angel (H. A. Jones), 120–1, 162, 175

Midas (O'Hara), 67

Mid-Channel (Pinero), 117, 176

Midsummer Night's Dream, A, xii, 19, 140

Miller and His Men, The (Pocock), 46, 171

Millward, Jessie, xi

Minister and the Mercer, The (Bunn), xii

Misalliance (Shaw), 133, 176

Mollentrave on Women (Sutro), 145, 177

Mollusc, The (Davies), 127, 177

Monckton, Lionel, 144

Moncrieff, William Thomas, 57, 164, 172

Money (Bulwer-Lytton), 52, 63, 157, 173

Monkhouse, Allan, 139

Montépin, Xavier de, 54

Moore, Eva, xiii

Moore, Mary, 126

Moreau, Charles-François, 61

Morley, Henry, 166

Morton, John Maddison, 65, 66, 158, 173

Morton, Michael, 176

Morton, Thomas, 40, 43, 63, 163, 171

M.P. (Robertson), 78, 81, 113, 174

Mr. Buckstone's Ascent of Mount Parnassus (Planché), 69, 173

Mr. Buckstone's Voyage Round the Globe (Planché), 69, 173

Mrs. Dane's Defence (H. A. Jones), 123–4, 161, 175

Mrs. Gorringe's Necklace (Davies), 126–7, 177

Mrs. Warren's Profession (Shaw), 130, 176

Much Ado About Nothing, xi, 24, 107

Munden, Joseph, 25, 26, 160, 166
music: and burletta, 10, 66: and spectacle, 39, 42; melodrama and, 43, 46; and burlesque, 72; for musical comedy, 144
Music Hall, 71; evolution of, 83, 143; expansion of, 144–5

National Theatre, 107, 149, 167, 168
New Hay at Old Market (Colman the younger), 29, 171
New Haymarket Spring Meeting, The (Planché), 69, 173
New Men and Old Acres (Taylor), 84–5, 174
New Theatre, 105
New Woman, The (Grundy), 91, 175
Nineteenth Century Theatre Research, 169
Notorious Mrs. Ebbsmith, The (Pinero), 116, 176

Oberon (Planché), 70, 172
Octoroon, The (Boucicault), 55, 56, 57, 174
O'Hara, Kane, 67
Ohnet, Georges, 112
Old Drama and the New, The (Archer), 52
Old Price riots, 3–4, 6, 83, 105
Old Vic, 107, 141
Olivia (Wills), 99, 174
Olivier, Laurence, Lord Olivier, 161
Olympic Devils (Planché), 67, 172
Olympic Revels (Planché), 67, 172
Olympic Theatre, 10, 12, 152, 153: Vestris and the 18, 19, 27, 28, 29, 68, 70
On Bail (Gilbert), 159, 175
Only Way, The (F. Wills), 162
opera, 1, 4, 8, 11, 13, 39, 70, 83: comic, 101, 144
Orpheus in the Haymarket (Planché), 68, 173
Othello, 4
Othello Travestie, 72
Our American Cousin (Taylor), 63, 164, 174
Our Betters (Maugham), 148
Our Boys (H. J. Byron), 89, 174
Ours (Robertson), xiii, 76, 78, 79, 174

Our Theatres in the 'Nineties (Shaw), 130

Pair of Spectacles, A (Grundy), 92, 154, 175
Palmer, John, 9, 10
pantomime, xii, 11, 20, 39: Planché and, 70; the Conquests and, 70 n2
Paolo and Francesca (Phillips), 100, 177
Paphian Bower, The (Planché), 67, 68, 172
Passers By (Chambers), 126, 177
patents, theatre, 8–9, 9ff: abolition of, 13
Patrick's Return (Byrne), 4
Pavilion Theatre, Whitechapel, 12, 161
Peer Gynt (Ibsen), 128, 129
Peg Woffington (Reade), 61
Pelissier Follies, 145
Pepys, Samuel, 3
Perfect Lover, The (Sutro), 145, 177
Perplexed Husband, The (Sutro), 146, 177
Peter Pan (Barrie), 128, 176
Petits Oiseaux, Les (Labiche and Delacour), 92
Petticoat Perfidy (Young), 90, 175
Phelps, Samuel, 12, 53, 156, 166: acting of, 160–1
Philanderer, The (Shaw), 130, 176
Phillips, Stephen, 100, 106, 177
Pie Voleuse, La (Caigniez), 46
Pilot, The (Fitzball), 47–8, 172
Pinero, Sir Arthur Wing, 79, 102, 105, 106, 108, 128, 176: as director, 81, 136; as dramatist, 112–18, 120, 126, 127, 145, 146; Court farces, 159; earnings from The Second Mrs. Tanqueray, 165; revivals of his plays, 168
Pink Dominos (Albery), 87, 159, 175
Pixérécourt, René Charles Gilbert de, 45–6
Pizarro (Sheridan), 44, 171
Planché, James Robinson, xiii, 17, 20, 145, 152–3: and extravaganza, 18, 29, 69–71, 94; and magic, 45; and burlesque, 66; and Vestris, 67–8

Play (Robertson), 78, 174
play, the: the actor and, 2; Robertson and, 84, 90; the audience and, 92; Irving and, 96; acting and reading editions of, 108
playbill, the, 4–5, 17
Play of the Future, The (Grundy), 92
Plays of the Passions (Baillie), 31
Plays Pleasant and Unpleasant (Shaw), 108
playwright, the: and the Victorian theatre, 1–2, 38, 64; and the pleasure gardens, 9; and public demands, 31; as stage-manager, 80–2; his rising status, 107–8, 136, 149; and Society drama, 108ff; Shaw as, 133–5; repertory and, 139; Barker and, 140–1; earnings of, 163–4
pleasure gardens, 9
Plot and Passion (Taylor), 58, 174
Pocock, Isaac, 46, 171
Poel, William, 142
Pollock, Benjamin, 46
Poole, John, 163
Poor Gentleman, The (Colman the younger), 42, 171
Poor of New York, The (Boucicault), 55, 57, 174
Poor Vulcan (Dibdin), 67
Potter, Paul, 175
Prefaces to Shakespeare (Barker), 142
Prince, Richard Archer, 142 n
Prince of Wales's Theatre, ix, 29, 73, 144: Robertson and, xiii, 75, 76, 78, 81, 82; the Bancrofts and, 82, 102, 153; standards at, 153
Princess's Theatre, xii, 118: Kean and, ix, 13, 16, 17, 17 n2, 20, 53, 76: Queen Victoria visits, 152; repertoire under Kean, 160
Prisoner of Zenda, The (Rose), 162
problem play, 108–17: Shaw and, 130–1
producer, the, 81, 136
Profligate, The (Pinero), 113, 162, 176
Progress (Robertson), 76, 77, 174
Prometheus Unbound (Shelley), 32, 35, 172
Prunella (Housman and Barker), 134, 177
Pückler-Muskau, Prince, 21, 22

Punch, 20, 53, 58
Pushkin, Alexander, 38, 101
Puss in Boots (Planché), 69–70, 172
Pygmalion (Shaw), 133, 134, 176
Pygmalion and Galatea (Gilbert), 94, 175

Quality Street (Barrie), 127, 176
Queen Mary (Tennyson), 37, 100, 173
Queen's Theatre, 73, 105
Quintessence of Ibsenism, The (Shaw), 129, 130

Raising the Wind (Kenney), 64–5, 172
Raleigh, Cecil, 162
Räuber, Die (Schiller), 44
Reade, Charles, 58, 61, 98, 174
Regency Theatre, ix
Rehearsal, The (Buckingham), 66
Reinhardt, Max, 140
Rejected Addresses (Smith), 7–8
Remorse (Coleridge), 33, 34, 36, 172
Renascence of the English Drama, The (H. A. Jones), 118–19
Rent Day, The (Jerrold), 50, 173
repertory movement, 138–40, 142, 157: and Shakespeare, 141
Return of the Prodigal, The (Hankin), 147, 177
Reveillon, Le (Meilhac and Halevy), 159
revues, 145, 148
Reynolds, Frederick, 163
Rich, John, 6, 8, 70
Richard II, 106
Richelieu (Bulwer-Lytton), 51, 52, 99, 173
Rigoletto (Verdi), 154
Rip Van Winkle (Boucicault), 55, 174
Riquet with the Tuft (Planché), 69, 172
Ristori, Adelaide, 166
Road to Ruin, The (Holcroft), 41, 171
Robertson, Agnes, 55
Robertson, Sir Johnston Forbes, xi, 97, 105, 106, 159, 166
Robertson, Thomas William, 29, 73–4, 116, 153, 154, 161, 174: as stage-manager, xiii, 78–81, 136; as a dramatist, 75–8, 113,

Robertson, *(cont.)*
147; and the actor, 81–2; his successors, 84–92, 100–2; Gilbert and, 94; plays on tour, 157; at the Prince of Wales's, 159; earnings, 165; tribute by the National Theatre, 168
Robespierre (Sardou), 100
Robins, Elizabeth, 135, 177
Robinson, 'Perdita', 153
Robson, Frederick, 71: in Windsor theatricals, 152; favourite of Queen Victoria, 153; at the Olympic, 160
Rogue's Comedy, The (H. A. Jones), 124, 175
Romantic Movement: the theatre and, 32–8, 71, 100; and comedy, 64; Barker and, 136–7
Romeo and Juliet, 19, 20
Rothenstein, Albert, 141
Royal Academy of Dramatic Art, 107
Royal Circus, 9, 12
Royal Shakespeare Company, 168
Royalty and the theatre, 18, 83, 103, 134
Royalty Theatre, 9
Royal Victoria Theatre, 12
Rubens, Paul, 144
Runaway Girl, A, 144

Sacred Flame, The (Maugham), 148
Sadler's Wells, 4, 9, 160: Phelps and, 13
St. James's Theatre, 12, 82, 83, 91, 102, 162: Alexander and, x, xiii, 105, 112, 113, 117
Saints and Sinners (H. A. Jones), 119, 175
Salvini, Tommaso, 166
Sans Pareil Theatre, 12
Sardanapalus (Lord Byron), 17, 34, 34, 36, 172
Sardou, Victorien, 76, 85, 100, 109, 131, 159
Saturday Review, 130
Savoy Operas, 72, 93–5, 97, 101, 107, 167
Savoy Theatre, 84, 95, 143, 144, 153, 157; Barker and, xii, 140, 141
scenery, ix: development of, x, 14–17;

Kean and, xi; Barker and, xii, 140; Vestris and, xiii, 18–19; Macready and, 16; Taylor and, 59–60; Robertson and, 79–82
Schiller, Johann Christoph Friedrich, 32, 33
School (Robertson), 77, 78, 80, 174
Schoolmistress, The (Pinero), 112, 168, 176
Scott, Clement, 85, 129, 155, 166, 167
Scott, Sir Walter, 50
Scrap of Paper, A (Simpson), 159
Scribe, Eugène, 53, 58, 75, 109
Second Mrs. Tanqueray, The (Pinero), 103, 105, 113–14, 117, 120, 176: literary qualities of, 161; Pinero's earnings from, 165
Settling Day (Taylor), 58, 174
Seven Champions of Christendom, The (Planché), 69, 173
Shadows (Young), 90, 175
Shaftesbury Theatre, 144
Shakespeare, William, 33, 38, 63, 72, 150, 152, 160: Barker and his texts, 140–1
Shakespeare production: in the Victorian theatre, 13, 14, 15, 20, 83, 105, 148, 149; Macready and, x, 16–17; Kean and, ix, 16, 17, 20; antiquarianism, 17; Vestris and Mathews and, 19–20; Irving and, xi, 97, 98, 100; Tree and, xi, 106–7; Barker and, 140–1; Benson and Greet and, 141; Poel and, 142
Shaughraun, The (Boucicault), 55, 168, 174
Shaw, George Bernard, 81, 100, 108, 139, 145, 150, 176: Archer and, 128–9; and Ibsen, 129–30; his dramatic progress, 130–3; and the Court Theatre, 133–5, 167; estate, 165; attacks Irving, 165; plays revived, 167
Shelley, Percy Bysshe, 32, 33, 38, 172
Sheridan, Richard Brinsley, 6, 44, 63, 67, 72, 150, 160, 163, 171
Shop Girl, The, 144
Siddons, Sarah, 24, 159, 166
Sign of the Cross, The (Barrett), 162
Silver Box, The (Galsworthy), 135, 177

Silver King, The (H. A. Jones and H. Herman), 118, 175
Silver Shield, The (Grundy), 90, 175
Siraudin, Paul, 61
Skin Game, The (Galsworthy), 136
Sleeping Beauty in the Wood, The (Planché), 70, 173
Smith (Maugham), 147, 177
Smith, James and Horatio, 7
Society (Robertson), 73–4, 75, 76, 77, 78, 79, 84, 113, 174
society and the theatre, 83–4, 89, 92, 103–4, 108–9
Sorcerer, The (Gilbert), 95, 175
Sothern, Edward Askew, 63, 75
Spanier in Peru, Die (Kotzebue), 44
spectacle: demand for, 11, 15; in the Victorian theatre, 14, 18, 31, 38–9, 43, 64; and gas-lighting, 21; acting styles and, 22; and pantomime, 70
Speed the Plough (Morton), 40, 171
Squire, The (Pinero), 113, 176
stage, the: its design, ix, x, xi, xiii, 6–8; and the pleasure gardens, 9; and Victorian spectacle, 14, 18, 20; development of, 14–15; Vestris and, 19; its mechanical devices, 20–22; and acting styles, 22; the Bancrofts and, 101; Craig and, 139; Barker and, 140
stage-manager, the: Kean, 26; Robertson, 78–82, 86; Albery, 86
Stage Society, 134, 136, 137, 147
Standard Theatre, Shoreditch, 12
Stanfield, Clarkson, x, xii, 16
Stephenson, B. C., 85, 175
Still Waters Run Deep (Taylor), 59, 153, 157, 174
Stirling, Fanny, 98
stock company, 83, 84, 139
Strafford (Browning), 36, 37, 173
Strand Theatre, 12, 72, 73
Stranger, The (Thompson), 44, 58, 172
Stratford-on-Avon Shakespeare Festivals, 141
Strife (Galsworthy), 136, 177
Stuart, Leslie, 144
Sullivan, Barry, 25, 83
Sullivan, Sir Arthur, 66, 90, 144, 168: his scores, 93, 95

supernatural, the, in English drama, 45
Surreyside theatres, 9, 10, 47
Surrey Theatre, ix, 9, 12, 13, 46, 48
Sutro, Alfred, 177: as a Society dramatist, xiii, 145–6, 147
Sweethearts (Gilbert), 94, 175
Sweet Lavender (Pinero), 113, 127, 176
Swinburne, Algernon Charles, 32, 175

Tale of Mystery, A (Holcroft), 41, 46, 171
Talfourd, Francis, 66, 71, 72
Talfourd, Sir Thomas, 31, 172
Taming of the Shrew, The 64
Tarbe, 91
Taylor, Tom, 58–61, 63, 136, 153, 164, 174: as a dramatist, 84–5, 90, 118
Telbin, William, xi, xii, 17, 141
Telemachus (Planché), 67, 172
Tempter, The (H. A. Jones), 119, 175
tennis-court theatre, 3, 14
Tennyson, Alfred, Lord, 32, 173: as a dramatist, 37–8, 100
Tenth Man, The (Maugham), 147, 177
Terriss, William, xi, 26, 49, 90, 97, 142 and n, 161
Terry, Edward, 143
Terry, Ellen, xi, 20, 21, 96, 161: Hare and, 82, 99; Irving and, 97, 99, 100, 104; Shaw and, 131, 132
Terry, Fred, 26
Thackeray, William Makepeace, 51, 52
That Wretch of a Woman (Melville), 143
Theatre, The, 166–7
Theatre
  Elizabethan: its design, 3, 7, 14, 17, n2, 20, 140, 142; the Romantics and, 33, 38, 64
  English: evolution of, 2–3, 4ff; rioting in, 3–4; its changing design, 6–8; and the pleasure gardens, 9–10; and acting styles, 22–9; and the new drama, 31, 91; the Romantics and, 32–8; Boucicault and, 55–7; and burlesque, 66–9, 72; pantomime in,

Theatre, (cont.)
69–71; Robertson and, 75–81, 85, 87; the Bancrofts and, 82–4, 89, 103; Society and, 83–4, 89, 92, 103–4, 108–9; Savoy Operas and, 93; after Robertson, 101–2; the actor-manager and, 104–7, 136; Archer and, 128–9; and Ibsen, 128–9, 135; Shaw and, 133–5; the Repertory movement and, 138–40; its war-time prosperity, 148; post-war changes in, 148–9

Georgian: its design, ix, x, 14, 15, 20, 79, 96; its audience, 4, 5, 7; patents, 8; drama in, 11, 22, 31, 39, 40, 61, 63, 64

provincial, 5–6, 22, 83–4, 104, 138–9: changes in, 154–7

Restoration: its design, 3, 6, 7, 14; its audience, 4, 5

Victorian: its changing design, x, 6–8; its mechanical devices, xii, 20–2; the playwright and, 1–2, 38; its development, 2–3; Kean and, 13, 17–18; and spectacle, 14, 15, 20; antiquarianism in, 15, 17; the interior scene, 18–19; acting styles in, 22–9; tragedy in, 31–8; Dickens and, 50–1; its changing taste, 52–3; and Romantic drama, 54, 58, 100; its prudery, 58, 59; comedy in, 63–4; Robertson and, 75ff; the dramatist-director, 81; the Music Hall and, 83; the touring companies, 83, 139; Gilbert and, 93–5; Irving and, 95–100, 101; verse-drama in, 100; the last chapter, 104ff, 142; and Society drama, 108ff; Jones and, 125; Barrie and, 127; and intellectual drama, 128; Galsworthy and, 135–6; its popularity, 149

Theatre Regulation Act, 13, 83, 160
theatres, minor, ix, 12, 66
Theatres Royal, 5–6
Theseus and Ariadne (Planché), 68, 173
Thespis (Gilbert), 93, 94, 175
Thomas, Brandon, 112, 176
Thompson, Benjamin, 44, 172

Three Plays for Puritans (Shaw), 130
Thunderbolt, The (Pinero), 117, 176
Ticket-of-Leave Man, The (Taylor), 59–61, 136, 174
Times, The (Pinero), 113, 176
Timour the Tartar (Lewis), 44, 172
Tobin, John, 64, 172
Tom and Jerry (Egan), 47
Tom and Jerry (Moncrieff), 164, 172
Tom Jones (German), 144
Tom Thumb the Great (Fielding), 66
Toole, John Laurence, 127, 143, 153
Tosca, La (Sardou), 159
touring companies, 83–4, 139, 141, 156–7
tragedy, in Victorian drama, 31–8
Traviata, La (Verdi), 154
Tree, Ellen, 17; see also Kean, Charles
Tree, Sir Herbert Beerbohm, 82, 95, 105, 119, 126, 134, 136, 143, 166: his Shakespeare productions, xi, 106–7, 141; acting in Shakespeare, 160; preference for melodrama, 161
Trelawny of the 'Wells' (Pinero), 79, 116, 168, 176
Trial by Jury (Gilbert), 95, 175
Trilby (Potter), 105, 106, 175
Triumph of the Philistines, The (H. A. Jones), 121, 175
Two Foscari, The (Lord Byron), 35, 172
Two Gentlemen of Verona, The, 140
Two Loves and a Life (Taylor), 58, 62, 174
Two Mr. Wetherbys, The (Hankin), 146, 177
Two Roses (Albery), 86–7, 175
Two Virtues, The (Sutro), 146, 177
Tyranny of Tears, The (Chambers), 126, 177

Used Up (Boucicault), 53, 174
Utopia (Limited) (Gilbert), 93, 144, 175

Vampyre, The (Planché), 45, 172
Vanbrugh, Sir John, 53, 105
Vance, Alfred, 145
Vandenhoff, George, 25

Vanderdecken (Wills), 99, 174
Vedrenne-Barker management, 134, 138, 140
Venice Preserv'd (Otway), 35
Vestris, Madame, 12, 53, 70, 161: and scenic reform, xiii, 18–20, 79; and acting reform, 27, 28; and burlesque, 67, 68, 69; as male impersonator, 70
Vicar of Wakefield, The (Goldsmith: adapted by Wills as *Olivia*), 99
Victoria, Princess, later Empress of Germany, 152
Victoria, Queen: interest in opera and ballet, 151; preference for French drama, 152; extends her theatregoing, 152–3; favourite plays and players, 153; commands performances at Windsor, 152–3; and at Balmoral, 153–4
Virgin Goddess, The (Besier), 100, 177
Virginius (Knowles), 32, 64, 172
Votes for Women (Robins), 135, 177
Voysey Inheritance, The (Barker), 137–8, 177

Walker, London (Barrie), 127, 176
Walkley, Arthur Bingham, 167
Waller, Lewis, 105, 107, 143, 161
Walls of Jericho, The (Sutro), 146, 177
Walpole, Horace, 39
War (Robertson), 77, 82, 174
Ward, Geneviève, 98
Waste (Barker), 137, 177
Webster, Benjamin, 17 n2, 26
Webster, John, 33
Wedding Guest, The (Barrie), 127, 176
Wedding March, The (Gilbert), 159, 175
Werner (Lord Byron), 35–6, 172
Werther (Schiller), 44
West, William, 46
What Every Woman Knows (Barrie), 128, 176
When We Dead Awaken (Ibsen), 130
White Cat, The (Planché), 70, 173
White Devil, The (Webster), 33

Whitewashing Julia (H. A. Jones), 124, 175
Widowers' Houses (Shaw), 129, 130, 133, 176
Wife, The (Knowles), 64, 172
Wife's Sacrifice, A (Grundy), 91, 175
Wigan, Alfred: in Windsor Theatricals, 152; manager of Olympic, 153, 160; favourite of Queen Victoria, 153
Wilde, Oscar, 105, 176: and Society drama, 109–12, 113, 161; revivals of his plays, 167
Wild Oats (O'Keeffe), 168
Wilkinson, Norman, xii, 141
William Tell (Knowles), 32, 172
Wills, William Gorman, 38, 99–100, 153, 174
Wilton, Marie, 72–3, 76, 113, 143; *see also* Bancroft
Windsor Castle, 152, 153
Winki the Witch, 4
Winter's Tale, The, 140: Kean and, xi, 16, 17
Woman of No Importance, A (Wilde), 110, 176
women: in Society drama, 109–10, 123, 127, 135, 146; in Shaw, 130, 131, 132
Wordsworth, William, 33–4, 38, 172
World of Sin, A (Melville), 142
Worst Woman in London, The (W. Melville), 143
Wren, Christopher, ix, 6
Wright, Edward, 160
Wyndham, Sir Charles, 82, 101, 106, 122, 126, 166: as actor-manager, 104–5
Wyndham's Theatre, 105

Yellow Dwarf, The (Planché), 70, 173
You Never Can Tell (Shaw), 132, 176
Young, Charles, 25
Young, Sir Charles L., 89–90, 175
Younger Generation, The (Houghton), 139, 177

Zola, Émile, 61